Self-Perception

Self-Perception

The Psychology of Personal Awareness

Chris L. Kleinke

Wellesley College

W. H. Freeman and Company
San Francisco

A Series of Books in Psychology

Editors: Jonathan Freedman
Gardner Lindzey
Richard F. Thompson

Library of Congress Cataloging in Publication Data

Kleinke, Chris L.
Self-perception.

Includes bibliographical references and index.
1. Self-perception. 2. Mind and body.
3. Personality change. I. Title.
BF697.K58   155.2   78-1370
ISBN 0-7167-0063-8
ISBN 0-7167-0062-X (pbk.)

Printed in the United States of America

1   2   3   4   5   6   7   8   9

To my family

Contents

Preface

My aim in writing this book was to present an organized discussion of research conducted by psychologists on a topic that is dear to all of our hearts: *ourselves.* I have found the research described in this volume fascinating and relevant to our everyday lives.

Studies of self-perception can be divided into two general categories: (1) the perception and interpretation of bodily states, and (2) the perception and interpretation of overt behaviors. Research studies in the first category shed light on such issues as how people learn to experience emotions like romantic love, anger, and guilt; the conditions under which they recognize bodily needs such as hunger and thirst; and methods people can learn for dealing more effectively with anxiety, depression, and pain. Chapters One through Three review research in these areas. The second category of research studies covers a wide range of topics including how people form attitudes, how they learn to be assertive or helpless, the ways in which they perceive their lives as being under internal or external control, and the reactions people have to success and failure. Chapters Four through Nine examine the perception and interpretation of overt behaviors.

I have written the book with the hope of reaching several audiences. Nonpsychologists will appreciate the informal writing style. Students will benefit from the book's extensive reference list and comprehensive coverage of journal articles. Persons interested in therapeutic applications will find a useful integration of research on self-perception with recent developments in self-control training and cognitive behavioral modification.

The study of self-perception implies different things to different people. The approach taken in this book is experimental. Information, examples, and conclusions are based on research studies that have appeared in professional journals, rather than on intuitive or experiential reports. I have attempted to integrate these research studies within the theoretical frameworks of Stanley Schachter and Daryl Bem from a behavioristic perspective. It is possible that the research reported here could also be interpreted according to other theoretical points of view.

Many of the experiments included giving subjects false or misleading information. The American Psychological Association specifies that all subjects must be fully debriefed at the conclusion of their participation in psychological studies. The reader can be assured that subjects in the research summarized in this book were always informed about the nature and purpose of the study in which they participated and the reasons for any possible misleading information or deception. Colleges and universities have committees for regulating research with human participants according to ethical standards set forth by the American Psychological Association. Federal funding agencies require that researchers intending to use human subjects receive a positive endorsement from an ethics committee before applying for a research grant. Readers who are interested in the issue of ethical standards in psychological research may wish to consult the American Psychological Association publication, *Ethical Principles in the Conduct of Research with Human Participants.*

I wish to thank my sister, Katharine, for her encouragement and helpful comments and suggestions. I would also like to express appreciation to Mrs. Ruth Church and Mrs. Nancy Shepardson for typing and editing the manuscript.

Chris L. Kleinke

January 1978

Self-Perception

ONE

Interpreting
the Messages
of Our Bodies

The perception and interpretation of bodily states and overt behaviors constitute the underpinnings of self-perception. To gain an insight into the orientation of the research presented in this book, we will analyze the strong influence of learning and experience on the self-perception of bodily states. Examples from everyday life of rather specific experiences such as pain and hunger, and of more general experiences such as guilt and mental or emotional disturbance, will help clarify how culture, circumstances, and personal motivation affect the labels people apply to their physiological arousal.

Recognizing Our Emotions

Imagine that you come home one night and a friend of yours jumps out from behind the door and shouts, "Boo!" What emotion would you experience? You might say you were scared; or surprised; or angry. If your friend happened to be your lover you might even say you experienced heightened sexual attraction.

How do you feel when you are riding on a roller coaster? Possibly you feel afraid. You might also label your feelings as joy or delight. If you are with a close friend you might feel strong personal attraction.

A measure of your physiological responses in the above situations would show that your heart was beating faster than usual, your breathing was accelerated, and your palms were sweaty; in short, it would reveal that you were physiologically aroused. There would be nothing in the physiological recording instruments, however, that would suggest what emotional label you should attach to this physiological arousal. Whether you are scared, joyful, angry, or emotionally attracted to another person, your body is aroused in essentially the same manner. The labels or interpretations you give to your physiological arousal depend on the particular situation and what you have learned or experienced in the past.

Consider a young child who goes to the circus for the first time. Bombarded with new sights, smells, and sounds, the child is in a state of general physiological arousal, experiencing a faster-than-usual heartbeat, slight tremors, accelerated breathing, and possibly cold or sweaty hands. How does the child interpret this arousal? What emotion does he or she feel? Let us look a bit further. As the child walks by the lions' cage his or her parent most likely says, "Oh, that lion is so big. I bet you're *scared*. Don't be *scared*, the lion can't hurt you." Later when the trapeze artists are performing the parent helps the child interpret his or her arousal by exclaiming, "Isn't that *exciting!*" Then the clowns appear and the parent "instructs" the child by laughing and commenting on how *funny* and *happy* they are. Before leaving the circus the child is likely to confront the smell of animals and learn from the parent that arousal in this context is a sign of *unpleasantness* and *disgust*. During all this time the child has been in essentially the same state of physiological arousal. However, the child has learned to label or interpret this arousal as different emotions according to the particular stimuli or events in the immediate situation.

The examples of the friend jumping out at you, the ride on the roller coaster, and the child at the circus illustrate a theory of emotion that was originally formulated by Stanley Schachter and his colleagues.[1] Schachter argues that people's emotions are made up of two basic components: physiological arousal and the labeling of that physiological arousal. He proposes that the quality of physiological arousal associated with different states of emotion is pretty much the same. What distinguishes emotions such as *anger, fear, love, elation, anxiety,* and *disgust* is not what is going on inside the body but rather what is happening in the outside environment. The implication of Schachter's theory is that specific emotions are learned rather than innate. The notion that the self-perception of arousal can be influenced by learning has fascinating personal applications. Before exploring these applications we will look briefly at the research Schachter and his colleagues conducted to test and validate their theory of the self-perception of emotion.

To substantiate their hypotheses, Schachter and his co-workers devised a way to vary the degree of physiological arousal subjects experienced and at the same time affect the possible labels the subjects would give to this physiological arousal. Participants in one research study were divided into four groups. The first three groups were injected with adrenalin, a drug that produces increased rates of heartbeat and respiration, an increase in blood pressure, and some palpitation, tremors, and flushing. The fourth group of participants in the study was injected with a harmless saline solution. Schachter and his colleagues included this fourth group to show that the potential effects of adrenalin were not due to the experience of being injected but rather to the arousal caused by the drug itself. This kind of control group is called a *placebo group*. The participants in the first three groups were under the same conditions of physiological arousal, but Schachter and his co-workers had arranged the experimental circumstances so that the subjects' explanations, or labels, for this arousal would be very different. The first group of participants (informed group) was instructed that the adrenalin would arouse them as described above. They had no reason to look to the environment for an explanation for their arousal because they clearly knew it was due to the injection. The second group of participants (ignorant group) was given no information about the possible effects of the adrenalin, and the third group (misinformed group) was falsely told that the adrenalin injection might make them itch a bit. The ignorant and misinformed participants were of greatest importance in testing Schachter's theory because they were highly aroused but had no immediate explanation for the cause or meaning of this physiological arousal.

After receiving their respective injections and instructions, the participants were placed in the company of another person (who was actually a confederate of the experimenter). For half of the participants in each group the confederate acted in a happy and euphoric manner. He doodled briefly on a piece of paper, crumpled it up, shot it at the wastebasket, and attempted to engage the participant in a "basketball game;" constructed a paper airplane and sent it flying around the room; then constructed a tower out of manila folders and used a rubber-band slingshot to shoot wads of paper at it until it fell; and finally spotted a hula hoop and danced wildly around the room. For the other participants, the confederate acted in an angry manner, complaining about having agreed to participate in the research study, becoming increasingly angry about a questionnaire he and the participant were asked to fill out, and finally tearing up the questionnaire and stomping out of the room.

The results of the study supported Schachter's theory of emotion by showing that participants in the ignorant and misinformed groups, who were physiologically aroused with adrenalin and given no explanation for this arousal, were strongly influenced by the behavior of the confederate in interpreting their own emotional states. When confronted with a happy and euphoric confederate, ignorant and misinformed participants evaluated themselves on a rating form as being happy, and they acted in a happy manner. When confronted with an angry confederate, ignorant participants (misinformed participants were not exposed to the angry confederate) evaluated themselves as angry and acted in an angry manner. Participants in the informed group, who were injected with adrenalin and clearly informed about the drug's effects, were less influenced by the behavior of the confederate because they could use their knowledge of the effects of the adrenalin to label or interpret their arousal. Participants in the placebo group were less influenced by the behavior of the confederate because they were not physiologically aroused.

A 1953 study of marijuana users also supports the theory that people designate physiological arousal in various ways as a result of cues from the environment.[2] Interviews with marijuana users from a variety of social backgrounds led to the conclusion that in order to have the feeling of being "high," a person must experience the physiological symptoms caused by marijuana and also recognize and label these symptoms as a "high." People smoking marijuana for the first time often do not experience the feeling of being high until they learn from more experienced users some of the appropriate cues, such as rubbery legs, cold hands and feet, lightness in the head, and increased hunger. An example of a person learning to label increased hunger as a high is seen in the following excerpt from one of the interviews:

> They were just laughing the hell out of me because like I was eating so much. I just scoffed [ate] so much food, and they were just laughing at me, you know. Sometimes I'd be looking at them, you know, wondering why they're laughing, you know, not knowing what I was doing. [Well, did they tell you why they were laughing eventually?] Yeah, yeah, I come back, "Hey, man, what's happening?" Like, you know, like I'd ask, "What's happening?" and all of a sudden I feel weird, you know. "Man, you're on, you know. You're on pot." I said, "No, am I?" Like I don't know what's happening.[3]

In addition to recognizing the physiological symptoms of marijuana, the experienced marijuana user has also learned to label these symptoms as pleasurable:

> Marijuana-produced sensations are not automatically or necessarily pleasurable. The taste for such experience is a socially acquired one, not different in kind from acquired tastes for oysters or dry martinis. The

user feels dizzy, thirsty; his scalp tingles; he misjudges time and distances; and so on. Are these things pleasurable? He isn't sure. If he is to continue marijuana use, he must decide that they are. Otherwise, getting high, while a real enough experience, will be an unpleasant one he would rather avoid.[4]

An experienced marijuana user gave this description of how he introduces newcomers to marijuana:

> Well, they get pretty high sometimes. The average person isn't ready for that, and it is a little frightening to them sometimes. I mean, they've been high on lush [alcohol], and they get higher that way than they've ever been before, and they don't know what's happening to them. Because they think they're going to keep going up, up, up till they lose their minds or begin doing weird things or something. You have to like reassure them, explain to them that they're not really flipping or anything, that they're gonna be all right. You have to just talk them out of being afraid.[5]

Because of the importance of appropriate labeling for enjoying marijuana, most marijuana users prefer not to drink alcohol while smoking marijuana. It is difficult to distinguish between the effects of marijuana and the effects of the alcohol and if they are taken together the proper cues for a good high become confused.

Self-labeling is also a critical factor in alpha rhythm experiences. Research has shown that people can learn to increase their alpha rhythms with special training and physiological feedback about their brain waves.[6] The experiences reported by people in an "alpha state," however, are primarily a function of their expectations. In other words, it is not alpha rhythms that cause a difference in feelings or experience. Feelings or experiences of people undergoing alpha training are a result of the training procedure which consists in paying close attention to one's body, being in a dark soundproof laboratory, and receiving encouragement and learning positive expectations from the experimenter. The same argument has been made about meditation. It is not a *state of mind* that causes a person to have favorable experiences. Favorable experiences in meditation come from the positive labeling of behaviors that result from the *practice* of relaxation, imagination, and attention to one's body.

Schachter's experiment, the study of marijuana users, and research in alpha training provide a theoretical framework for understanding how people learn to interpret the messages from their bodies by first recognizing physiological changes and then labeling those changes according to their past experiences in similar situations. We can use this theoretical framework to explore some interesting examples of how people learn to label the messages from their bodies in everyday life.

Experiencing Pain

One thing is certain: We have all experienced pain. Our bodies clearly communicate physiological reactions to injury, abuse, and all other varieties of physical trauma. However, the manner in which a person interprets or labels these physiological reactions resulting from physical injury or trauma strongly influences the experience of pain. One way of appreciating the importance of self-labeling on experiences of pain is to compare reactions of people from different cultures. Experimental studies in which people are exposed to pain have also demonstrated how self-labeling affects reactions to pain. The people in the following studies presumably suffered similar physiological responses to painful stimulation, but because they interpreted these responses in different manners their ultimate experiences were remarkably different.

Comparing Reactions of Hospital Patients

Mark Zborowski conducted a series of interviews with hospital patients in New York City and found that patients from various backgrounds and cultures reacted to pain in quite different manners.[7] Although it is not appropriate to make generalizations about religious and ethnic groups on the basis of interviews, the responses of patients in this study give interesting examples of the relationship between self-perception and reactions to pain. Protestant patients whose families had lived in the United States for several generations had a strong reluctance to express feelings of pain. These patients were unemotional and attempted as much as possible to inhibit any overt manifestations of pain, such as crying or complaining. The "Old American" Protestants talked about pain in the following ways:

> I don't cry for help, I just pull myself together and bite my lip. I like to control my reactions. Crying and screaming can't do you any good.
>
> I don't cry—I want to take my pain like a man—I want to be a real man and not to show my pain.
>
> I don't scream or cry. Just sit there and take it. I don't fight, just sit there. What can you do? No use in hollering or fighting it. The energy that you put out for screaming, and yelling, and fighting and exerting yourself—screaming and yelling and twisting and in combating pain is just wasted and makes it only worse.[8]

The reactions of Jewish patients to pain were strikingly different. The Jewish patients interviewed had no inhibitions against reacting negatively to pain. They expressed the following feelings:

> I loosened down—I let out the emotion. Because I know it's best to let it out than to keep it within yourself. Cry it out and be better off.
>
> Yesterday it hit me like hell. I was crying like a baby. So the nurse came in. I don't know what I would have done if she hadn't helped me.
>
> I cried once when I was in severe pain. It was a helpless feeling, more like tears came to my eyes with the light. I felt so helpless.[9]

Italian patients also had no inhibitions about expressing pain:

> No, no, no, you can't hide it. It's too tough. Yeah, you can't hide it. You know you have got it, because you got to moan or scream or do something.
>
> Oh, when the pain came in, I—I—I, mean, I just can't stand the pain. It's—it brings tears to my eyes. . . .
>
> I cried like a God-damned baby. I cried early in the morning. The first day I couldn't go to work in the morning.[10]

Americans from Irish backgrounds were similar to the third generation Protestants. Their reactions to pain were nonexpressive and non-vocal:

> Oh, no, I wouldn't complain. I'd just wait till it went away, that's all. I'm not that bad about it.
>
> I wouldn't complain much. Complaining, cursing, that's—isn't going to do you any good. I'd say, "Oh, I got a pain—hurt" or something like that, but I can never see much sense to laying there and moan and groan. It doesn't help.
>
> I can take it pretty well. Sometimes I might have a pain and nobody will know it. I'll suffer myself.[11]

Tonsillectomies in China

A rather dramatic example of how people differ in their learned reactions to pain is seen in the following description by British physician P. E. Brown of tonsillectomies in China:

> While visiting a children's hospital we saw a queue of smiling 5-year-olds standing outside a room where tonsillectomies were being carried out in rapid succession. The leading child was given a quick anaesthetic spray of the throat by a nurse, a few minutes before walking into the theatre unaccompanied. Each youngster in turn climbed on the table, lay back smiling at the surgeon, opened his mouth wide, and had his tonsils dissected out in the extraordinary time of less than a minute. The only

instruments used were dissecting scissors and forceps. The child left the table and walked into the recovery room, spitting blood into a gauze swab. A bucket of water at the surgeon's feet containing thirty-four tonsils of all sizes was proof of a morning's work.[12]

Children in China are taught from an early age to view surgery with a positive attitude and to be confident that it will be successful and result in little or no pain. The labels used by Chinese children for their bodily responses to surgery are quite different from the labels employed by most American children.

Experimental Studies of Pain

Differences in people's responses to pain have also been investigated in experimental studies. In one experiment, women volunteers were encouraged to submit to increasingly stronger electrical shocks until they felt it was too uncomfortable to continue.[13] None of the shocks were severe enough to be of any danger to the participant's health. One purpose of the experiment was to see if differences would emerge between the women in their tolerance for electrical shock and in their perceptions of the intensities of shocks that were "painful" to them. The results of the experiment showed that women from Italian backgrounds reported discomfort at significantly lower intensities of shock than women from Irish and third generation Protestant backgrounds. The third generation Protestant women were significantly more relaxed (in measures of palmar skin potential) than the other women as they were receiving the shocks. The researchers who conducted this experiment suggested that the matter-of-fact attitude of this group of people toward pain ("you take things in your stride") might have helped them achieve greater physiological relaxation. The Irish women did not show similar signs of physiological relaxation during the time they were being shocked. The experimenters felt that the Irish attitude of "keeping a tight upper lip" but "fearing the worst" is not as adaptive as the Protestant attitude in helping the body to relax.

Another group of researchers interested in how people experience pain recruited Jewish and Christian college students as volunteers and exposed them to pain from a pressure cuff placed around the upper arm.[14] The cuff was designed with hard rubber projections which could be pressed into a participant's arm with increasing force until the participant asked for the pain to be terminated. The most interesting result of this experiment was that both Jewish and Christian participants significantly increased their pain tolerance when they were told beforehand that their religious group was thought to be inferior in its tolerance for pain. Apparently, not only cultural background but also motivations can influence the perception and labeling of pain.

Offering another example of how motivations influence reactions to pain was an experiment in which two groups of participants were exposed to electric shock under different motivational situations.[15] Participants in one group were made to feel that it was completely their choice to take a series of shocks while attempting to complete a learning task. Participants in the second group were given the feeling that they had no choice in the matter, but that there was good reason for them to take the shocks while attempting to complete the learning task. The first group of participants, who had agreed to be shocked "of their own free will," reported less pain and less disturbance from the shocks received during their work on the learning task than the second group of "forced" participants. The "free will" participants had been given no good reason for the shocks and therefore could attribute their suffering to their own willingness to volunteer. One way for them to rationalize their willingness to be shocked was to play down the pain caused by the shocks. The second group of participants did not need to rationalize why they were taking shocks because it wasn't really their choice and there was supposedly a good reason for including the shocks in the experiment. The "forced" participants could admit that the shocks were painful.

Experiencing Thirst and Hunger

Just as the human body sends messages about physical injury and abuse, it also communicates clear reactions to prolonged lack of liquids and food. We have seen that both motivation and learned cultural patterns influence the labeling of bodily messages from physical trauma as "pain." Motivations and experiences also affect the manner in which people perceive and label physiological messages as "thirst" and "hunger." We have all had the experience of being so wrapped up in something we are doing that we miss a meal without ever thinking about it. Research studies provide other examples of how self-perceptions of thirst and hunger are affected by external factors that influence the labels applied to bodily reactions. The people in the following experiments experienced similar deprivations of liquids or food. However, differences in motivation and experience caused them to interpret and label their bodily deprivations in very different manners.

Labeling Thirst

Male and female participants in an experiment went without liquids for about fourteen hours.[16] Half of the participants were paid $1.00 for going without liquids; the remaining participants were paid $5.00. The male participants who were paid only $1.00 for their inconvenience experienced less thirst and drank less water when it was offered after the experiment than the male participants who were paid $5.00. This is probably because the $1.00 participants had to rationalize why they agreed to suffer the inconvenience of going without liquids for so little money; the simplest way to do this was to convince themselves that going without liquids wasn't so bad and that they weren't really thirsty. The participants who were paid $5.00 could admit that they were thirsty because they were being paid a fair amount for their trouble. The results of the experiment showed, however, that the female participants did not make the same distinctions as the males. Females who were paid $1.00 did not evaluate themselves as being less thirsty than the females who received $5.00; they seemed to feel $1.00 was a fair payment for going without liquids. Females who were paid $1.00 and $5.00 were equally willing to use the money as a justification for their inconvenience.

Male participants in another experiment were fed crackers and a spicy hot sauce and then led to believe that they would go without liquids for twenty-four hours.[17] Half of the participants were given a good reason for their inconvenience with the explanation that they were participating in a valuable scientific study. The remaining participants were led to believe that there was no good reason for their inconvenience. As you would expect, the second group of participants rated themselves as being less thirsty and drank less water after the experiment than the first group of participants. Because they had no good reason to justify the discomfort of the hot sauce and expected deprivation, participants in the second group were more motivated to underestimate their self-perception of thirst.

Labeling Hunger

Similar studies have shown how motivation influences the self-perception of hunger. A group of male college students went without food for a day and were then placed in a situation where they worked on a series of learning tasks.[18] Half of the students were paid $5.00 for their participation. The remaining students received no payment. At the end of the experiment, the participants who received no payment rated themselves as significantly less hungry than the participants who were paid $5.00. Participants in another part of this study went without food from 4:30 P.M. one day until 9:00 A.M. the next day. Half of these participants were given good justification for their inconvenience; they were led to believe that the experiment would be very valuable to medical research and that their participation would greatly contribute to the success of the project. The remaining participants were led to believe that the experiment was not particularly important and that their participation would be of no real scientific value. You can predict the results. Participants with great justification for going without food could admit that they were very hungry because they were suffering for a good cause. Participants with little justification for going without food had to rationalize their inconvenience by perceiving themselves as not being hungry. Another interesting finding in this experiment was that the participants with little justification for going without food not only rated themselves as less hungry, but also showed fewer physiological signs of hunger when measured for plasma-free fatty acids in the blood stream. This result shows how motivation can influence not only the labeling of bodily states, but also the bodily states themselves.

Deciding When to Eat

Differences Between Overweight and Normal-Weight People

We have seen that motivation and the particular situation in which a person is involved strongly influence the self-perception of hunger. Since the self-perception of hunger in turn affects eating behavior, it seems possible that overweight and normal-weight people differ in how and when they label themselves as hungry. This indeed appears to be the case. After an extensive program of experimental research, Stanley Schachter concluded that normal-weight people rely on internal cues from their bodies to determine when they are hungry and overweight people rely on external cues from the environment to determine when they are hungry.[19]

Let us look at some of the research that led Schachter to this conclusion. He found that overweight people do not interpret physiological signs as hunger in the way that normal-weight people do. In other words, overweight people do not recognize the bodily messages that they are "full" when they have just eaten and that they are "hungry" when they have not eaten for a long time.[20] Researchers have demonstrated this difference by having both overweight and normal-weight people swallow a balloon that is connected to instruments allowing precise measurement of stomach contractions. Data obtained by this method indicate that people of normal weight are quite accurate in correlating "hunger" to contractions of their stomachs but overweight people are not. The stomachs of overweight people contract in the same way as the stomachs of normal-weight people after food deprivation, but the overweight people have apparently not learned to recognize or label these contractions as "hunger."[21]

Normal-weight and overweight college students were recruited to participate in another study pointing out the differences between the ways in which overweight and normal-weight people label hunger. The researchers arranged it so that half of the students had not eaten for at least six hours before the experiment. The remaining students were given food to eat immediately before the experiment. The experiment was described to the participants as a study of taste preference. The students were given an assortment of crackers to eat and then rate for taste on a rating form. It was left to the participants' discretion to eat as many or as few crackers as they desired. The experimenters were not interested in the participants' ratings of the crackers, but rather in how many crackers each participant would eat. Normal-weight students who hadn't eaten for six hours ate significantly more crackers than normal-weight students who had just been fed; but overweight students who had just been fed ate as many crackers as overweight students who had gone without food for six hours. Apparently, the presence of the crackers, rather than the recognition of internal hunger, triggered the eating behavior of the overweight students.

In a second part of the study, the participants were threatened with electrical shock, which would either be very slight and hardly noticeable or rather severe and quite painful.[22] When the normal-weight students were made extremely fearful by threat of shock, their consumption of crackers greatly decreased. The fear reaction to shock inhibited their stomach contractions so that the fearful normal-weight students no longer felt hungry. Manipulation of fear had little effect on the eating behavior of the overweight students. Again, the eating behavior of overweight students appeared to be under control of the external presence of the crackers rather than the internal bodily reactions to fear. Related to this result is the finding in another study that overweight college students do not appear to increase their eating during times of stress such as examination periods.[23]

Who Will Eat Bland Food?

A somewhat different approach toward comparing the eating habits of overweight and normal-weight people has been to contrast their reactions to tasty and bland foods. According to Schachter's theory, since taste is an external cue it should have a greater effect on the eating behavior of overweight people. Research has found this to be true. One study compared overweight and normal-weight patients before and after they entered a hospital.[24] Before entering the hospital, the overweight patients ate an average of 1200 calories per day more than the normal-weight patients. After they had been in the hospital for several days on a bland diet similar to Nutrament or Metrecal, the caloric intake of the overweight patients dropped far below that of the normal-weight patients. The normal-weight patients regulated their eating behavior according to their bodily cues. They ate enough food to maintain their normal body weight, whether or not it tasted good or bad. Overweight patients, apparently guided by external cues of taste, ate significantly less food when it tasted bad than when it tasted good.

Overweight and normal-weight participants in another study were offered milkshakes that had either a good taste or a rather bad taste.[25] Both overweight and normal-weight participants preferred the good-tasting milkshake, but the normal-weight participants drank one-and-a-half times as much good milkshake as bad milkshake whereas the overweight participants drank more than five times as much of the good milkshake.

A study of students at Columbia University found that overweight students were significantly more likely to drop out of dormitory food contracts than normal-weight students.[26] With the not too far-fetched assumption that dormitory food is untasty, we see another example of taste affecting the eating behavior of overweight students more than normal-weight students.

Clocks Versus Stomachs

Knowing that the eating behavior of overweight people is influenced by external cues, we might predict that overweight people would pay more attention to the clock in deciding when to eat and normal-weight people would pay more attention to the cues from their stomachs. In one study, overweight and normal-weight college students were placed in a rather boring situation involving various kinds of physiological measures which lasted thirty minutes.[27] These physiological measures were only important to the experiment because they gave the experimenter an excuse for removing the participants' watches (the watches might be damaged by the electrode paste). After submitting to the physiological measurements, the participants were given some learning tests to complete and offered a box of crackers to eat while they worked on the tests. For half of the participants a clock in the room falsely showed that only twenty minutes had passed during the previous physiological measurements and that the time was only 5:20 P.M. (the true time was 5:30 P.M.). The remaining participants were led to believe that it was already after 6:00 P.M. The experimenters were interested in seeing if the doctored clocks would influence how many crackers the participants ate. As you might expect, overweight participants ate significantly more when they thought it was late rather than early; they apparently relied on the external cue of the clock to tell themselves, "It's past dinner time. I must be hungry." The normal-weight participants actually ate fewer crackers when they thought it was late rather than early because, as they reported, "they didn't want to spoil their dinner."

In another study researchers compared the eating behavior of overweight and normal-weight flight crew members of a trans-Atlantic airline company.[28] Leaving Paris at noon after eating lunch and arriving in New York eight hours later, these people reached their destination when their stomachs told them it is dinner time, but the New York clocks told them it is only early afternoon. Because the overweight crew members gauged their eating behavior by the clock and the normal-weight crew members gauged their eating behavior by their stomach, it was the normal-weight crew members who suffered the greatest conflict: Their stomachs said it was dinner time, but the clocks said it was not. They wanted to eat dinner when everyone else in New York had just eaten lunch. By contrast, the overweight crew members could more easily wait until the New York clocks told them it was time for dinner.

Teaching Overweight People to Regulate Their Eating

One way to help overweight people regulate their eating behavior is to teach them to identify their internal hunger cues. Research has shown that it is possible to teach overweight people to recognize their stomach contractions by providing them with feedback about what their stomach is doing and helping them to label or interpret their stomach contractions in an accurate way.[29]A second way to help overweight people change their eating habits is to control the taste of their food. Overweight people will eat less food if it is unappealing. A third way to regulate the eating behavior of overweight people is to control the external cues for eating. These external cues include a time schedule for eating, the effort required for eating, and the presence or absence of food itself.

A time schedule to regulate the eating behavior of overweight people could be set up by having them agree to eat only at certain specified times. A study of eating habits showed that overweight and normal-weight college students had similar lunch and dinner schedules on weekdays.[30] Morning classes would be followed by a scheduled lunch period and a dinner period was customary before an evening of studying. On weekends the eating schedules of normal-weight students did not change much. Overweight students, on the other hand, showed a great deal of variation in the times they would eat on weekends because the externally determined weekday schedule did not apply.

Overweight people usually eat less if eating requires a certain amount of unaccustomed effort. One study showed that overweight people ate more almonds than normal-weight people if the almonds were preshelled.[31] If the almonds had to be shelled, the overweight people did not eat more than the normal-weight people. In a second study, overweight people did not eat more food than normal-weight people if eating the food required effort that was not part of their usual experience.[32] However, if the work required for eating was something that the overweight people were used to (such as unwrapping candy kisses), they did eat more than normal-weight people.

A simple study showing how the presence of food affects the eating behavior of overweight people was conducted in the following manner.[33] Overweight and normal-weight people were given a plate containing either one or three sandwiches and told that they were welcome to go across the room to a refrigerator for more sandwiches if they desired. When the plate contained one sandwich, both the overweight and normal-weight people ate the sandwich, but more normal-weight people were more willing to go to the refrigerator for another half-sandwich or so. When the plate contained three sandwiches, overweight people ate significantly more than normal-weight people. Apparently, the eating behavior of the overweight people was regulated by the external presence of the sandwiches on the plate. If overweight people had to expend the effort of going to the refrigerator for food that was not immediately present, they ate significantly less. The influence of food on a plate is also shown by the fact that overweight people are more likely than normal-weight people to clean their plates during a meal.[34]

Experiencing Guilt

Do Sociopaths Feel Guilty?

Most people more or less agree on what sorts of acts society would label as acceptable or unacceptable. There is probably even more certainty about which acts society would consider criminal. If you committed an act labeled by society as a crime you would be aware of this both from your knowledge of the laws and from the guilt you felt about the crime. According to Schachter's theory of emotion you would experience heightened physiological arousal after committing the crime and, being aware of this arousal and the laws of society, you would label this arousal as guilt. What about sociopathic criminals? Do they experience guilt in the same way? Many psychologists have suggested that they do not. Clinical psychologists have characterized sociopathic criminals as having an emotional flatness and an apparent inability to experience positive as well as negative emotions. An analysis of the non-emotionality of sociopathic criminals in terms of Schachter's theory of emotion points to two possible explanations for the phenomenon. On the one hand, it is possible that sociopaths do not become physiologically aroused; without physiological arousal they would not experience emotions. Another possibility is that sociopaths do become physiologically aroused but they fail to recognize this arousal or interpret it with the socially appropriate emotional label.

Stanley Schachter and Bibb Latané conducted an extensive research program comparing prison inmates who had been clinically diagnosed as sociopathic with inmates diagnosed as nonsociopathic.[35] Results of this research showed that sociopathic criminals experience the same physiological arousal as nonsociopathic prisoners. Because of this finding, Schachter and Latané concluded that sociopathic criminals are capable of becoming physiologically aroused but they do not apply appropriate emotional labels to their arousal. One interesting finding supporting this conclusion is that sociopathic criminals engage in a much higher proportion of nonemotional crimes (such as burglary, forgery and con games) and a much lower proportion of emotional crimes (such as murder, rape, and assault) than nonsociopathic criminals. Before commiting emotional crimes people usually become physiologically aroused and apply some sort of label such as *jealousy, passion, hate,* or *anger* to that arousal. It is on the basis of experiencing these emotions that they commit emotional crimes. Because sociopaths are less likely to label their arousal states as emotions, they are less likely to commit emotional crimes.[36]

Another study supporting Schachter and Latané's analysis of sociopathic criminals showed that sociopathic prisoners were much less likely than either nonsociopathic prisoners or non-prisoners to learn how to solve a problem and thereby avoid electrical shocks.[37] All of the participants in this study were physiologically aroused at the threat of being shocked. The nonsociopathic participants apparently interpreted their arousal as anxiety and were motivated to reduce this anxiety by learning how to solve the problem. The sociopaths apparently did not label their arousal as anxiety and felt no particular motivation to solve the problem. This conclusion is supported by an extension of the study in which sociopathic criminals were given an injection of adrenalin that increased their physiological arousal and then asked to learn a problem to avoid being shocked. The sociopathic criminals were not told that the injection would arouse them and they therefore experienced an inexplicable added boost of arousal that was very new to them. Apparently this unique physiological arousal was enough to gain their attention and cause them to perceive themselves as anxious. With the new experience of arousal from the adrenalin the sociopathic criminals became significantly more successful in solving the shock-avoiding problem.

When Will People Cheat?

Two other experiments showing how people learn to label physiological arousal as guilt were conducted with college students. In one experiment students volunteered to participate in a study of the effects of a particular vitamin on perception.[38] The students were given a pill, thinking it was the vitamin. In reality, half of the students were given a drug (clorpromazine) that would make them feel very relaxed and the remaining students were given a placebo. (You will remember that *placebo* is the term used by psychologists for a fake pill that is usually made from sugar or some other neutral substance.) After taking the pill, the students were given an examination on which they would be motivated to perform well. It was arranged that participants would have the possibility of cheating with the idea that no one would ever find out if they did. In reality, the experimenters had a secret way of determining who cheated and who didn't. The students who had been secretly relaxed by the "vitamin pill" cheated significantly more than the students who had taken the placebo. From the point of view of Schachter's theory of emotion, people who take an exam while physiologically aroused are apt to label that arousal as guilt; they are less likely to cheat because they feel guilty. If they are not aroused or do not label their arousal as guilt they are more likely to cheat because they do not feel guilty. In this study, the students who were secretly relaxed by the "vitamin pill" felt much less aroused than the students who had taken the placebo "vitamin pill." Because the secretly relaxed students did not feel physiologically aroused they were much less likely to label themselves as guilty and they cheated significantly more.

College students in a second study were placed in a situation where they were motivated to cheat.[39] Half of the students had been given a placebo pill with the false expectation that it would relax them. The other students were given a placebo pill with the false expectation that it would arouse them. Which group of students cheated more? The students who took the "relaxing" pill experienced a certain amount of physiological arousal from the temptation of cheating. Feeling the arousal from the temptation of cheating, the students most likely said to themselves, "That pill was supposed to relax me, but I still feel aroused. I must *really* be aroused!" These students, perceiving themselves as highly aroused and apparently labeling this arousal as guilt, cheated very little. The students who took the "arousing" pill probably interpreted the arousal they felt from the temptation of cheating by saying to themselves, "That pill was supposed to arouse me. I do feel aroused and that's probably because of the pill." These students could attribute the arousal they felt from the temptation of cheating to the pill. They were much less likely to perceive themselves as feeling guilty and they therefore cheated considerably more than the "relaxed" students.

Moral Behavior in Children

The tendency to label arousal resulting from temptation as guilt is learned. When children misbehave, they are commonly confronted by a parent who responds with "disappointment" and withdrawal of affection. The children are taught to appease the parent by saying, "I am sorry I did that. I feel bad about it." In order to regain the parent's approval, the children learn to label the feelings associated with misbehavior and consequent disapproval as *guilt*. Children who have learned to associate temptation with feelings of guilt will be motivated to alleviate this guilt by avoiding temptation in the future. It is possible that children with very punitive parents learn to label the arousal associated with temptation in a very different way. These children are taught to associate misbehavior with direct physical punishment. They learn to label the feelings associated with misbehavior and consequent physical punishment as *shame* from being caught. In future situations of temptation, children with very punitive parents might interpret their arousal as fear of shame and misbehave as long as they think they can get away with it.[40]

Self-Perception
and Personal Adjustment

There are a number of ways in which self-perceptions can influence feelings of personal adjustment. Schachter and Latané suggest that highly neurotic people overreact to their physiological arousal in the same way that sociopaths underreact to physiological arousal. Neurotic people, according to Schachter and Latané, have an exaggerated tendency to apply emotional labels to their bodily states in situations that would be interpreted by most people as nonemotional and part of everyday life.[41]

Another example of the relation between self-perception and personal adjustment can be seen in the practice of teaching growing children to interpret their experiences with culturally appropriate labels.[42]

Children are taught not to equate dreams with waking life. Imagine a person who grew up believing that nightmares were real! Young girls are told in advance about menstrual periods. The experience of menstrual bleeding without advance explanation would be quite traumatic. The pleasure of sexual orgasm is probably also influenced by learning. Unexplained or unexpected orgasm could be disconcerting, if not aversive. Although most of human development requires children to absorb explanations from an adult point of view, some experiences are specifically characteristic of children. For example, an adult with absolutely no knowledge of children might interpret a child's fantasy play as a sign of severe pathology.

Brendan Maher has suggested that people who appear to be suffering from delusions may actually be searching for labels to explain unusual or extreme perceptual experiences. Let's say you are with a person who has an unusual or unexpected perceptual experience as a result of certain physiological idiosyncracies connected with his or her body. Because you are not aware of the cause of this perceptual experience and have no direct knowledge about what it feels like to the person, you cannot be of assistance in finding an explanation. At worst, you may influence the person to label the experience as something "abnormal." If no medical or physiological explanation for the perceptual experience can be found, the person will be motivated to search for other explanations. He or she may then attribute the unusual perceptual experience to things like cosmic rays, ESP, demons, or divine powers. Maher gives the example of an elderly person who is becoming hard of hearing. If the person is unaware of this hearing loss, it may appear that other people in the same room are whispering. When the elderly person attempts to validate this perception by asking the people why they are whispering, they say that they are *not* whispering. Since the other people have not been helpful in supplying an accurate label for the apparent whispering, the elderly person may explain it as a sign of some sort of conspiracy. Many of us have had unusual experiences that we have been fortunate enough to explain in a comforting and satisfactory manner. People who have unusual perceptual experiences because of physiological idiosyncracies within their bodies can be helped if they are taught to label these experiences as perceptual anomalies rather than signs of mental illness or irrational forces in the outside world.[43]

Stuart Valins and Richard Nisbett have described situations in which people would benefit from attributing bodily symptoms to *external* causes.[44] Stress from problems in work or school might be viewed as a natural response to a life crisis instead of a personal weakness. Shyness and nervousness could be understood not as an inadequacy but as a common and natural reaction to groups. Many college students would be happier if they attributed average grades in college to the highly selected college population rather than to loss of intelligence since high school. There are other situations in which it is most adaptive to attribute bodily reactions to *internal* causes. It is usually advantageous to attribute experiences of success to one's own efforts and abiltiy rather than to chance or luck. The ability to cope is better attributed to oneself than to a drug. Psychological addiction to stimulating or tranquilizing drugs may occur because people learn to attribute feelings of enthusiasm or relaxation to the drug and lose the sense that they can control their feelings from within. Research has shown that people who have learned to tolerate stress under the influence of tranquilizing drugs suffer reduced tolerance for stress when they no longer use the drugs.[45]

Some Implications and Applications

In this chapter I have introduced Schachter's theory of emotion and pointed out how it can help us understand the self-perception of experiences such as pain, thirst, hunger, guilt, hallucinations, and "madness." The studies summarized showed how people under presumably similar states of physiological arousal were influenced by their culture, past experiences, and motivations to label this arousal in very different ways. After learning about the importance of labeling in the self-perception of bodily states it has probably occurred to you that people can be taught to relabel certain "negative" bodily reactions in ways that are more culturally adaptive. Psychologists have developed a variety of techniques for teaching people to interpret intense arousal and stress with appropriate and adaptive emotional labels. Before presenting some of those techniques, I will review several research studies that analyze how people use their bodily states to interpret both attitudes toward certain issues and positive or negative affection for other people.

TWO

Attitudes,
Evaluations,
and Love

In Chapter One we learned that people perceive their bodily states by recognizing physiological messages from their bodies and then labeling these messages according to past experiences. People also use their bodily messages to interpret their attitudes toward objects and issues as well as to identify their feelings of positive or negative affection for others. In the first part of this chapter I will summarize research investigating the ways in which people label their bodily states as attitudes and feelings; this research was designed to measure how people perceive themselves as they experience varying amounts of arousal and are provided with different cues for labeling that arousal. Later in the chapter I will describe how people are influenced by their cultures to label their feelings as romantic attraction and love.

There are several different methods for manipulating people's experiences of arousal. The participants in Stanley Schachter's research were aroused with injections of adrenalin (see Chapter One). It is also possible to arouse people by threatening them with fear-provoking stimuli, such as electric shock, or by inducing them to engage in different types and degrees of antisocial behavior, like telling lies. Another method used by psychologists to manipulate people's perceptions of their arousal is to provide them with false feedback about their bodily states. Studies using this method place participants in a situation that leads them to believe they will be given accurate feedback about their physiological responses. Participants are hooked up to a physiological recording device and provided with an "arousal meter" that indicates their present state of physiological arousal. The meter readings are not real and can be manipulated by the experimenter to make participants perceive themselves as experiencing "high, medium, or low" physiological arousal. Because most people are not very accurate in discriminating their true physiological states, they find the fake arousal meter quite credible. Researchers can also deliver false feedback about arousal by telling people they are listening to their heartbeats over a speaker. The "heartbeats" can then be faked to appear very fast, medium, or very slow. This technique is also usually believable because most people are unable to discriminate what their heart is *really* doing.

It is obvious that changing people's actual arousal with drugs or experiences such as threat of electric shock is very different from changing people's perceived arousal with false feedback. Nevertheless, both of these methods are useful for testing Schachter's theory of emotion because Schachter's theory emphasizes that people label emotional states verbally according to how much they *believe* they are aroused in various situations. In this chapter we will explore how people label their perceived arousal in the immediate situation. Experiments using false feedback and experiments using actual arousal will be considered interchangeably. In Chapter Three, when we review research showing how false feedback has been used to study long-range adaptation to bodily responses, I will analyze important distinctions between real and perceived arousal, arguing that false feedback is more useful for influencing people's verbal responses than for altering their actual bodily states.

Self-Perception of Attitudes

According to Schachter's theory, people form attitudes by interpreting their arousal according to both past experiences and whatever positive or negative labels are available in the situation. A number of experiments have studied this notion by exposing people to various combinations of perceived (or real) arousal and external labels and measuring the attitudes they ultimately express.

One group of participants in an experiment was shown a film of Russia containing many cues that would imply danger to the United States.[1] The film contained scenes showing Russian armies and weapons that were designed to make the audience feel threatened. A second group of participants looked at slides of Russian scenery and architecture that were designed not to be threatening. All of the participants in the experiment were given false feedback with an "arousal meter" to make them think they were highly aroused. Then they were asked to specify their attitudes toward Russia on a questionnaire. Participants who viewed the non-threatening slides had no way to explain their "arousal" so they interpreted it as a negative reaction toward Russia. They were very unfavorable toward Russia on the questionnaire. Participants who viewed the threatening film could explain their "arousal" by attributing it to the scenes in the film they had just viewed. They were not as negative toward Russia because they interpreted their ostensible arousal as coming from the film rather than from the experience of evaluating Russia on the questionnaire.

Female participants in an experiment were asked to listen to tape recorded passages and rate them according to how much emotion the speaker was expressing.[2] While they were listening to the passages, the participants received false feedback from a meter that they were either aroused or relaxed. When the participants were led to believe they were aroused, they were more likely to perceive the passages as emotional. This was apparently because no other explanation had been provided to explain their "arousal" and it was therefore interpreted as a reaction to emotion in the spoken passages.

Female participants in a study were shown color slides of people who had experienced a violent death.[3] While viewing the slides the participants were led to believe they were listening to their heartbeats through a speaker. Participants who were given false feedback indicating that the rate of their heartbeat had increased in reaction to the slides rated the slides as being significantly more unpleasant and discomforting than participants whose "heart-rates" were supposedly not influenced by the slides. The participants receiving false feedback apparently interpreted their false heart-rates as an indication of their attitudes toward the generally negative slides. Male participants in a similar study were given false feedback about their heart-rates as they looked at a series of pictures.[4] Half of the participants were told by the experimenter that increased heart-rates were an indication of a positive reaction. These participants rated the pictures associated with false increases in heart-rate more favorably than pictures shown while their false heart-rates were stable. The remaining participants were told by the experimenter that increased heart-rates were a sign of a negative reaction. These participants rated the pictures associated with false increases in heart-rate less favorably than pictures shown while their false heart-rates were stable.

Male participants in an experiment were insulted by another male (who was a confederate of the experimenter), and an "anger meter" led them to believe that they experienced either very great, moderate, or very little anger toward the insulting person.[5] Participants were then given the opportunity as part of a learning test to deliver electric shocks to the person who had insulted them. Those participants who supposedly felt moderate anger delivered significantly more shocks than participants who supposedly experienced very slight anger. The participants who were supposedly very angry did not deliver particularly severe shocks. This was probably because they felt a bit guilty for feeling so much anger toward a person whose insult had been relatively minor. In all cases the false feedback influenced the participants' self-perception of anger.

White college students who evaluated themselves as unprejudiced were placed in a situation where they looked at a series of slides while receiving false feedback about their heart-rates.[6] Half of the participants were falsely led to believe they were prejudiced by making it appear that their heart-rates increased disproportionately to slides showing interracial interactions. It was thought that these students would feel guilty because they were shown to be "prejudiced" when they didn't think they really were. When the students left the building after receiving the false feedback about their "prejudice," they were confronted by a black student who asked, "Can you spare some change for some food?" The students who had been falsely made to feel prejudiced gave significantly more money to the black student than the students in the study who were not led to believe they were prejudiced. Unprejudiced college students in a second experiment were led to believe they were prejudiced with false heart-rate feedback.[7] Half of the students were confronted by a black panhandler immediately after the experiment and half of the students were not. Two days later, all of the participants were contacted by an organization called the "Brotherhood Society" and asked if they would be willing to volunteer some time to work for a fund raising drive. Students who had not been confronted earlier by the black panhandler volunteered significantly more time than students who had. This is probably because the students who were confronted by the black panhandler were able to alleviate the guilt they felt from the possibility of being prejudiced by giving him some money. The remaining students did not have this chance to alleviate their guilt from the threat of being prejudiced and therefore were more motivated to reduce their guilt by donating time to the "Brotherhood Society."

Changing People's Attitudes

The above research studies provide good examples of how people's attitudes can be influenced by their interpretation and labeling of perceived changes in their bodily states. This principle of self-perception has served as a basis for studies designed to modify people's attitudes. The strategy for changing people's attitudes toward certain issues or objects is to manipulate the degree to which they are aroused (or *believe* they are aroused) when they are thinking about or in the presence of these issues or objects. Researchers have attempted to change people's attitudes by placing them in situations where there are actual changes in their bodily states and also by giving people false feedback about ostensible changes in their bodily states.

False Feedback and Attitude Change

Female participants in an experiment were led to believe with an "arousal meter" that they were either very aroused or quite relaxed while listening to a tape-recorded speech.[8] Participants who perceived themselves as highly aroused were more influenced by the message in the speech than participants who perceived themselves as relaxed. This is apparently because the first group of participants interpreted their "arousal" as a sign that they were very involved with the speech and that it had a strong effect on them. The second group of participants apparently interpreted their "relaxation" as a sign of low interest and lack of involvement in the speech.

Female participants in another experiment listened to a tape recording containing a fear-arousing message about the dangers of pesticides.[9] After hearing the fear-arousing information about pesticides, the participants listened to a list of recommendations for coping with the problem. The experimenters, who wanted to see if they could influence the degree to which participants would accept the recommendations for dealing with pesticides, gave them false feedback about their bodily states during the messages with an "arousal meter." One group of participants was led to believe that they were highly aroused when they listened to the message about the dangers of pesticides and that they became fairly relaxed after hearing the recommendations for dealing with these dangers. Participants in a second group perceived themselves as being aroused by the message about pesticides but not relaxed by the recommendations. Participants in a third group were led to believe that they were relaxed throughout the entire experiment. As you can guess, it was the first group of participants who showed the greatest acceptance of the recommendations for coping with the dangers of pesticides. They could interpret their "arousal" during the message about the pesticides as fear and concern over the possible dangers. The "relaxing effect" of the recommendations convinced them that the recommendations must be valid. Participants in the second group, who were led to perceive themselves as fearful and concerned about pesticides but not to see their fear reduced by the recommendations, found the recommendations much less valid. The third group of participants did not perceive the message about pesticides as especially alarming because it had not "aroused" them and they therefore did not feel the recommendations were particularly important.

Manipulated Bodily States
and Attitude Change

Participants in an experiment were given a persuasive message to read and then tested to see how much the message had changed their attitudes.[10] Two groups of participants were given a caffeine pill before reading the message. One of these groups was told honestly what the pill was and that it would increase their physiological arousal. The second group of participants taking the caffeine pill was falsely told that it would have no affect on their feelings of arousal. A third group of participants in the experiment took a fake pill (a placebo) made up of powdered milk and sugar with the understanding that it would not affect their feelings of arousal. The second group of participants in this experiment showed the greatest change in attitude in response to the persuasive message. The people in this group were aroused and didn't know why. They were therefore in a position to attribute their arousal to the written message. The second group of participants apparently interpreted the arousal they felt as a deep involvement in the persuasive message. They showed significantly more agreement with the message than participants in the other two groups. Participants in the first group felt aroused but they knew this arousal was due to the caffeine pill. They had no reason to interpret their arousal as involvement with the persuasive message. The third group of participants was not aroused and also had no reason to feel involved with the persuasive message.

Male college students were asked to write an essay that would argue against their beliefs about free speech on campus.[11] All of the students were given a placebo pill. One group of students was falsely told that the pill would make them feel aroused and somewhat tense. A second group of students was falsely told that the pill would make them feel relaxed. The experimenters were interested in seeing which group would be most influenced by writing the counterattitudinal essay. The experience of writing an essay that goes against a person's beliefs is likely to cause feelings of tenseness and discomfort. Students in the first group could attribute the tenseness and discomfort they felt from writing the essay to the pill. Because they were likely to think it was the pill rather than the experience of writing the essay that made them feel uncomfortable, they had no reason to feel involved with the essay. For students in the second group, the tenseness and discomfort from writing a counterattitudinal essay was in direct conflict with the relaxation they expected to feel from the pill. These students were in a position to say to themselves, "I feel tense. If that pill was supposed to relax me and I still feel tense, I must *really* be tense." These students were led to believe that they were highly involved with the essay they had been asked to write. To reconcile or rationalize this perceived involvement with the essay, they were motivated to be influenced by its content. The second group of students who perceived themselves as emotionally involved with the counterattitudinal essay were more likely to change their attitudes to agree with the essay than the first group of students who felt very little emotional involvement with the essay.

Female college students in a similar experiment were told to make a brief speech in favor of a tuition increase.[12] It was known ahead of time that all the students opposed an increase in tuition, which means that delivering the speech would cause quite a bit of discomfort. The students were also led to believe that they would be in a second experiment where they would be given electric shock. At this point the female students have two reasons to be emotionally aroused: the anticipation of making a counterattitudinal speech and the threat of being shocked. The students were then exposed to another female who was supposedly a participant in the experiment but was actually a confederate of the experimenter. Half of the time the confederate said that she was really nervous about making the speech because other people would see it and she was worried about how it would turn out. The students who were exposed to this confederate had a reason to interpret the arousal they felt much more to the experience of making the speech than to the threat of electric shock. For the remaining students, the confederate acted in a way that would influence them to interpret most of their arousal as a reaction to the threat of being shocked. Which group of students was more likely to change their attitudes in favor of a tuition increase? The students who could attribute their arousal to the threat of shock had no reason to feel particularly involved with the experience of making a counterattitudinal speech. They paid little attention to the arguments they were asked to make in the speech and did not change their attitudes very much. The students who were influenced to interpret their arousal as a sign of involvement in the speech showed significantly more attitude change in favor of a tuition increase. They were led to believe that the experience of making the counterattitudinal speech was very emotionally involving. To explain or rationalize this emotional involvement to themselves, they were motivated to pay attention to the speech and to be influenced by its content.

Arousal in Personal Interactions

When people interact with each other they attempt to maintain a comfortable degree of personal intimacy.[13] If one person comes on too strongly by sitting very close, engaging in too much eye contact, or discussing personal feelings, the second person will back off a bit to compensate. If one person is very distant, the second person will generally attempt to increase the intimacy of the interaction by moving closer, looking more, or engaging in more personal conversation. Most people make small changes in their behaviors to maintain a comfortable degree of intimacy without any particular awareness of what they are doing. If a person makes a relatively large change affecting his or her intimacy with another, it is likely to cause an abrupt increase in the second person's arousal. If the second person labels this arousal in a positive manner, he or she will most likely be willing to reciprocate with greater intimacy toward the first person. If the second person labels the arousal in a negative manner, his or her most likely reaction will be one of escape or avoidance.[14]

Reactions to Physical Closeness

A series of experiments was conducted to demonstrate that reactions to physical closeness depend on how that closeness is interpreted within the particular context or situation.[15] Participants in these experiments interacted with an experimenter who sat either very close to them (less than one foot) or at what would be considered a moderate distance (about three feet). Results of these experiments showed that participants increased their liking for experimenters who sat close and who were friendly and complimentary. Participants decreased their liking for experimenters who sat close and acted unfriendly and uncomplimentary. In other words, physical closeness intensified participants' reactions to both the positive and negative behaviors of the experimenter. In another study, males using urinals in a lavatory were confronted by a male experimenter who stood either at the urinal right next to theirs or at a urinal further away.[16] Participants in this experiment were not specifically influenced to label the experimenter's physical closeness in a positive or negative manner. The experimenters had assumed that arousal from physical closeness by a strange man in a lavatory would be perceived as negative. Their reasoning was supported by the finding that males left their urinals faster when the experimenter was physically close.

Reactions to Gaze

Research has also shown that people are likely to interpret the arousal they feel from another's gaze according to the context or situation. Participants in two experiments increased their liking for experimenters who gazed at them in a positive interaction and decreased their liking for experimenters who gazed at them in a negative interaction.[17] People confronted on the street by an experimenter asking for help were most likely to comply when the experimenter gazed at them persistently and the type of help needed was well defined.[18] People were least likely to comply when the experimenter gazed persistently but described the request for help very ambiguously. When people receive a persistent gaze from another person in an ambiguous context they have no clear way of labeling their arousal and are motivated to escape from the situation. Subway riders in New York City were less likely to help an experimenter who "accidently" dropped a stack of papers if the experimenter had stared at them during the previous four minutes between stops.[19] Automobile drivers went through an intersection significantly faster when the traffic light turned green if an experimenter standing on the corner had gazed at them persistently while the traffic light was red.[20] In another study, experimenters asked people to give them a dime with either a legitimate or illegitimate explanation.[21] The legitimate explanation was that the experimenter needed to make a phone call; the illegitimate explanation was that the experimenter wanted to buy some gum. People were more willing to supply the dime for a phone call when the experimenter gazed persistently. In the context of a legitimate excuse, gaze was apparently interpreted positively. When the experimenter's excuse was illegitimate, people were less likely to supply the dime when the experimenter gazed persistently. In this illegitimate context, gaze from the experimenter was apparently interpreted negatively.

Perceiving Positive and Negative Feelings for Other People: An Explanation for Romantic Love

Ellen Berscheid and Elaine Walster have suggested that Schachter's theory of emotion may be useful for understanding how people interpret and label their feelings of positive and negative affection and romantic love.[22] Berscheid and Walster point out that people usually like someone who does things to them that are positive and dislike someone who does things that have a negative effect on them. However, they can feel romantic love for someone who does *either* positive *or* negative things to them.

Consider the example of the lover in an Associated Press story who explained tearfully, after kidnapping his former sweetheart, "The fact that she rejected me only made me want to love her more."[23] According to Schachter's theory, the lover experienced a good deal of arousal after being rejected by his girl friend and apparently interpreted this arousal as a strong feeling of *romantic love*. We know that the labels people give to feelings of arousal are learned and depend on their culture and past experiences. Other people might have labeled the arousal resulting from being rejected by a former lover as *hate* or *bitterness*. Margaret Mead has suggested that the arousal resulting from rejection by a loved one might be more appropriately labeled as *jealousy:*

> Jealousy is not a barometer by which the depth of love may be read. It merely records the degree of the lover's insecurity. It is a negative, miserable state of feeling, having its origin in a sense of insecurity and inferiority.[24]

Berscheid adds:

> Jealous people, however, usually interpret their jealous reactions in quite another way: jealous feelings are taken as evidence of passionate love rather than inferiority. Thus, in this culture, a jealous man is a loving man rather than an embarrassed man.[25]

Most of us have more than once perceived ourselves as feeling romantic love because we were physiologically aroused and the situation was conducive to labeling that arousal as romantic love. To study how Schachter's theory of emotion relates to romantic love, it is necessary to vary people's real or perceived states of physiological arousal as well as the situational cues that influence them to label their arousal as positive affection or love. There are a number of research studies that relate in one way or another to Berscheid and Walster's explanation of romantic love. In some of these studies researchers manipulated people's perceptions of their arousal with false feedback. In others, psychologists manipulated participants' actual states of arousal by placing them in different sorts of arousing or nonarousing situations. In discussing these studies I am using the term arousal in a very general sense because the participants' actual physiological states were seldom measured. In addition, the measures used evaluated liking or attraction rather than romantic love. Nevertheless, by analyzing these studies as an integrated body of research, we can relate them to Schachter's theory to elucidate further how people interpret their feelings of positive and negative affection for other people.

False Feedback and Reactions
Toward Other People

Male participants in two experiments were asked to look at photographs of women and rate how attractive the women were to them.[26] While they were looking at the pictures, the participants were led to believe they were listening to their heartbeats amplified through a loudspeaker. The heartbeats were fake and arranged so that they would speed up for some of the pictures and remain stable for others. Results of the experiments showed that participants were much more favorable toward the pictures associated with "increased" heart-rates rather than "stable" heart-rates. In terms of Schachter's theory, the participants perceived that some of the pictures had aroused them, and because the pictures were of attractive women, they interpreted this perceived arousal as positive attraction.

Male participants in a similar study were hooked up to a physiological recording instrument and asked to give their impressions of a number of photographs.[27] The participants were falsely told by the experimenter that some of the photographs had aroused them and that other photographs had not aroused them. When the photographs were of nude women, the participants evaluated them as more attractive and appealing when they thought they were aroused. When the photographs were somewhat repulsive, showing gory scenes of accident victims, the participants evaluated them as less attractive and appealing when they thought they were aroused. This experiment supports Schachter's theory by showing that people will label perceived arousal as a positive emotion when it is associated with attractive stimuli and they will label it as a negative emotion when it is associated with unattractive stimuli.

A third study using false feedback was set up so that 18- to 20-year-old female college students were interviewed by 23- to 25-year-old males about various aspects of college life.[28] During the interview the females were hooked up to a physiological recording instrument and falsely led to believe that they were either very aroused or relaxed. In addition, the females were given an evaluation from the interviewer which made them think he liked them very much, he liked them somewhat, or he strongly disliked them. The experimenters hypothesized that the females would label their perceived arousal as positive affection when it was associated with a positive interviewer and as negative affection when it was associated with a negative interviewer. This prediction was corroborated by the fact that females led to believe their interviewer disliked them were much less willing to return for a second interview if they thought his negative evaluation had caused them to be aroused. Females not led to believe they were aroused by the negative evaluation from the interviewer were not so reluctant to see him again. "Aroused" and "relaxed" females were equally willing to return for a second interview with an interviewer who gave them a positive evaluation.

Studies using false feedback about arousal are useful for theoretical purposes because they demonstrate how people can be influenced to label their arousal by cues and stimuli in the environment. However, because false feedback studies rely on a deception that people might eventually question, their value for changing people's self-perceptions over a long period of time is limited. Experiments in which participants' actual states of arousal are manipulated are also of theoretical value for demonstrating how people learn to label their bodily states according to cues in the environment. Experiments varying actual arousal also provide a test of Berscheid and Walster's explanation of romantic love that generates less suspicion on the part of people who are participating. One group of research studies using manipulated bodily states investigated how the labeling of *positive* feelings influences reactions toward other people. A second group of research studies *compared* the effects of positive and negative feelings on reactions toward other people. A third group of research studies investigated how the labeling of *negative* feelings influences reactions toward other people.

Positive Feelings and Reactions Toward Other People

In a study showing the influence of positive feelings on reactions toward other people, participants were shown a series of possible tasks they could do.[29] One group of participants actually worked on the tasks and it was arranged that they would be successful and receive a compliment from the experimenter. A second group of participants learned about how the tasks worked, but did not have the opportunity to experience success and receive a compliment from the experimenter. After this positive or neutral exposure to the tasks, the participants were confronted by a person who was in need of a favor. In one case, the person was collecting for a charity. In another case, the person was carrying a stack of books and needed help opening a door. In a third case, the person was carrying an armload of books and "accidently" dropped one of the books and needed help in picking it up. Results of the study showed that participants who had just experienced a positive feeling of success were significantly more likely to help the person in need than participants whose immediate feelings were neutral. In other words, participants' reactions toward other people become more positive with the "warm glow of success."

Positive reactions toward other people can be influenced by other favorable experiences besides success. In one study, experimenters tended telephone booths in San Francisco and Philadelphia shopping malls so that half of the people using them would "accidently" find a dime in the coin return slot.[30] The other half of the people using the phone booths did not find a dime. Immediately after leaving the phone booths, the people were confronted by a female experimenter who "accidently" dropped a manila folder full of papers in their path. Results showed that 87 percent of the people who had just found the dime would help the experimenter pick up her papers. Only 4 percent of the people who had not found a dime would help the experimenter pick up her papers.

In another study showing the effects of favorable experiences on reactions toward other people, a group of experimenters went to a university and distributed cookies to a random group of students who were studying.[31] A second group of students in the library did not get cookies and were not aware that the cookies were being distributed. A short time later, a person who appeared to be unrelated to the experimenters approached the students and asked if they would help him with a project he was doing for a psychology course. The confederate asked half of the students to help with the psychology project by volunteering to be friendly and helpful to other people. The remaining students were asked to volunteer to be unhelpful and annoying to other people. The students who had received the cookies were more willing than the other students to volunteer to be helpful to other people and less willing to volunteer to be unhelpful to other people. Apparently, the favorable experience of receiving cookies increased the students' willingness to volunteer as an assistant if the job they were asked to do was consistent with their internal positive feelings. They were not willing to volunteer for a job that was inconsistent with their internal feelings.

Research by Bernice Lott and Albert Lott has shown that when people have a positive experience in the presence of others they increase their liking for those who witnessed their success. In one study, elementary school students were given a task to complete.[32] It was arranged that some of the students would succeed and win a prize and that others would not succeed and would not win a prize. The successful children felt significantly more liking for other children who were present while they were working on the task than the unsuccessful children. A second study found that children who received attention and rewards from their teacher increased their liking for their classmates significantly more than children who were ignored by their teachers.[33] A third study was arranged so that some children would help other children play a game.[34] Children playing the game who won a prize were liked significantly more by the helping children than children playing the game who did not win a prize. This was true even though the helping children knew they would not share any of the prizes. Apparently, the vicarious positive experience of seeing another child win a prize and the knowledge that they had helped this happen were sufficient to enhance the helpers' feelings of liking for the successful children.

Adults also increase their liking for other people as a result of positive experiences. An experiment was set up so that college students would receive either a high or a low payment for participating in a psychology study.[35] The students given the high payment showed significantly more liking for a stranger who was present than the students receiving the low payment, even though the stranger had nothing to do with the payment. A similar study showed that college students had significantly more liking for a stranger when they received positive evaluations from an experimenter even though the stranger had nothing to do with the evaluations.[36]

It is clear that a person will increase his or her liking for other people if he or she has a positive experience while they are present, even if they are not directly responsible for that positive experience. We will now look at research investigating the effects of mixed feelings and negative feelings on reactions toward other people. Before reading on, it is important to remember that self-perceptions are influenced not only by bodily states, but also by the labeling and interpretation of those bodily states. Therefore it is not *necessarily* true that people dislike others after being aroused in a negative way.

Comparing the Effects of Positive and Negative Feelings

Female participants in an experiment were exposed to a movie that would arouse them either in a positive or a negative way.[37] Females in the positively aroused group saw a happy film, *Good Old Corn*. Females in the "negative" group saw a rather sad film, *John F. Kennedy 1917–1963*. After viewing their respective films, participants were asked to read some information about another female with whom they were unacquainted and to give their impressions of her on a rating form. The results of the experiment showed that participants who had viewed the positive film were significantly more favorable toward the female they were rating than participants who had viewed the negative film. Apparently, the participants' perceptions of how they felt toward the female were strongly influenced by the positive or negative nature of their arousal from the films.

Participants in a similar experiment were asked to read a series of statements and attempt to experience the feelings in the statements.[38] One group of participants was given statements that would promote positive feelings, such as, "I'm full of energy," and "God, I feel great!" A second group of participants read statements that would promote negative feelings, such as, "All of the unhappiness of my past life is taking possession of me," and "I want to go to sleep and never wake up." Later, all of the participants were asked to do a favor for someone who was supposedly unrelated to the experiment. Participants who had placed themselves in a positive mood were more willing to do the favor than participants who had placed themselves in a negative mood.

One group of males in a research study was given an article to read that depicted a romantic seduction scene.[39] A second group of males read a neutral article about herring gulls. After reading their article, the males were given a photograph of an attractive female and asked to give their impressions of her on a rating form. The males who had read the article with the seduction scene evaluated the female as being significantly more attractive than the males who had read the neutral article. Males who felt they would have an opportunity to date the female in the photograph rated her as more sexually receptive after reading the seduction article than after reading the neutral article. In terms of Schachter's theory, the males who had read the seduction article were more aroused than the males who had read the neutral article and were provided with the appropriate cues from the attractive female in the photograph to label this arousal as positive attraction.

Participants in another experiment were introduced to a person of the same sex (actually a confederate of the experimenter) who either expressed similar or dissimilar opinions as they discussed issues such as interracial marriage, homosexuality, marijuana, and birth control.[40] While the participants were interacting with the confederate their physiological arousal was recorded by measures of skin conductance. Results of the experiment showed that participants liked an agreeing confederate more when their physiological arousal was high rather than low. When participants interacted with a disagreeing confederate, they liked the confederate less when their arousal was high rather than low. One possible explanation for these results is that participants interpreted their physiological arousal as positive affection for a person who agreed with them and as negative affection for a person who disagreed with them. An explanation based on Schachter's theory would contend that agreement and disagreement from the confederate served as different kinds of cues for participants' labeling of arousal during the interaction.

Male participants in an experiment were given a series of personality tests.[41] Half of the participants received false results from the personality tests that would raise their self-esteem: They were told that they were extremely well adjusted. The remaining participants received false results that would lower their self-esteem: They were told that they were poorly adjusted. The participants were then placed in a situation where they received either a positive, neutral, or negative evaluation from a female. Compared with males whose self-esteem had increased, males with lowered self-esteem expressed more liking for the positive female and less liking for the negative female. We can explain this result by assuming that the males with lowered self-esteem were under a fairly high state of arousal. When they received an evaluation from a female that was favorable, they interpreted this arousal as positive affection. When they received an evaluation from a female that was unfavorable, they interpreted their arousal as negative affection.

Participants in an experiment were aroused with erotic literary passages and slides.[42] It turned out that some of the participants interpreted their arousal from the erotic material in a positive way by viewing themselves as sexually aroused, entertained, interested, and curious. These participants perceived themselves as being more attracted toward a person of the opposite sex to whom they were introduced than participants who had not been exposed to the erotic materials. Other participants reacted to their arousal from the erotic materials in a negative way by viewing themselves as sexually "turned off," disgusted, and bored. These participants were not any more or less) attracted toward a person of the opposite sex to whom they were introduced than participants who had not been exposed to the erotic materials. It appears that participants in this experiment only used arousal as a cue for liking if they could interpret it in a positive manner.

Harvey Hornstein has summarized a number of studies showing how a person's feelings often become positive toward other people upon hearing good news and negative toward other people in the presence of bad news.[43] A few hours after John F. Kennedy was killed, a group of men and women who were participating in a scientific study were asked to record their views of humanity.[44] Those people who were most fond of President Kennedy reported feeling very pessimistic about human nature and the general moral-ethical disposition of other people. Four months later, when the passage of time had attenuated the negative experience of the murder, the supporters of President Kennedy were considerably less negative in their outlook toward humanity. The grief from Kennedy's death had at least temporarily affected their feelings toward other people.

College students who had signed up to take part in a study of decision-making were seated alone in a room to wait until the experimenter was ready for them.[45] While the students were waiting they could hear music coming from a radio. After a few minutes there was a news report. The news report, designed to be part of the experiment, was not real. An announcer reported one of the following two stories in a trained professional voice. Half of the students heard a rather positive news story:

> A middle-aged man will be saved thanks to a person he has never met. The man, who suffers from a fatal kidney disease, had only a short while to live without an emergency kidney transplant. WWBG had broadcast pleas for help. Late last night a respected clergyman came to the hospital and offered to help. The donor has refused the family's offer to pay his hospital costs. Even in this day and age, some people hear a call for help.[46]

The remaining students heard a negative news story:

> A seventy-two-year-old sculptress, beloved by neighborhood children for her statues of Winnie-the-Pooh, was strangled in her apartment last night by what appears to be a self-styled executioner. The murderer, who has been identified as a respected clergyman, was a long-time neighbor of the victim. He had the keys to the apartment because he occasionally babysat for the victim's grandchildren and was in the habit of bringing up her mail and packages.[47]

After the news story the radio continued playing music until it was turned off by the experimenter who then asked the students a series of questions about their views of human nature. Because the students who had heard the two different news reports believed the broadcasts were real, they were influenced to feel quite differently toward humanity. Students who had heard the good news were more likely than students who had heard the bad news to believe that people lived clean and decent lives, were basically honest, and tried to apply the Golden Rule even in today's complex society. Two other groups of students who had heard one of the above news reports were given the opportunity to play a game with a stranger in which there was a chance to make money. The students were told that they and the stranger could either compete and try to beat each other or cooperate and share whatever they earned by working together. Students who had heard the good news report expressed significantly more trust and willingness to cooperate with the stranger than students who had heard the bad news report.

A group of middle-aged women was placed in a situation where they "overheard" either a good or bad news report.[48] The women were then asked to read summaries of two law suits. In one case a man was being accused of murder. In the second case a man was being sued for injuries sustained by a passenger in his car during an accident. The women who had heard the good news were far more likely to judge the man innocent in both cases than the women who had heard the bad news.

Negative Feelings and Reactions Toward Other People

The research studies summarized in the last two sections support Berscheid and Walster's application of Schachter's theory to romantic love and positive affection by showing that favorable reactions toward other people increase when a person's feelings are positive and the cues in the environment are appropriate for labeling those positive feelings as liking. In this section we will review experiments showing that favorable reactions toward other people can also increase as a result of negative feelings. These experiments are especially important for supporting Berscheid and Walster's theory because they demonstrate that it is not our bodily states *per se* that govern our reactions toward other people, but rather the manner in which we interpret and label these bodily states. Berscheid and Walster point out that people aroused by a negative experience may perceive this arousal as positive affection for someone they are thinking about or as positive affection for an attractive or desirable person who is in their presence. Negative experiences might also lead to positive affection because thinking about or being with another person is calming and reassuring.[49]

One group of males in an experiment was aroused with the threat of electrical shock.[50] A second group of men was not threatened with electrical shock. The men were then introduced to an attractive female. The men who had been threatened with shock were significantly more favorable in their evaluations of the female on a rating form than the men who had not been threatened with shock. Even though threat of shock is a somewhat negative event, the males apparently interpreted the arousal they felt from threat of shock as a sign of attraction toward the female.

Unaccompanied male tourists between the ages of 18 and 35 years were approached by a male or female experimenter on one of two bridges over the Capilano River in British Columbia.[51] The experimenter explained that he/she was doing a project for a psychology class to study the relationship between exposure to scenic attractions and creative expression. The male tourists were asked to fill out a questionnaire and give their free associations to a series of pictures. After assisting with the ostensible psychology project, the males were given a telephone number they could call if they wanted to learn about the results of the study. Half of the males approached by the experimenter were on a high suspension bridge, constructed of wooden boards attached to wire cables. This bridge is constructed in a way that is likely to induce physiological arousal in people who cross it because it has a tendency to wobble and sway. The bridge also has low handrails that permit a clear view of the 230 foot drop to the rapids below. The remaining males were approached by the experimenter on a solid wooden bridge that is only 10 feet above the water. We can see that the males on the suspension bridge were in a position to be considerably more physiologically aroused than the males on the solid bridge. Males on the suspension bridge gave significantly more free associations to the pictures that included themes of sexual imagery than males on the solid bridge. Males on the suspension bridge were also significantly more likely to call the female experimenter to "find out about the experiment." Apparently, the males interpreted their arousal on the suspension bridge as attraction in the presence of a female experimenter. When the experimenter was a male, there was no difference between males on the suspension bridge and solid bridge in either their free associations or frequency of calling. Not surprisingly, males did not interpret their arousal on the suspension bridge as positive attraction when the experimenter was a male.

Because it is possible that men who are willing to cross the suspension bridge are different from a random group of men on the solid bridge, the experiment was repeated in a different way. One group of males was approached by a female experimenter while they were on the suspension bridge. A second group of males was approached by a female experimenter 10 minutes after crossing the suspension bridge. It was thought that the men on the suspension bridge would be more aroused than the men who had 10 minutes to relax. The results of this experiment were similar to those of the first experiment. Males gave more free associations with sexual imagery and were more likely to call the female experimenter if they were approached while on the suspension bridge than if approached after they had already crossed it.

To complete their study of how anxiety affects sexual attraction, the researchers looked at the influence of arousal on males' responses to females in a more controlled way. They arranged it so that one group of male participants in an experiment would be threatened with strong electrical shock and a second group of males would be threatened with weak electrical shock. Results of this experiment were similar to the experiment just described. Males who were threatened with strong shock said they were more attracted toward a female who was present and gave more sexual imagery in the free associations to pictures than males who were threatened with weak shock. In terms of Schachter's theory of emotion, the males who were threatened with strong shock were more aroused than the males threatened with weak shock and therefore more likely to perceive themselves as attracted to the female.

Elaine Walster and her colleagues hypothesized that an interesting example of how negative feelings can lead to increased positive attraction is found in the strategy of "playing hard-to-get."[52] A woman who plays hard-to-get increases a man's frustration and it is traditionally thought that this frustration will be interpreted by the man as increased desire and attraction for the woman. Socrates gave the following advice to a woman over two thousand years ago:

> They will appreciate your favors most highly if you wait till they ask for them. The sweetest meats, you see, if served before they are wanted seem sour, and to those who had enough they are positively nauseating; but even poor fare is very welcome when offered to a hungry man. [The woman inquires] And how can I make them hunger for my fare? [Soc-

rates' reply] Why, in the first place, you must not offer it to them when they have had enough—by a show of reluctance to yield, and by holding back until they are as keen as can be for them the same gifts are much more to the recipient than when they are offered before they are desired.[53]

Ovid, the Roman poet, gave similar advice:

Fool, if you feel no need to guard your girl for her own sake, see that you guard her for mine, so I may want her the more. Easy things nobody wants, but what is forbidden is tempting. . . . Anyone who can love the wife of an indolent cuckold, I should suppose, would steal buckets of sand from the shore.[54]

Bertrand Russell argued more recently:

The belief in the immense value of the lady is a psychological effect of the difficulty of obtaining her, and I think it may be laid down that when a man has no difficulty in obtaining a woman, his feeling toward her does not take the form of romantic love.[55]

With the inspiration of these writers, Walster and her colleagues set out to test the influence of playing hard-to-get on interpersonal attraction.[56] Male college students who were participating in a computer dating program were given the name and telephone number of a female who randomly played easy-to-get or hard-to-get. When the males called the easy-to-get female, she immediately accepted their offer for a date. The hard-to-get female made it somewhat more difficult for the males by saying:

Mmmm (slight pause) No, I've got a date then. It seems like I signed up for the Date Match thing a long time ago and I've met more people since then—I'm really pretty busy all week.[57]

Finally, the hard-to-get female also accepted the date. When the males were asked to evaluate their attraction for the easy-to-get and hard-to-get females there was no difference. In this situation, playing hard-to-get had no effect on liking.

Walster and her colleagues next attempted to test the influence of playing hard-to-get by enlisting the assistance of a prostitute. For half of her clients the prostitute played hard-to-get and said:

Just because I see you this time it doesn't mean that you can have my phone number or see me again. I'm going to start school soon, so I won't have much time, so I'll only be able to see the people that I like the best.[58]

For her other clients, the prostitute did not communicate this message. Results of the experiment showed that playing hard-to-get was not successful in increasing the clients' attraction toward the prostitute. When the prostitute played hard-to-get her clients were no more likely to call her back, offer her more money, or say they liked her than when she played easy-to-get.

These two failures to show that playing hard-to-get can increase the attraction of men toward women prompted Walster and her co-workers to refine their approach. After interviewing a number of men it became clear that although women may appear less desirable when they are very easy-to-get, they may also appear too threatening and distant when they play very hard-to-get. To test out this possibility, a third study was designed in which male college students were placed in a situation where they were given the choice of dating one of three women. To control for physical appearance, the men did not actually meet the women but were given the following information about how the women supposedly felt. The first woman appeared easy-to-get. She made it clear that she was equally willing to date any of the men. The second woman appeared hard-to-get. She stated that she was not enthusiastic about dating any man in the group. The third woman gave information to the effect that she was interested in dating the particular man in question but was not interested in dating any of the other men in the study. The third woman who was selectively hard-to-get was overwhelmingly preferred. The men felt that the easy-to-get woman was friendly and warm, but also unselective and possibly unpopular and overdependent. In short, the easy-to-get woman appeared to be "just another date." The hard-to-get woman appeared to the men as very selective and popular, but also as cold, rigid, and unfriendly. The hard-to-get woman was seen as a challenge, but also as someone who might be picky and hard to get along with. The selectively hard-to-get woman appeared to the men as friendly and warm and also as popular and selective. The men thought she would be easy to get along with and they liked her because she had specifically chosen them as a date rather than "just anybody."

Although a hard-to-get woman may be arousing, she apparently does not provide the proper cues for most men to label this arousal as positive attraction. It is true that men with very high self-esteem may be more likely to be attracted to a hard-to-get woman than men with low self-esteem. I will discuss the question of individual differences in self-perception of attraction later in the chapter. First, let us look at an example of how frustration may lead to increased feelings of romantic attraction.

Throughout history there have been countless instances where external threats have increased the solidarity of people in danger. The same process often holds for romantic couples. We need only consider Romeo and Juliet as an example of love blossoming under opposition. A psychological study of what could be called "the Romeo and Juliet effect" was conducted in the following manner.[59] A total of 49 dating couples and 91 married couples were studied during the course of about a year. During this time the experimenters took measures of how much each couple felt they were in love and how much interference was imposed upon the relationship by either the male's or female's parents. Results of the study showed a fairly strong correlation between the amount of parental interference in the relationship and the couples' ratings of romantic love for one another. Although it is true that parents can often break up a relationship, this study provides an example of how the frustration and challenge from parental opposition can lead couples to have perceptions of increased romantic love for one another.

Self-Perception of Love

While reading about Berscheid and Walster's theory of romantic love and the related research studies, you probably thought of times when you experienced the influence of learning on your labeling of feelings as love. We can understand how people learn to label their feelings as love on a broad scale by comparing differences between cultures. We can also understand how people learn to label feelings as love by looking at research that has studied individual differences between people.

How Cultures Teach Love

One has only to attend a Hollywood movie to be reminded how deeply American culture is preoccupied with the experience or wish to experience feelings of romance and love. It is true that people in many other cultures also learn to appreciate romantic love. Few cultures, however, go to the same extremes as American culture in emphasizing romantic love as a necessary and often *sufficient* condition for marriage.[60] The following description gives a fairly clear characterization of the American "Romantic Dream":

> The telling of the myth is begun in the nursery with fairy tales: Cinderella, Sleeping Beauty, Snow White, Frog Prince, and half a hundred less famous stories. Hardly a child *believes* the tales, but they all have the same message: A handsome prince overcomes obstacles to marry the poor maiden with whom he has fallen in love; they are married and live in bliss. Alternately, the handsome but poor peasant boy overcomes ob-

stacles to marry the princess, with whom he has fallen in love; they are married and live in bliss. Always beauty, always obstacles, always love, always a class barrier (presumably changing from frog to human leaps an ethnic barrier), always married bliss. The unsaid last line of each story is "some day this may happen to you." Parents set the proper example for their children by relating to the child their own prince-and-beauty story. "Why did you marry Daddy?" "Because we fell in love."[61]

The practice of basing marriage on feelings of passion is not practical because physiological arousal (and the labeling of that arousal as love) is a temporary state. Marriage should be based on something more enduring. The European social critic Denis de Rougemont expressed the following analysis of the practice of marrying for love:

> We are in the act of trying out one of the most pathological experiments that a civilized society has ever imagined, namely, the basing of marriage, which is lasting, upon romance, which is a passing fancy.[62]

Isn't everyone who gets married in love? Not necessarily. We all know of societies where marriages are prearranged for practical rather than romantic reasons. A Kwakiutl Indian of Vancouver Island gave the following description of his marriage:

> When I was old enough to get a wife—I was about twenty-five—my brother looked for a girl in the same position that I and my brothers had. Without my consent, they picked a wife for me—Lagious' daughter. The one I wanted was prettier than the one they chose for me, but she was in a lower position than me, so they wouldn't let me marry her. I argued about it and was very angry with my brother, but I couldn't do anything. . . . Anyway, my older brother made arrangements for my marriage. He gave Lagious, the head chief of the Nimkis, two hundred blankets to keep Lagius from letting others have his daughter.[63]

A Baiga woman in India was married in a similar manner:

> In Dadaragon I was forcibly married to Marru. None of us wanted the marriage. I was too young, only ten years old, and my father didn't like Marru. But my brother Chaitu had run away with Marru's wife, and Marru said he must have a girl in return.[64]

In Japan, arranged marriages are known as *miai:*

> I was the youngest among my brothers and sisters. They were all married and I was left alone as a single woman. My mother got high blood pressure from worry about my being unmarried. My family were anxious to arrange a marriage as soon as possible and showed my mother the picture of my prospective husband. I was thus in haste to marry. After

the *miai,* I did not love my partner but I married him. It was not for my sake but because I wanted to relieve my mother and my family of their anxiety that I decided to marry.[65]

Although most of you will agree that marriages should not be based strictly on romantic love, you are unlikely to accept the practice of arranged marriages as a suitable alternative. There are two important questions that arise at this point. First, how does it happen that cultures differ so widely in the process of mate selection? Second, how have we in American culture learned to compensate for the dangers involved in basing marriage primarily on the existence of romantic love?

Paul Rosenblatt and his colleagues studied some 60 societies throughout the world and arrived at the following conclusions about when love and affection are most likely to be used as a basis for marriage.[66] Love is useful for marriage in societies where people have little freedom in choosing a mate because it gives couples in arranged marriages some justification for why they were married and increases their commitment to each other. Love is useful in societies where it is difficult for young people to escape the parental home. "Falling in love" gives motivation for breaking away from the parents. Love is used as a basis for marriage when economic dependence between partners is weak. If both members of a couple have jobs and don't depend on each other for the necessities of living, they need something like love to hold them together. Love is also useful for holding together couples who live with kin because much of their economic support comes from other members of the family. Love between marriage partners is valuable if it is needed to protect marriages from the intrusion of kin. When other members of the family are constantly visiting or calling on the telephone the couple can maintain a close relationship with feelings of love.

We can see from Rosenblatt's research that American society is characterized by many of the factors that encourage the inclusion of romantic love in marriage relationships. To understand how American culture has attempted to solve the problems of basing marriage on love we must remind ourselves of the influence of learning on the self-perception of emotion. Schachter's theory argues that emotions are labels people learn for physiological states of arousal. But how do people learn to label arousal as romantic love? Our society gives us a good deal of help. There are "eligible" and "ineligible" potential marriage partners for all of us and we find out at a very young age to recognize who they are. Our parents influence us by teaching us to label strong attractions toward ineligible people as *infatuation* and strong attractions toward eligible people as *love.* When we get older we often learn to label a relationship in retrospect. If the relationship flowers and is long-lasting, we interpret our involvement as *love*. If the relationship dies, we conclude that we were merely *infatuated*.[67] Our culture is fairly clear in specifying who is eligible for the label of love. An eligible person is usually from a similar background. Research has shown that whites in the United States marry other whites 99.8 percent of the time and that blacks marry blacks 99 percent of the time.[68] Marriage partners in the United States belong to the same religion 93.6 percent of the time.[69] A study of dating couples found that couples who agreed closely on personal values were more likely to progress toward a permanent relationship than couples whose agreement was not so close.[70] Another study found that college students were significantly more attracted toward dates who had similar rather than dissimilar attitudes on issues such as belief in God, birth control, drinking, women's liberation, and preferred entertainment.[71]

Our society teaches us to be more liberal with self-perceptions of romantic love for people who are physically attractive. We must search for other justifications before we can label our feelings as romantic love toward physically unattractive people.[72] Ralph Linton described the American preoccupation with physical attractiveness in the following manner:

> All societies recognize that there are occasional violent emotional attachments between persons of the opposite sex, but our present American culture is practically the only one which has attempted to capitalize on these and make them the basis for marriage. The hero of the modern American movie is always a romantic lover, just as the hero of an old Arab epic is always an epileptic. A cynic may suspect that in any ordinary population the percentage of individuals with capacity for romantic love of the Hollywood type was about as large as that of persons able to throw genuine epileptic fits.[73]

Our society has traditionally taught different labeling processes to males and females. Females from traditional backgrounds learn that "nice" girls don't have sexual relations unless they are in love. They are therefore under a cultural obligation to label feelings of sexual arousal as love and also to seek similar labels from the male. Males are taught that they must be in love to get married, but not necessarily to have sexual relations. Males from traditional backgrounds usually do not learn to label sexual arousal as love.[74] In fact, it was not uncommon for middle class men in the 1960s to say that they would have sexual relations with an "undesirable" female but not with someone they really wanted to marry.[75] It may surprise you that one study found college men to be less willing than college females to marry a person they did not love (if the person had other suitable qualities).[76] Presumably, this is because females have learned more than males to give weight to factors such as education, social background, and future employment in choosing a marriage partner. It would be interesting to determine whether traditional differences between the ways in which men and women label love have been modified in the last ten years by the sexual revolution and movements toward male and female liberation.

Individual Differences

Whether or not people interpret their feelings as love depends on past experiences and how they perceive themselves. What makes some people more romantic than others? Research has shown that people who are not defensive and who are willing to admit personal shortcomings are more likely to experience romantic love than people who are highly defensive. People who are not defensive and who also have high self-esteem have the greatest tendency to experience romantic love.[77] Research has also shown that people who see themselves as having a large amount of control over their fate are less likely to experience romantic love than people who perceive their fate more strongly influenced by external factors.[78] This is probably because romantic love is commonly seen as something mysterious that "happens to us" or "engulfs us" rather than as an emotion that we "choose to experience." It is also likely that people who view love as reflecting dependency and weakness are less likely to experience romantic love than people who do not.[79]

We can influence how people label their feelings toward us by how we respond to them. Berscheid and Walster give the example of insecure men or women who habitually complain, "You don't love me, you just think you do; if you loved me, you wouldn't treat me this way."[80] The men or women who then go on to itemize evidence for this conclusion are helping their partners to label these behaviors as a reflection of rather negative feelings. Berscheid and Walster suggest that men or women with a great deal of tact and self-confidence could help their partners to label the same behaviors as a reflection of positive feelings. You might want to ponder the question of how you have learned to label your feelings of romance and affection toward other people.

Some Conclusions

Attitudes toward issues, objects, and other people are influenced by a person's awareness and self-labeling of bodily arousal. Self-awareness of bodily states can be influenced by the manipulation of actual arousal with drugs or fear-provoking stimuli, or by the control of perceived arousal with false feedback. Labels for bodily states can be influenced by changes in the context or apparent causes of arousal. If researchers can alter the manner in which other people label their feelings, we can certainly learn to control the ways in which we label our own feelings. Chapter 3 will present a more generalized discussion of the self-perception of bodily states, including an analysis of reactions to such experiences as fear, anxiety, and pain. It will also suggest ways in which we can use our knowledge of awareness and labeling of bodily states to live with our bodies in a more adaptive manner.

THREE

Learning to Live
with Our Bodies

Our examination of how people interpret messages from their bodies has revealed that learning can influence the self-perception of bodily states. If people label their bodily messages the way they do *because* of learning, it stands to reason that they can change those labels as a *result* of learning. The understanding of how people learn to label their bodily states has led to some exciting research into methods for teaching people to live with their bodies in more adaptive ways. In one group of research studies, experimenters attempted to modify people's perceptions of their bodily states through false feedback and misattribution. False feedback and misattribution are theoretically useful because they can demonstrate the influence of self-labeling on reactions to experiences such as anxiety, pain, and insomnia. However, the therapeutic value of false feedback and misattribution is limited because the effects of these techniques are often temporary. In another group of studies, psychologists attempted to teach people methods of self-relaxation that they could rely on for coping with anxiety and for enhancing self-control in difficult situations. In a third group of studies, researchers directed people to actively relabel or reinterpret their bodily reactions. This approach has much in common with procedures employed in hypnotism and acupuncture. Based on the development of positive motivation and effective cognitive strategies, the techniques of adaptive relabeling have been applied to research in pain tolerance, learning, sexual behavior, and personal adjustment.

False Feedback and Misattribution

Changing Labels for Anxiety and Pain

False feedback has been used not only to influence people's attitudes toward various issues and modify their feelings of positive or negative affection for other people (see Chapter Two), but also to change people's perceptions of pain and anxiety.

Participants in one experiment looked at a series of color slides and at the same time listened to what they thought were their heartbeats being played through a speaker.[1] Half of the slides projected pictures of snakes and half of the slides projected the word "SHOCK." The false heartbeats were arranged so that the participants would think their heart-rates were dramatically increased by the word "shock," but not by the pictures of snakes. Basing their predictions on Schachter's theory of emotion, the researchers assumed the participants would say to themselves: "My heart-rate really sped up when I saw the word 'SHOCK,' but it did not increase when I saw the pictures of snakes. I must be a lot more scared of shock than I am of snakes." The participants were later significantly more willing to approach and touch a live (nonpoisonous) snake than another group of participants who had also seen the slides but had been told that the sounds from the speaker were meaningless noise they should try to ignore.

A group of 60 college students who reported experiencing considerable fear when they had to speak in front of other people volunteered to participate in a study during which they would give three short speeches.[2] All of the students gave the first three-minute speech under the same practice conditions. Before giving the second three-minute speech the students were randomly divided into five different groups. The first three groups of students were given a small earphone and led to believe that they would be listening to their heartbeats. The "heartbeats" were falsely arranged to either increase, decrease, or remain stable during the course of the second speech. The fourth group of students was told that they would hear meaningless sounds in the earphone and the fifth group of students wore an earphone that remained silent. The third three-minute speech was given by all students under the same conditions with no earphone.

Results of the study showed that there were no apparent differences between the five groups of students during the second speech. During the third speech, some interesting effects of the false heart-rate feed-back appeared. Students who believed their heart-rates had increased during the second speech rated themselves as significantly more anxious and showed significantly more signs of anxiety in their behavior than students who believed their heart-rates had decreased or remained stable during the second speech. Reactions of students who had supposedly heard meaningless sounds or no sounds at all were similar to those of students who believed their heart-rates had decreased or remained stable. The authors of this study concluded that people can learn to reduce their anxiety about giving speeches if they practice making speeches and at the same time are taught to view themselves as relaxed. It is much less likely that people who are anxious about giving speeches will benefit from practice speeches if they continue to view themselves as anxious and aroused.

False feedback alters people's interpretations of their bodily states by influencing the perceived *intensity* of bodily reactions to various objects, experiences, and situations. A second method of influencing people's interpretations of their bodily states is to alter their perceptions of the *causes* of various bodily reactions. This method relies on a type of mis-attribution generated by influencing people to attribute their bodily states to causes that are provided by the experimenter rather than to the real causes in the original situation. Many experiments have attempted to convince people to misattribute the causes of various bodily reactions to a placebo. You will remember from Chapter One that a placebo is a harmless substance given to people in a pill or an injection to make them think they are taking a drug of some sort when they really are not. A necessary control factor in all drug studies, the placebo can produce some very interesting psychological effects.

Male participants volunteered to take part in a series of studies investigating tolerance for electric shock. Participants were exposed to increasingly intense electric shocks until they reported that the shocks were becoming painful and they wished them discontinued. This arrangement assured participants that they would not have to suffer excessive discomfort.

In one study, half of the participants were given a placebo pill and told that it would cause them to be physiologically aroused.[3] It was explained that the pill would cause shaking in the hands, an increase in heart-rate and rate of breathing, and a feeling of "butterflies" in the stomach. The remaining participants were given a placebo pill with the expectation that it would cause them to be generally relaxed and possibly itch. Because participants were being given electric shocks, they were in reality under a fairly high state of physiological arousal. Participants in the first group had been given a pill that would supposedly arouse them in the same way as the shocks. They could attribute the actual arousal they experienced from the shocks to the false descriptions of the pill. They were willing to tolerate significantly more shocks than participants in the second group because they did not perceive the shocks as bothering them very much. Participants in the second group were not willing to tolerate as many shocks. They could not use the pill to explain the arousal they felt from the experience of being shocked. They interpreted their arousal as a sign that the shocks were aversive.

Participants in two other studies were given a series of electric shocks that were secretly made less intense over time.[4] This secret reduction of the intensity of the shocks gave participants the impression that they were increasing their tolerance for the shocks. Half of the participants were told that this "increased" tolerance for shocks was due to a placebo pill they had taken earlier. The pill was described as a drug that would help them tolerate pain. The remaining participants were told that the placebo pill would have no effect on their pain tolerance. They were led to believe that the "increased" tolerance for shock they had experienced was just that.

Results of these studies showed that participants in the second group were willing to tolerate more shocks in a second testing session than participants in the first group. In a third testing session, there was no difference in amount of shocks tolerated by participants in the first and second groups. Apparently what happened was that participants in the second group were led to believe after the first testing session that their "increased" tolerance for shock was due to themselves. Thinking that they had successfully increased their tolerance, they were willing to take more shocks during the second testing session. Because the shocks were not secretly reduced during the second testing session, these participants quickly realized that the shocks were still unpleasant. By the time of the third testing session the false perception of increased tolerance for shock had been disproved and the participants reacted toward the shocks as they had at the beginning.

Female participants in a study were given the choice of working on one of two puzzles.[5] Successful performance on the first puzzle would supposedly enable the participants to avoid a painful electric shock. Successful performance on the second puzzle would supposedly earn the participants a reward of money. At this point, we can understand that the participants would generally be scared of receiving a painful shock and would prefer to spend most of their time on the first puzzle. In this study researchers did not use a placebo to influence participants to misattribute their fear of shock. Instead, they arranged for the participants to be exposed to a fairly loud noise. One group of participants was told that they could expect the noise to cause their hands to shake, their heart to pound, their breathing to speed up, and a feeling of "butterflies" in their stomach. Because these are the same reactions people experience when threatened with shock, the experimenters thought that the participants in this group would misattribute a good deal of their original fear from the threat of shock to the loud noise. A second group of participants was told that the noise would cause dizziness, a dull headache, a ringing sensation in the ears, and weariness. These participants would not be able to attribute their fear from the threat of shock to the noise.

The results of the study supported the above expectations. Participants in the first group spent the greatest proportion of their time working on the money-reward puzzle, apparently because they misattributed their bodily reactions from threat of shock to the loud noise and consequently did not see the threat of shocks as particularly aversive. Participants in the second group spent the greatest proportion of their time on the shock-avoidance puzzle. These participants could not use the presence of the loud noise to reinterpret the bodily reactions they were experiencing from threat of shock. They had apparently interpreted their bodily reactions as a sign that the threat of shocks was aversive, which motived them to decrease the threat.

Female college students were asked to perform a series of problem-solving tasks after their anxiety had been aroused with the threat of electric shock.[6] One group of students was told that it would not be unusual for them to feel a bit nervous in the face of receiving electric shocks. A second group of students was given a placebo pill and told that the pill would make them feel somewhat anxious and nervous. A third group of students was given no explanation to go along with the original threat of electric shock. Results of the experiment showed that students in the first two groups performed significantly better on the problem-solving tasks than students in the third group. The first two groups of students felt anxious while performing the tasks but they could explain this anxiety to themselves by attributing it to their awareness of fear of shock or to the placebo pill. Students in the third group had no apparent explanation for their anxiety and presumably convinced themselves that they were anxious because they were weak in performing the problem-solving tasks. A second related experiment showed that women were more successful with problem-solving tasks under threat of electric shock if they were in menstruation. This effect was especially prevalent for women who experience relatively high menstrual discomfort. Apparently, women who experience great menstrual discomfort were able to attribute the anxiety they felt from the threat of electric shock to the fact that they were in menstruation; women who do not experience menstrual discomfort or who were not menstruating evidently attributed their anxiety to self-doubt about their ability to perform successfully on the tasks. Students in the above experiments were under the same states of physiological arousal caused by threat of electric shock. The attributions or labels they gave to this arousal (threat of shock, a placebo pill, menstrual discomfort, the tasks) significantly influenced their performance on the problem-solving tasks.

A group of dental patients was given a placebo injection and told that the injection would increase their heart-rate and cause them to feel physiologically aroused.[7] It was predicted that these patients would be influenced to misattribute their dental anxiety to the placebo and they would therefore feel less anxious about the dental treatment. A second group of dental patients was given a placebo injection and told that the injection would decrease their heart-rate and cause them to feel physiologically relaxed. These patients were expected to feel very anxious about the dental treatment because they would say to themselves: "That injection was supposed to relax me. But I still feel aroused, so I must be really anxious about the dental treatment." The results of the study showed that the manipulation toward misattribution did not change the perceived anxiety of most patients because they could not be convinced to believe in the false effects of the placebo injection. Some success with the misattribution treatment was achieved with patients who came into the dental office with very high anxiety about dental treatment. It is possible that highly anxious people are more likely to search for and believe in explanations for their anxiety such as the "arousing" placebo used in this study. The results for highly anxious patients may also be due to the fact that anxious people are probably more aware of their true bodily states and therefore pay more attention to their anxiety in a situation where a placebo is supposed to relax them but really doesn't.

The fact that the study with dental patients was not fully successful in changing self-perceptions of anxiety suggests that the use of misattribution techniques for therapeutic applications may be limited. I will discuss this inference in greater detail later in this chapter. First it will be worthwhile to learn how clinicians have applied misattribution techniques to therapy for insomnia and cigarette smoking.

Changing Labels for Insomnia

People who reported they suffered from insomnia were divided into three groups.[8] The first group of insomniacs was given a placebo pill and told that the pill would physiologically arouse them. They were led to believe that the pill would increase their heart-rate and body temperature and cause their body to feel generally activated. The second group of insomniacs was told that the placebo pill would calm and relax them. The third group of insomniacs was not given a placebo pill. Insomniacs who were given the "arousing" pill reported they fell asleep much faster when they had taken the pill than when they had not. They could attribute the arousal they felt from insomnia to the pill. They went to bed expecting the pill to arouse them. Upon going to bed and not feeling aroused, they were in a position to say to themselves: "That pill was supposed to arouse me. I don't feel particularly aroused and that is quite a relief. My insomnia must not be bothering me so much tonight." Insomniacs who were given the "relaxing" pill went to bed expecting to be relaxed. Upon going to bed and not feeling relaxed, they might have said to themselves: "The pill was supposed to relax me. I don't feel very relaxed. My insomnia must really be bothering me tonight." Insomniacs who had taken the "relaxing" pill reported that it took significantly longer to get to sleep when they had taken the pill than when they had not. As would be expected, the reported time to get to sleep did not change for insomniacs who were not given a placebo pill.

A slightly different explanation can also be given for the results of this study.[9] It is possible that insomniacs who took the relaxing pill interpreted the act of taking the pill as a sign that their insomnia was severe and necessitated them taking a pill that would help to relax them. Insomniacs who took the arousing pill may have interpreted this act as a sign that their insomnia was mild enough to permit them to take a pill that actually might arouse them. In other words, it might have been the perceived reasons for taking the pill rather than the effects misattributed to the pill that were responsible for the reported differences in onset of sleep. More research is necessary to clarify the applications of misattribution techniques in the treatment of insomnia.

Changing Labels for Smoking

It is clear that cigarette smoking increases physiological arousal. All you have to do is hook yourself up to a physiological recording machine and watch your heart-rate, blood pressure, and respiration increase as you begin to puff on a cigarette. To be precise:

> Smoking one to two cigarettes causes in most persons, both smokers and non-smokers, an increase in resting heart-rate of 15 to 25 beats per minute, a rise in blood pressure of 10 to 20 mm hg systolic and 5 to 15 mm hg diastolic, and an increase in cardiac output of about 0.5 l/min/sq m.[10]

Male college students who had smoked at least 20 cigarettes a day during the past year and male college students who did not smoke cigarettes were recruited to participate in a study of tolerance for electric shock.[11] Participants were given electric shocks of increasing intensity until they asked for the shocks to be discontinued. Before the shock sessions began, all participants were divided into three groups. The first group of participants smoked a cigarette with high nicotine content (Belair—19.0 mg tar and 1.6 mg nicotine). The second group of participants smoked a cigarette with low nicotine content (Cascade—8.0 mg tar and 0.3 mg nicotine).[12] Care was taken to insure that all participants properly inhaled the cigarette so that they would maximize the potential effects of the nicotine. Participants in the third group were asked to simulate smoking a cigarette that was not lit.

Results of the study showed that participants who were regular smokers were willing to tolerate more shocks as their consumption of nicotine increased. Nicotine consumption had no effect on the shock tolerance of nonsmokers. The author of the study concluded that nonsmokers experienced considerable physiological arousal from smoking both the low nicotine and the high nicotine cigarettes. However, it was clear to these participants *why* they were aroused and they were not at all influenced to attribute their arousal from the cigarettes to the experience of being shocked. The finding that regular cigarette smokers perceived themselves as more relaxed as their nicotine consumption increased is interesting and was explained by the author of the study in the following way. It is possible that cigarette smokers have learned to attribute any arousal they experience while smoking a cigarette to that cigarette. When they are smoking a cigarette they will perceive a particular experience as being less arousing because they can attribute the arousal they feel to the cigarette. When they are not smoking a cigarette they will attribute the arousal they feel to the experience itself. It is also possible that heavy smokers have a higher threshold for arousal. Because they are used to the physiological arousal they experience from smoking cigarettes, it takes a more severe arousal to have a noticeable physiological effect on them.

Female cigarette smokers volunteered to go without smoking for a day.[13] Half of the volunteers were given a placebo pill and were told that it would physiologically arouse them, increase their appetite, and make them feel irritable and restless. The remaining volunteers were given a placebo pill and told that it would have no particular effect on how they felt. Females in the first group reported less difficulties in going without cigarettes during the day and expressed less desire to have a cigarette than females in the second group. Apparently, female smokers in the first group could attribute their withdrawal symptoms from not smoking to the placebo pill. They did not perceive themselves as suffering as much from lack of cigarettes as female smokers in the second group.

Evaluating Techniques of
False Feedback and Misattribution

We have seen many examples of false feedback and misattribution techniques that were successful in altering people's interpretations of their bodily states. False feedback and misattribution techniques are useful for studying how people label their bodily states and for exploring ways in which people can be influenced to alter these labels. Research has shown that false feedback techniques are most effective when the verbal responses that are influenced are of minor importance and of small consequence for a person's future behaviors.[14] False feedback is also more influential on people in situations of low rather than high arousal. People who are greatly aroused are more likely to interpret their feelings according to their true bodily states.[15]

We have also reviewed several attempts to apply false feedback and misattribution techniques to therapy for such problems as anxiety, pain, insomnia, and smoking. The research data provide a number of reasons for arguing that the therapeutic applications of false feedback and misattribution techniques are of limited value. The main weakness of false feedback and misattribution techniques is that they influence verbal but not necessarily physiological behaviors. What typically happens in studies using false feedback and misattribution is that people are at first convinced to perceive and interpret their bodily states in a different way; after they have changed their perceptions and interpretations, they begin to behave in a way that is consistent with this new point of view. The problem is that since the labels provided by false feedback and misattribution are based on deception, the new behaviors reveal that the new labels are invalid. To explain it in a different way: During the first stage of altering their perception of arousal, people are convinced to believe the information about their bodily states provided by the false feedback or misattribution and change their self-perceptions accordingly. During the second stage, however, they discover that their new self-perceptions are not supported by the world around them because the false information provided by false feedback and misattribution can only be maintained for so long. Contact with reality then forces them to change their self-perception back to its original form. A good example of this process is seen in the failure of a number of researchers who attempted to use false feedback for reducing snake phobias.[16] People who are scared of snakes can be given false feedback showing that snakes do not cause an increase in their heart-rates. As a result of this false feedback, they will often evaluate the snakes as less fearful on a rating form. With a bit of encouragement these people can usually be influenced to test their supposed lack of fear by touching or picking up a live nonpoisonous snake. As soon as they touch the snake the participants discover that their heart-rates actually do increase and that the snake is indeed aversive. After this experience with reality they no longer rate the snake as less fearful on a rating form.

Another limitation of false feedback and misattribution techniques is that they rely on people making the same conclusions the experimenter intended them to make about their bodily states. In the insomnia study discussed earlier, for example, the researchers expected the participants to interpret an "arousing" placebo as a sign of relaxation and label a "relaxing" placebo as a sign of arousal. Two experiments failed to replicate the original insomnia study, possibly because participants were not inclined (or properly influenced by the experimenter) to make such complex attributions.[17] We will consider this point later in the chapter in our discussion of methods for training people to actively relabel or reinterpret their bodily states.

There is some evidence that false feedback or manipulation toward misattribution can increase people's arousal if it creates expectations about their bodily states that they are unable to confirm. False feedback and misattribution can also make people less aroused for short periods of time by distracting them from thoughts or objects that are uncomfortable. There is little evidence, however, that false feedback and misattribution techniques can change people's arousal over an extended period of time. Most studies have found no relationship between false feedback or misattribution treatments and actual arousal.[18]

Changing Our Bodily States with Self-Relaxation

Fortunately we do not have to end our discussion of how to live with our bodies on a discouraging note. Psychologists have developed techniques for teaching people to reduce their bodily arousal with self-relaxation. Techniques of self-relaxation enable people to learn to cope with their actual bodily reactions. Self-relaxation is more durable than false feedback and misattribution because it is real and therefore not subject to disproof.

Learning to Relax

Most of us are aware of the practices of Yoga and Transcendental Meditation, and have some familiarity with the ability of masters in these disciplines to control various functions of their bodies. Some of you may have studied these or related disciplines and learned to become more sensitive to your bodies and to develop methods for self-relaxation. Athletes, dancers, actors, and musicians also learn to be aware of what their body is doing and to relax themselves at critical points in their performance. The study of self-relaxation has been of considerable interest to psychologists and has found widespread therapeutic application in situations where people seek help in dealing with anxieties that are interfering in one way or another with their everyday lives. We will explore some of the research in relaxation training that psychologists have carried out and learn how to apply the findings of this research to our study of self-perception. Since Yoga, Transcendental Meditation, and other such disciplines have been the topic of numerous books and articles I will not include them in this discussion. You may wish to read about these disciplines in other sources and then compare their methods and procedures with those that have been developed by psychologists. You will find that the definitions and explanations for self-relaxation are different. The procedures and practices, however, are often very much the same.

The general procedure used by psychologists for teaching relaxation was developed by Joseph Wolpe. Wolpe modified a rather lengthy relaxation procedure originally used by Edmund Jacobson, so that people could practice it at home.[19] Self-relaxation is a very simple procedure. It may be accomplished while sitting in a comfortable chair or while lying down. Wolpe recommends that his clients practice self-relaxation during two 15-minute periods each day. The goal is to learn to concentrate on a specific area of your body, such as your right hand, and let it relax. Next, concentrate on your left hand and let it relax. Then, while both of your hands are still relaxed, concentrate on your right foot and let it relax. Now concentrate on your left foot and let it relax. Continue this procedure as you relax your right and left arms and legs. Then, with your hands and legs relaxed, you concentrate on your chest and back. After relaxing your chest and back, you concentrate on your neck and let it relax. Finally, you concentrate on your facial muscles, such as your jaws and forehead, and let them relax. In the end you may concentrate on your breathing muscles and allow them to work in a relaxed and tension-free manner.

One technique that will aid you in relaxing a particular muscle is to first tense it and then slowly let it relax. If you tense your hand by bending it back you can then let it relax very slowly and help yourself to sense the difference between tense and relaxed muscles. Similarly, you can tense your neck muscles by bending your head back and then slowly relax your neck muscles by letting your head fall gradually forward. You can tense your facial muscles by gritting your teeth, frowning, or wrinkling your brow. As you slowly relax these muscles you will learn to appreciate the difference between muscles that are somewhat tense and muscles that are fully relaxed. Saying to yourself, or having someone else say, the words "relax . . . relax" as you proceed is often helpful. You can also help yourself relax by imagining images of lying in the warm sun or floating on a cloud.[20]

Self-relaxation takes practice and you shouldn't be discouraged if it takes you a number of sessions to master the techniques. I wouldn't be surprised, however if you were somewhat more relaxed after reading this description than before you started.

Associating Self-Relaxation with Anxiety

Wolpe's general method for helping people deal with uncomfortable anxiety reactions is to teach them self-relaxation procedures and then have them practice associating their feelings of relaxation with the thoughts or events that were making them anxious. Wolpe's treatment is generally referred to by psychologists as a process of systematic desensitization. This process of systematic desensitization has to be carried out slowly; otherwise the anxiety from the feared events would overcome the newly developed feelings of self-relaxation. For example, a person with a strong fear of heights may go through the self-relaxation procedure and then start to think about grassy hills or porch steps. If the person can remain relaxed, he or she may be ready to think about a stairway in a house, weather balloons, or beautiful mountains. It may take several weeks, but sooner or later the person will be able to associate self-relaxation with thoughts about air planes, amusement park rides, and steep fire escapes.[21]

A student with severe anxiety about examinations can learn to associate self-relaxation with thoughts about an exam that will take place in a week. Remaining relaxed, the student can then think of the exam being three days away, one day away, and that very day. With time, the student will progress to the point where he or she can associate self-relaxation with actually taking the examination and finally getting the examination returned with a grade.[22]

A person who has strong anxieties about arguments between people can learn to become relaxed and then think about an argument between two strangers. Still remaining relaxed, the person can imagine a quarrel between two friends. In future sessions, relaxation can be associated with thoughts of arguments between siblings and parents. Finally, the person can learn to feel relaxed while imagining actual involvement in a quarrel with a sibling or parent.[23]

The treatment of anxiety with systematic desensitization has received a good deal of attention by psychologists during the past 30 years and has been the subject of hundreds of articles and books. There have been many different theories developed to explain how systematic desensitization works and numerous additions and modifications to Wolpe's original procedure. It is impossible to summarize all of the literature devoted to the clinical treatment of anxiety in this book.[24] Since our main interest here is self-perception, it will be useful to look at recent developments in systematic desensitization therapy that focus on the way people label and interpret their bodily states. When threatened with danger, it is appropriate and adaptive for people to label their resulting bodily states as fear or anxiety. Sometimes, however, we experience physiological arousal and suffer feelings of anxiety for no good reason. It is this unnecessary distress and discomfort from the maladaptive labeling of bodily states that we would like to learn to reduce.

Self-Relaxation as a Form of Self-Control

As we have seen, the general strategy of systematic desensitization therapy is to teach people to use anxiety-provoking objects or events in the outside world as cues or signs to begin to relax. The disadvantage of this approach is that it requires people to go through separate self-relaxation procedures for each object or event in the environment that causes inappropriate reactions of anxiety. Marvin Goldfried has proposed that systematic desensitization therapy would be more effective if it could teach people to use their own bodily states as cues or signs for self-relaxation.[25] Goldfried's approach is to teach people to become aware of their bodily reactions. When they feel themselves becoming anxious they can learn to use this recognition of anxiety as a sign to relax. The advantage of basing self-relaxation on bodily awareness rather than on environmental cues is that people can learn one general anxiety-reducing skill and then apply it to all situations in which they may find themselves.

One study using Goldfried's technique was conducted with college students who experienced anxiety when they had to speak in front of an audience.[26] The students were instructed to relax themselves in much the same way we learned about earlier. The students were then taught to use their skills in self-relaxation whenever they noticed themselves becoming tense or anxious. After practicing this anxiety-reducing strategy for five weeks, the students were given the opportunity to make a speech in front of an audience. The students' anxiety during these speeches was measured with both ratings made by observers and reports from the students about how anxious and uncomfortable they felt. Results of the study showed that training in self-control of anxiety had significantly decreased the students' anxiety and enhanced their ability to speak before an audience.

Training in self-relaxation can be used successfully by children as well as adults. An eleven-year-old girl who suffered from anxiety and insomnia when she was left with a babysitter was taught the procedures we learned for self-relaxation.[27] After about five weeks of practice, the girl was able to fall asleep with very little difficulty, even when she was with a babysitter. The girl's piano teacher reported a noticeable improvement in her lessons during the period of relaxation training. Her mother spontaneously commented: "It's another Susan! It's as if she matured three years in one year."

Adaptive Relabeling of Bodily States

We have seen that false feedback and misattribution techniques are theoretically useful because they give us a good understanding of how people learn to label and interpret their bodily messages. This increased understanding of self-perception has enabled psychologists to develop techniques for helping people to actively find adaptive ways of perceiving and interpreting their bodily states. Techniques for adaptive relabeling usually attempt to satisfy two goals: first, to encourage people to have positive motivations and expectations about their abilities to view certain typically negative interpretations of bodily messages in a more positive light; second, to train people to use relabeling strategies that they can actively incorporate into their everyday lives. The advantage of adaptive relabeling techniques is that they are not based on deception. People who learn these techniques have a feeling of active involvement. They are not merely passive participants in a psychological experiment.

Albert Ellis has developed a theory of psychotherapy emphasizing the ways in which people talk themselves into feeling positive or negative about themselves.[28] Ellis gives the example of a man who wants to ask a woman for a dance. The man most likely feels his heart beating a bit faster. He may also notice a slight shaking or coldness in his hands. The question is, how does he label these bodily reactions? The man may take a rather negative attitude and say to himself:

> She's very attractive and I would like to ask her to dance with me. But if she refuses, that would be awful! I would feel bad about it. I feel really nervous and not very confident at all. The way I feel, all nervous and upset, if I ask her to dance I don't think it will work out.[29]

On the other hand, the man could interpret his feelings in a positive manner:

> She's very attractive and I would like to ask her to dance with me. If she refuses, that would be too bad, but I don't really have anything to lose. I feel excited because if I take a chance and she says "Yes" it will be really great. If she says "No" I won't be any worse off than I am now.[30]

Ellis argues that "human thinking and emotion are *not* two disparate or different processes, but that they significantly overlap and are in some respects for all practical purposes, essentially the same thing."[31] You will notice how similar this viewpoint is to Schachter's theory, which defines emotion as a combination of labeling and arousal. It is interesting that Ellis and Schachter, coming from different professional backgrounds and training, have arrived at quite similar conclusions. Ellis has based his therapy, which he calls Rational-Emotive Psychotherapy, on the notion that people often talk themselves into beliefs that are irrational and cause them to be unnecessarily unhappy. Some of the irrational ideas that people talk themselves into at various times are that everyone must like them, that they must be perfect and never fail, that it is awful if things don't go exactly their way, that unhappiness is externally caused and they have no control over their feelings, that they always need to depend on someone stronger, and that they should constantly dwell on problems and be preoccupied with the negative aspects of their lives.[32] In his psychotherapy sessions, Ellis attempts to help clients talk themselves out of these irrational beliefs. Why should people make themselves unhappy if certain wishes (that were unrealistic in the first place) don't materialize? Ellis doesn't want people to kid themselves into being happy or to rationalize away problems that genuinely deserve attention. The point is not to become bogged down by applying negative appraisals and labels in situations where they won't do any good.

You probably have many ideas about how to apply Ellis' theory to our discussion of the ways in which people label and interpret their bodily states. Goldfried has incorporated Ellis' theory into his procedure of systematic desensitization in the following manner. When a person starts to feel excessively anxious, he or she can implement self-relaxation procedures and also ask the following questions: "I feel myself becoming physiologically aroused. Am I going to interpret this arousal in an irrational or unnecessarily negative manner? Or can I rather label my feelings in a more realistic or positive way?"[33]

Again, it would not be productive to use Goldfried's strategies to rationalize away a bodily reaction to something that poses a genuine threat. There are many times, however, when people feel aroused or agitated unnecessarily, and it is in these situations that self-relaxation and adaptive relabeling strategies can be of real value. In one study, people who were strongly committed to the kinds of irrational ideas outlined by Ellis were compared with people who had not talked themselves into holding such unrealistic expectations.[34] People who were preoccupied with irrational beliefs had a much greater tendency than people not preoccupied in that way to harbor anxiety about being in social situations and be afraid that others wouldn't like them. The people with many irrational beliefs had more fears that interfered with their ability to speak in front of groups and perform successfully on tests. People who were preoccupied with irrational beliefs were also found to be significantly more anxious about situations in which they might experience lack of attention or rejection from other people.

Another interesting application of Ellis' theory was made in a study of hospital patients who were about to undergo surgery.[35] The operations included hysterectomies, hernia repairs, and cholecystectomies. All of the patients had a favorable prognosis. They were randomly assigned to four different groups, equated for type of operation, seriousness of operation, and patients' sex, age, and religious affiliation. One group of patients was given training in adaptive relabeling of their reactions to the hospital experience. They were taught that many of the anxieties they felt were caused by their self-perceptions and that they could learn to reduce unnecessary fears by learning to label their bodily reactions in a more adaptive way. The patients were asked to imagine how differently they would react if they received a minor cut while they were engrossed in an interesting task or project rather than when they were bored and had nothing better to do than fuss about it. The patients also learned to see positive as well as negative sides to threatening situations in their lives. They practiced imagining events such as losing their job, suffering damage to their home, or wrecking their car and searching for positive ways in which to interpret these events. They also practiced giving attention to positive aspects of their hospital experience, such as receiving attention, losing weight (if appropriate), and the rare opportunity to relax, take stock of themselves, and have a vacation from outside pressures. Patients were taught to rehearse these positive thoughts whenever they felt themselves becoming anxious or upset about the impending surgery.

The second group of patients received preparatory information about the surgery but did not have training in adaptive relabeling. The patients in this group were given information about the surgery and what it would involve, as well as reassurance that it would be done with utmost care and expertise. The communication of preparatory information and reassurance is not related to the procedure of adaptive labeling, but has been shown to be useful to patients who have to undergo surgery or spend time in a hospital. There has been a good deal of publicity about the value of preparing people for hospital or surgical experiences. The argument is that people should be allowed to visit the hospital and learn from the surgeon and other staff members exactly what will happen to them. If people know what to expect, they are less likely to invent unrealistic fears.

The third group of patients was given training in adaptive relabeling as well as preparatory information. The fourth group of patients was treated in the regular manner with no training in adaptive relabeling and no preparatory information.

To test the effects of the above treatments on the patients' "success" in surgery, the following measures were taken. The nurses made ratings of how anxious the patients appeared to be and how well they were coping with their stress and discomforts. To prevent bias, the nurses were not aware of which patients had received the various treatments. The nurses also kept track of the number of pain relievers and sedatives the patients requested.

Results of the study showed that training in adaptive relabeling significantly improved the success of the patients' surgical experience on all of the above measures. Preparatory information alone did not significantly heighten surgical success. These data indicate that people facing hospitalization or surgery will benefit the most by gaining as much information as possible beforehand and by labeling this information as well as their anticipated experiences in the hospital in a positive and adaptive manner.

Adaptive relabeling strategies have also been successful in helping people who are anxious about making speeches and taking tests. Two studies were conducted in which college students with anxieties about speech-making and test-taking were taught to become aware of their negative thoughts during these activities and to replace these negative thoughts with positive statements to themselves.[36] For example, instead of saying to themselves, "I am nervous and that is going to disturb my performance" the students were trained to say, "My nervousness will make me more attentive and help me do better." Results of these studies showed that students who practiced making positive statements to themselves significantly reduced their speech-making and test-taking anxiety. Data from these studies suggest that positive "self-statements" are most useful when the sources of anxiety are vague and the anxious person needs a generally more favorable outlook on life. By contrast, self-relaxation techniques are probably most appropriate when there is a clear source of anxiety with which self-relaxation can be directly connected.

Donald Meichenbaum has suggested that relabeling strategies can be taught to people as an adaptive skill they can use at appropriate times throughout their lives.[37] Training in adaptive relabeling is accomplished by explaining that unfavorable reactions to stress can often be diminished with positive self-statements. People are then given practice in developing and rehearsing positive self-statements they can use when they find themselves in stressful situations. For instance, we can prepare ourselves for stress by telling ourselves things like: "Don't worry; worry won't help anything." "Develop a plan; think positively." During the stressful experience we can make self-statements such as: " 'Psych' yourself up—you can meet this challenge." "Don't think about fear; just think about what you have to do." "Relax, you are in control; it will be over shortly." After successfully dealing with the stressful situation we can reward ourselves by saying: "It worked, you did it." "You can be pleased with your progress." Meichenbaum believes that skill in adaptive relabeling provides people with a feeling of control and resourcefulness in threatening, stressful situations.

Positive Motivation and Cognitive Strategies

Theodore Barber and his colleagues have conducted research to learn more about how techniques associated with hypnotism can be used to broaden people's capabilities for controlling their relation with their body.[38] Among the capabilities that Barber and his colleagues have attempted to enhance are the abilities to control pain, amnesia, dreaming, and skin temperature, and to enjoy a wider range of perceptual and sensory experiences. One of the most consistent conclusions reported by Barber and his co-workers is that successful hypnotic procedures rely strongly on teaching people to have positive motivation and to make effective use of cognitive strategies.

Hypnotism and Positive Motivation

Participants in one experiment were divided randomly into two groups.[39] Participants in the first group were instructed that they were going to be tested for their imagination and ability to control their "self-experiences." Participants in the second group were told they were involved in a study of gullibility. All participants were then given hypnotic suggestions to undergo various mental and physical experiences, such as hallucinating thirst and experiencing bodily immobility, inability to speak, and selective amnesia. Participants in the first group had significantly more success in realizing these experiences than participants in the second group.

In a similar experiment, nursing students who were serving as volunteers, were divided into three groups.[40] One group of nursing students was encouraged to relax and use their imagination to the best of their ability. The second group of nursing students was given instructions that would make them more or less neutral toward the experiment. Nursing students in the third group were given the following instructions that would make them feel negatively toward the experiment:

> It's being rumored by doctors and administrators, and I don't know who else, that nursing students are too easily directed and easily led in their responses to suggestions. It's kind of shocking and discouraging to hear that the students are so easily directed and can't decide things for themselves. We've got a job to do—to impress the administrators and doctors around here with the fact that nursing students are not as gullible and as easily directed as they appear to have been showing during this research study. Well it sure is up to each of you as to how easily led, people around here think, student nurses are.[41]

The results of this study were also in line with what you would expect. Students in the first group were most successful and students in the third group were least successful in responding to the suggestions for realizing the physical and mental experiences described in the previous experiment.

Thus, research indicates that the first rule for enhancing our abilities to undergo interesting mental and physical experiences is to be positively motivated. Participants in an experiment were divided into two groups.[42] Participants in the first group were given instructions that made them feel more or less neutral toward the experiment. Participants in the second group received the following instructions to make them feel positively motivated:

> How well you do on the tests that I will give you depends entirely on your willingness to try to imagine and to visualize the things that I will ask you to imagine. . . . What I ask is your cooperation in helping this experiment by trying to imagine vividly what I describe to you. . . . We're trying to measure the maximum ability of people to imagine. If you don't try to the best of your ability, this experiment will be worthless. . . .[43]

Results of this study showed that participants with the positive motivational instructions had significantly more success in realizing mental and physical experiences. The importance of positive motivation for undergoing new mental and physical experiences has led Barber and his colleagues to argue that hypnotism can be more accurately understood in terms of self-perceptions rather than the hypothetical existence of a "hypnotic trance." The notion of a "hypnotic trance" implies that an experimenter can take passive people and hypnotize them into undergoing mental and physical experiences. This does not seem to be true. As we have seen, it is difficult, if not impossible, to hypnotize people who are not positively motivated to experience the hypnotic suggestions. Hypnotic experiences, according to Barber and his colleagues, require positive motivation and active cooperation by participants. We have seen how Barber and his colleagues have learned to increase the positive motivation of participants by using motivational instructions. Barber and his colleagues have also enhanced the ability of people to realize new mental and physical experiences by teaching them to respond to suggestions actively with a variety of cognitive strategies.

Hypnotism and Cognitive Strategies

If you agreed to participate in a demonstration of hypnotism, one suggestion you would probably receive is that your arm is weightless and is beginning to rise. Your ability to experience this suggestion would be greatly increased if you were positively motivated and if you had practiced a number of relevant cognitive strategies. For instance, you could imagine that your arm is hollow and that someone is pumping air or helium into it. You could also imagine that a helium-filled balloon is tied to your arm and is pulling it up. Another cognitive strategy would be to imagine yourself sitting in a pool of water and allowing your hand to float to the surface. All of these cognitive strategies would help you to experience the experimenter's suggestion of a weightless arm.[44]

If you wish to experience the suggestion that you will have amnesia for the number 4, you can implement the following cognitive strategies. You can imagine a line of numbers in which the 4 is missing. You can imagine a series of numbers on a blackboard from which you erase the 4 and then rewrite the remaining numbers to fill in the empty space. Other cognitive strategies would be to imagine the number 4 disintegrating or being carried off into space. Alternatively, you could imagine the part of your brain containing knowledge of the number 4 being disconnected or taken away.[45]

The suggestion that you will experience extreme cold in your hand can be enhanced by imagining that you have put your hand into snow or very cold water.[46] You can increase your ability to hallucinate music by imagining a record being played or by imagining that you are sitting in a concert hall listening to a live musical performance.[47] You can increase the probability of dreaming about a specific topic at night if you focus your thoughts on that topic before going to bed, as you are falling asleep, and during periods of the night when you are awake or semiawake.[48]

After reading about some of these cognitive strategies for expanding mental and physical experiences you may have doubts about how effective they are. If you do have doubts, you are actually supporting Barber's emphasis on cognitive strategies as well as positive motivation. You cannot appreciate these cognitive strategies by just reading about them. You have to motivate yourself to think positively and then actually put the cognitive strategies into practice. Most of us use cognitive strategies that we have either learned from others or developed for ourselves when we are forced to undergo pain. Barber and his colleagues have incorporated their suggestions for positive motivation and cognitive strategies into methods for teaching people to increase their tolerance for pain.

Learning to Tolerate Pain

In Chapter One we compared the reactions to pain of people from different cultures and discovered how the labels people learn affect their perception of pain. Now we can see how the methods discussed in this chapter can be used for changing reactions to pain. Techniques of self-relaxation, adaptive relabeling, positive motivation, and cognitive strategies can all help people increase their tolerance for pain.

Hypnotism and Tolerance for Pain

An example of self-suggestion influencing people's tolerance for pain is shown in the following incident reported in 1889:

> There are few cases of this kind more remarkable than one related by Mr. Woodhouse Braine, the well-known chloroformist. Having to administer ether to an hysterical girl who was about to be operated on for the removal of two sebaceous tumors from the scalp he found that the ether bottle was empty, and that the inhaling bag was free from even the odor of any anesthetic. While a fresh supply was being obtained, he thought to familiarize the patient with the process by putting the inhaling bag over her mouth and nose, and telling her to breathe quietly and deeply. After a few inspirations she cried, "Oh, I feel it; I am going off," and a moment after, her eyes turned up, and she became unconscious. As she was found to be perfectly insensible, and the ether had not yet come, Mr. Braine proposed that the surgeon should proceed with the operation. One tumor was removed without the least disturbing her, and then, in order to test her condition, a bystander said that she was coming to. Upon this she began to show signs of waking, so the bag was once more applied, with the remark, "She'll soon be off again," when she immediately lost sensation and the operation was successfully and painlessly completed.[49]

At one time or another, you have probably heard stories about the power of hypnotism to eliminate or reduce pain in people undergoing surgery and other varieties of trauma. Before exploring techniques that might be used to increase a person's tolerance for pain, we must evaluate some of the anecdotes about the hypnotic reduction of pain which have been passed down during the last century. Barber and his colleagues make several points in arguing that hypnotism does not function as an unequivocal method of eliminating pain.[50] For one thing, the vast majority of subjects on whom hypnotism was successfully employed to reduce pain also received pain-relieving drugs of one kind or another, and it is usually impossible to separate the pain-reducing effects of hypnotism from the effects of the drugs. A second point is that there is less pain experienced in surgery than one might assume. Although the skin is sensitive to a knife cut, the muscles, bone, and most of the internal organs of the body are relatively insensitive to cutting. The following conclusions have been reached by researchers about the physiology of pain:

> The subcutaneous tissue gives rise to little pain when it is cut. Slight pain is elicited when muscles are cut. Compact bone can be bored without pain. The articular surfaces of joints are insensitive. The brain is quite insensitive. The lungs and visceral pleura are insensitive to puncture. The surface of the heart is insensitive. . . . Solid organs such as the spleen, liver, and kidney can be cut without the patient being aware of it. The stomach may be cut without pain. Lower portions of the alimentary canal, including the jejunum, ileum, and colon, are also insensitive to cutting.[51]

Because it is mainly the skin that is sensitive to cutting, many major operations can be performed with only local anesthetics to produce insensitivity of the skin. Local anesthetics have been used successfully in major operations such as amputation of limbs, removal of thyroid glands, removal of a female breast, removal of the appendix, cutting into and draining the gall gladder, suturing a hernia, excising glands in the neck and groin, and cutting the bladder.[52]

A third point made by Barber and his colleagues is that many reports of cases in which hypnotism was used to reduce pain exaggerate the extent of pain reduction. On some occasions the patients had also been given drugs that interfered with their ability to report accurately on how much pain they were experiencing. On other occasions patients gave signs of pain in grimacing and writhing that were not accurately reported.[53]

Researchers have conducted a number of controlled studies to learn about techniques for increasing people's tolerance for pain. You may be curious to see which of these techniques you have already tried and which ones you might wish to practice in the future.

Increasing Tolerance for Pain
with Self-Relaxation

One of the first strategies to employ when forced to undergo pain is to relax. The effects of pain are often exaggerated by the normally concomitant experiences of fear and anxiety. People can begin to increase their tolerance for pain by reducing their fears and anxieties.[54]

In one study, pregnant women taking special classes in childbirth were compared with similarly pregnant women who were not taking the special classes.[55] The classes included training for labor and practice in various postures, exercises, and breathing techniques to be used during delivery. Results of the study showed that the courses were successful in reducing fear and anxiety about childbirth. In addition, the women who participated in the special classes reported significantly less pain during childbirth than the women who did not participate in the classes.

There are two ways in which people can use the procedure of self-relaxation to increase their tolerance for pain: They can employ techniques of self-relaxation when they are experiencing pain; and they can develop their ability to label bodily states positively or rationally in painful situations.

Increasing Tolerance for Pain
with Distraction

A second strategy that appears to increase tolerance for pain is distraction. Participants in one study were asked to hold their hand in ice water for as long as they could stand the pain from the cold.[56] One group of participants was instructed to talk into a tape recorder during the experiment and verbalize all of their thoughts and sensations. A second group of participants was instructed to pay close attention to a clock as long as their hand was in the water. Participants in a third group were allowed to look at color slides of landscapes, buildings, and people. Participants in a fourth group were given no instructions for distracting themselves. Results of the study showed that participants who looked at the slides had the highest tolerance for pain. Participants who watched the clock also tolerated the pain more than participants who had no instructions for distracting themselves. The participants who were instructed to talk about their sensations during the painful experience had less tolerance for pain than participants in any of the other groups. By talking about how much the ice water was hurting, they focused on the pain they were experiencing and probably convinced themselves through self-labeling that the ice water was very painful.

In another study of the effects of distraction on tolerance for pain, participants endured pain from a finger pressure device that pressed a sharp Plexiglas wedge against a finger.[57] Participants who listened to an interesting tape-recorded story and participants who were given simple arithmetic problems to solve aloud were more successful in tolerating the pain than participants who were provided with no distraction. Participants in a third study were exposed to pain from a finger pressure device while they listened to a tape recording describing erotic escapades of an unnamed Hollywood actor.[58] They were asked to guess the identity of the actor and to remember as many of the details of his escapades as possible. People who were given this distracting task were more successful in tolerating pain than people who were not distracted from their pain. College students in a fourth study were threatened with electric shock.[59] Students who were given a book to read and evaluate manifested significantly less physiological stress than students who were not provided with this distraction.

The above research has shown that distraction increases tolerance for pain. Another interesting finding of these studies is that most people used their own strategies for distraction in addition to the ones provided by the experimenters. Some of the self-distracting strategies that participants brought with them to the experiments included thinking of other things, counting, clenching their teeth, looking at their watches, looking out the window, and concentrating on different objects or pieces of equipment in the room. Only practice can determine which strategies for distraction work best for you. You will probably achieve the most fruitful results if you combine distraction with some of the cognitive strategies reviewed in the next section.

Increasing Tolerance for Pain
with Cognitive Strategies

In addition to relaxing and distracting yourself when exposed to pain, it is also helpful to engage in certain kinds of cognitive strategies for perceiving pain in a less aversive manner. In one study, for example, a patient who was undergoing severe pain was taught to engage in self-relaxation and then to associate self-relaxation with the following cognitive strategy.[60] The patient would visualize his painful sensations as being caused by tightening steel bands, which he could loosen with self-relaxation. This combination of self-relaxation and cognitive strategies helped the patient relieve his pain. The above cognitive procedure was devised for the particular patient in question. There are other, more general cognitive strategies that can be of use to all of us.

One cognitive strategy for tolerating pain is to think pleasant thoughts about past or future experiences. A second cognitive strategy is to imagine that the affected part of your body is numb and insensitive. A third cognitive strategy, which might be successful for minor pain, is to try to imagine the pain as a new and interesting experience. Research has shown that all of these cognitive strategies can help people tolerate pain.[61] Participants in one study experienced less physiological stress under threat of shock when they actively imagined the shocks as harmless vibrations.[62] Participants in a second study were exposed to pain from a finger pressure device.[63] One group of participants was instructed to imagine pleasant events during their experience of pain. A second group of participants was instructed to vividly imagine that their finger was numb and insensitive. Participants in a third group were given no cognitive strategies but were instructed that with practice they could expect to experience a reduction in pain. Participants in a fourth group were given no instructions. The participants who were led to believe they could lessen their pain with practice reported significantly less pain than participants who were given no special instructions. However, the participants who were provided with either of the two cognitive strategies reported even less pain than the participants who were given only positive expectations.

At this point we can conclude that tolerance for pain is enhanced by positive expectations. Combining positive expectations with relaxation, distraction, and the active rehearsal of cognitive strategies can even further enhance a person's tolerance for pain. Some researchers have suggested that distraction might be most effective for tolerating concrete pain whereas cognitive strategies might work best for tolerating ambiguous threats of pain.[64]

Acupuncture and Tolerance for Pain

Since acupuncture has received so much attention during recent years, you are probably curious about how it works and whether or not it is of any value for increasing our tolerance for pain. Theodore Barber and his colleagues have summarized the ancient Chinese theory of acupuncture in the following manner:

> This theory . . . is based on the concepts of *Yin* and *Yang*. Yin is the weak, female, negative force; Yang is the strong, male, positive force. Health is viewed as a condition of harmony between Yin and Yang, while disease is thought to result from an imbalance of these two forces. Yin and Yang control life energy (*Ch'i*), which flows from organ to organ in the body through a network of meridians or channels (Ching-lo) that lie

beneath the skin. During treatment, acupuncture needles are placed along the meridians at points that are thought to correspond to specific organs.[65]

The major problem with this theory of acupuncture (beside being somewhat sexist) is that it has gained little or no support in medical research. Because physiological and anatomical evidence for a meridian theory of acupuncture has not been found, Barber and his colleagues have conducted research to see if the effects of acupuncture could be explained in other ways. The conclusions from their research are fascinating because they correspond so closely with what we have already learned about the self-perception of bodily states and strategies for tolerating pain.[66]

To clarify the effects of acupuncture, Barber and his colleagues make two points that are similar to those we learned for hypnotism. First, studies of acupuncture, both in China and the United States, show that acupuncture is rarely used alone without pain relieving drugs.[67] Second, the pain associated with acupuncture or regular surgery is not always as severe as people might think.[68] These points are important because they show that the effects of acupuncture on pain reduction may often be exaggerated. Nevertheless, in some instances the techniques of acupuncture can successfully increase the tolerance for pain by many of the same strategies that we have just explored.

The first strategy we learned for reducing pain is to relax and reduce our fears and anxieties. The same procedure is followed with acupuncture. Children in China grow up playing with acupuncture needles; as a result, they learn to regard the needles without fear. Patients are chosen for acupuncture in China only if they are positively motivated and enthusiastic. These "selected" patients (at the time of Barber's study) prepared themselves for acupuncture surgery by reciting quotations from Chairman Mao's book. Mao's picture was present in the operating room for "reassurance" and patients looked forward to thanking Chairman Mao when the operation was completed. Acupuncture patients in China are also given special preparation and indoctrination before undergoing surgery. The patients are encouraged to visit the hospital several days before the operation and meet the surgeons to learn exactly what is going to happen to them. Patients who have been selected for acupuncture with surgery also often talk with other patients who have had the same kind of surgery and are given a set of acupuncture needles with which they can become accustomed.[69] You can see from these descriptions that many of the techniques we have learned for positive motivation and self-relaxation are put into practice with acupuncture.

The second strategy for increasing our tolerance for pain is the use of distraction. Acupuncture needles are often quite painful. Sometimes an electrical current is applied to the needles. On other occasions the acupuncture needles are twirled mechanically. These treatments cause a range of experiences from slight aching to sharp pain. If acupuncture needles are manipulated in a way that produces pain, it is not surprising that they can successfully distract patients from the pain of surgery.[70]

The third procedure doctors commonly employ during acupuncture is the use of suggestions for pain relief. Researchers who have studied acupuncture report that surgeons spend a good deal of their time giving suggestions for pain relief that either provide patients with cognitive strategies or encourage patients to use cognitive strategies of their own.[71]

It is clear that much of the apparent success of acupuncture can be explained in terms of relaxation, distraction, and positive motivation. Does acupuncture do anything else? Forty-two adult patients suffering from shoulder pain caused by tendonitis and bursitis were divided randomly into two groups.[72] The first group of patients received traditional acupuncture therapy in which acupuncture needles were inserted into the points of the body that acupuncture experts believe are optimal for relieving shoulder pain. Patients in the second group received a simulated acupuncture treatment in which acupuncture needles were touched against the skin but not inserted in the manner believed necessary by acupuncture experts. After five treatment sessions, more than two-thirds of the patients reported they were experiencing less discomfort from shoulder pain. There was, however, no difference between patients receiving actual acupuncture and those receiving simulated acupuncture therapy. It is important to point out that patients who received simulated acupuncture therapy *believed* it was genuine. Apparently, the patients' feelings of improvement resulted from their belief in the acupuncture therapy rather than from any therapeutic value of the insertion of acupuncture needles. This conclusion is even more strongly supported by another part of the study in which patients were given either positive or negative expectations about acupuncture therapy. Patients who were told that acupuncture was an effective therapy and assured that it would lead to reduced shoulder pain reported less discomfort after treatment than patients who were led to believe that acupuncture is not a proven technique and that they should not expect it to reduce shoulder pain. This effect of positive or negative expectation occurred for patients receiving actual as well as simulated acupuncture therapy. There is a final discouraging note to this study. Regardless of acupuncture treatment or expectancy, patients experienced little or no improvement in ability to actually move their painful shoulders.

Other Applications of Cognitive Strategies

Cognitive Strategies and Sexual Experiences

In addition to increasing tolerance for pain, cognitive strategies have other applications. Daydreams, fantasies, and other imaginative excursions are all forms of cognitive strategies people use to enhance their experiences. If you think for a moment, you will be able to list a number of different ways in which you use cognitive strategies to make life more interesting. After reading about some of the suggestions in this chapter you might discover new ways of applying cognitive strategies. One idea that has undoubtedly occurred to you is the relationship between cognitive strategies and sexual experiences.

Most people have sexual fantasies. Examples of how people use imagination and fantasies during sexual experiences abound in the research of Kinsey.[73] From what we now know, we can interpret sexual fantasies as a variety of cognitive strategy that might serve to make a person's sexual experiences more interesting, if not more satisfying.

A group of 141 married women in a New York suburb were asked to report (anonymously) whatever sorts of fantasies they engaged in during sexual intercourse with their husbands.[74] Sixty-five percent of the women reported a moderate to high amount of fantasy. In addition, 37 percent of the women said that during sexual intercourse with their husbands they engaged in these fantasies "very often." The most common fantasies experienced by the women included thoughts of an imaginary lover, imagination of being overpowered or forced to surrender, thoughts about doing something wicked, being in a different place like a car, motel, beach or woods, reliving a previous sexual experience, feelings of delighting many men, thoughts about watching oneself or other people making love, and thoughts about being irresistible and then seduced. After interviewing over a third of the women, the authors of this study concluded that the women's sexual fantasies generally served to enhance their enjoyment of their sexual experiences. The researchers suggested that the women used sexual fantasies as a positive and adaptive strategy for adjusting to sexual relationships that otherwise might be less than satisfactory.

A study with men approached the issue of cognitive strategies for sexual arousal from the opposite direction.[75] Men were exposed to an erotic tape-recorded message consisting of a woman describing her part in a sexual encounter. The message included explicit descriptions of foreplay, oral-genital contact, and coitus. The sexual arousal of the men was recorded by an instrument designed to measure changes in penile tumescence. One group of men heard the erotic message with no distraction. Other groups of men heard the erotic message while they were being distracted with certain cognitive tasks. Results of the study showed quite clearly that as the men became more and more distracted from the erotic message they became less and less sexually aroused. The authors felt that this study has important implications for problems of impotence in males. It is likely that if a man worries too much about his immediate erection he may be distracted from erotic thoughts that would contribute to his sexual arousal.

We can see that increasing a person's attention with erotic materials and cognitive strategies can enhance sexual arousal whereas decreasing attention with distraction can retard sexual arousal.

Cognitive Strategies and Learning

Cognitive strategies can be used to enhance learning and recall. Most people probably use mnemonics to remember certain things. For example, children learn the sentence "Every good boy does fine" as a way of memorizing the notes *e, g, b, d, f* of the musical scale. Research has shown that people have greater success in memorizing a series of word pairs if they practice visualizing images about how the two words might go together.[76] For instance, a person wishing to remember that the words *cat* and *bicycle* went together could picture the image of a cat riding a bicycle. Research in learning has led to the conclusion that visual imagery is an important part of the memory process because visual images lend themselves to faster recall than more abstract verbal processes.[77]

Cognitive Strategies and Personal Adjustment

One way in which all people use cognitive strategies is by daydreaming. Jerome Singer has described how daydreaming can be adaptive by promoting imagination and creativity.[78] Daydreaming can also be maladaptive if it involves thoughts, beliefs, or perceptions that cause conflict with the outside world. One study compared fantasies of high school males who had been identified as normal on a psychological test with those of high school males who had been identified as abnormal.[79] The normal students had many more positive fantasies than the abnormal students and also looked forward to more positive events in the future. The authors of this study concluded that the normal students may have engaged in more positive fantasies because their lives were happier. The authors also argued that positive perceptions of life can *result* in a more positive life. Jerome Singer has suggested that a valuable goal in psychotherapy is to teach people to use cognitive strategies for enhancing positive experiences and for adapting more effectively to distressing events in life.[80]

Some Conclusions
About Perceived Bodily States

Our discussion so far has focused on the self-perception of bodily states. We have seen how self-perceptions of emotions, motivations, attitudes, affection, and well-being are influenced by bodily messages and the labels people give to them. We have learned how experimental research has studied the theoretical aspects of self-labeling with techniques of false feedback and misattribution. We have also learned how people can use self-relaxation, relabeling, and cognitive strategies to relate to their bodies in more adaptive ways.

The remaining chapters of this book will focus on the self-perception of behavior. Most of the understanding we have gained about the self-perception of bodily states also applies to the self-perception of behavior. However, instead of directing our attention to the labeling of internal bodily reactions, we will now concentrate on how people label their overt actions.

FOUR

Knowing Ourselves
Through Our Actions

We now understand that people perceive their emotions by interpreting their bodily states according to cues and labels in the environment. In a related process, labels and interpretations people give to their actions and behaviors directly affect their self-perceptions. This chapter will introduce the theory that people form their attitudes by observing their behaviors and making attributions about the causes of these behaviors. Research has shown that it is possible to influence attitudes with environmental cues, false feedback about behavior, reinforcement of behavior, and inducement to perform behaviors that are discrepant and thereby produce dissonance.

Attitudes as Labels for Behaviors

Imagine that someone asks you whether you like television. Your reply might be, "Yes, I like television. I watch quite a lot of it." Alternatively, you might answer, "I rarely watch television. I don't like it very much." If you were asked whether you liked Beer X you might reply, "I drink Beer X fairly often. I like it quite a bit." Or you might say, "I usually drink Beer Y. I like Beer Y better than Beer X." Similarly, to interpret the attitudes of other people, you usually watch what they do.

You would conclude, for example, that a friend *likes* the *New York Times* better than the *Boston Globe* if he or she buys the *Times* every day rather than the *Globe*. A person who plays chess every day *enjoys* chess. A person who always chooses orange juice instead of tomato juice *prefers* orange juice. A person who participates regularly in demonstrations for a cause *believes* in that cause. Because it is physically impossible to open people up to discover the attitudes inside them, it is necessary to infer people's attitudes by observing how they behave.

Our parents could not look inside of us when we were young; they taught us to perceive our attitudes by observing and labeling our behaviors. Our behaviors as young children provided sources of information that we and our parents could share. We learned that we *liked* the toys we played with often and *disliked* or were *bored* with the toys we ignored. We learned that foods we ate *tasted good* and foods left on our plate *tasted bad*. We ran to and hugged adults to whom we felt *close*. We hid from adults who scared us and made us feel *shy*. When we laughed we were *happy*. When we kicked and screamed we were *unhappy* and *frustrated*. Because our parents and other people around us could only label our attitudes by how we acted we also learned to perceive our attitudes according to our actions.

The notion that people use their behaviors as cues for perceiving their attitudes was proposed by Daryl Bem.[1] Bem's theory is useful because it helps to make our study of self-perception objective. If we focus our attention on the study of behavior, which is measurable, we need not get bogged down with explanations that are highly subjective and metaphysical. The more or less traditional explanation for behavior is that it is the manifest result of some sort of inner attitude. Bem and many other psychologists argue that people's behaviors are not caused by something inside of them, but rather by forces in the outside environment.[2]

To test Bem's theory of self-perception it is necessary to set up situations that will cause people to alter their behavior and then see if the change in behavior produces a change in attitude. There is another important factor which must also be considered. Bem explains that before people use their behaviors to interpret their attitudes they make discriminations about the causes of their behavior. If there are obvious external reasons that explain why they engaged in a certain behavior they do not label that behavior as an attitude. If a man is forced to make a statement, for example, he will not use his behavior of making the statement as a sign that he actually believed it. He will perceive that he made the statement because he was forced to do so. If a woman gets paid a large sum of money for working on a political campaign she will not necessarily conclude that she is in favor of the campaign. She may have just as likely done it for the money. If people change the way they act because a certain law was passed they will not necessarily change their attitudes. They can explain their behavior by saying they did it because of the law.

If we took the above examples and changed them so there was no coercion or external reason for making the statement, little or no payment for working on the political campaign, and a change in behavior without a change in law, we would then be able to interpret the respective behaviors as an indication of attitudes or beliefs. Observing no obvious external forces we could hypothesize: These people acted in this way. There was no external pressure or force to make them act this way. They must have done it because of their attitudes or beliefs. The strategy for testing Bem's theory involves changing people's behaviors and also varying the environmental cues so that people either attribute their behaviors to external forces or to themselves. It is the cases in which people attribute their behaviors to themselves where we would predict changes in their attitudes.

Bem would argue that all behaviors are *actually* caused by factors in the environment. The point is that sometimes people *perceive* these environmental causes and sometimes they do not.[3] This is what makes the study of self-perception so fascinating. How is it possible to change people's behaviors so that they attribute their behaviors to themselves rather than to external forces in the environment? In this chapter we will explore various types of research studies related to Bem's theory of self-perception. In Chapter Five we will consider practical applications of Bem's theory for changing people's attitudes in real life situations.

Influencing Attitudes with Environmental Cues

A series of studies conducted by Bem has shown that experimenters can influence people's self-perceptions by altering the cues available for labeling recently performed behaviors. Participants in one experiment were asked to rate a series of cartoons on how funny they were.[4] The participants were then placed in sort of a training session in which they were asked a series of questions. During each question, either a green light or an amber light was illuminated. Half of the participants were instructed to tell lies when the green light was on and to tell the truth when the amber light was on. The remaining participants used the amber light as a cue for lying and the green light as a cue for telling the truth. This was done to control for any intrinsic differences between the two lights. Bem's hypothesis was that he could train people during these sessions to have more faith in their responses in the presence of the "truth" light than in the presence of the "lie" light. After the training sessions, participants were again asked to give their honest opinions about the cartoons they had rated earlier. While participants were judging some of the cartoons, their previously learned "truth" light was illuminated. Participants judged other cartoons in the presence of their previously learned "lie" light. Because the participants had already rated the same cartoons, the influence of the "truth" and "lie" lights could be measured. Results of the experiment showed the participants were influenced significantly more by the judgments they gave in the presence of the "truth" light than by their judgments in the presence of the "lie" light. In other words, if participants gave somewhat different judgments of the cartoons during the second ratings than they had given during the first ratings they tended to believe these second ratings more in the presence of the "truth" light than in the presence of the "lie" light.

The results of the above study led Bem to propose that similar cues for self-perception might be operating in situations such as police interrogations. Arrested suspects must be informed by police that any responses they make to police questioning are completely a matter of their own free will. On the surface, at any rate, police interrogators are prohibited from using any coercion. According to Bem, conditions of freedom to answer or not answer and lack of overt coercion create cues or signals for "telling the truth." General experience teaches people to regard things they say out of free choice and in the more or less respectable surroundings of a police station as the truth. A skillful interrogator can inadvertently or deliberately add more "truth" signals to the situation by first asking questions that will guarantee truthful answers, such as where the suspect lives and where he or she was born. The interrogator can then slowly shift to somewhat more ambiguous questions and add "helpful" hints, such as, "You did see a man of average height getting into a late model car, didn't you?"[5]

A study in which college students volunteered to give a persuasive argument to people they encountered on the street illustrates how other people can influence self-perceptions.[6] After agreeing to make the arguments, one group of participants was exposed to a confederate of the experimenter who said that he was willing to give arguments to people in the street when the issue was something he really believed in. A second group of participants was exposed to a confederate who said that he was willing to deliver arguments when the arguments were generally reliable and made a valid point. The participants were then asked to evaluate how much they agreed with the argument they had committed themselves to make. The participants in the first group agreed with their arguments significantly more than the participants in the second group. Participants in the first group had apparently been influenced by the confederate to label their willingness to deliver an argument as a reflection of their own personal beliefs. Participants in the second group were presumably influenced by the confederate to disassociate their commitment to deliver the argument from their own personal beliefs.

To test his theory of police interrogations Bem conducted the following experiment.[7] Participants were asked to "commit a crime" by crossing out certain words on a list. Participants then went through a training session similar to the one described above, in which they learned to associate "truth telling" with a light of one color and "lying" with a light of a second color. Finally, the participants were interrogated. They were asked to say whether or not they had crossed out certain words on the list. During the interrogation, either the "truth" light, the "lie" light, or no light was illuminated. When the "truth" light was illuminated, participants were influenced to believe their confessions. If participants made a confession about crossing out a word that was not true they were significantly more likely to believe this confession in the presence of the "truth" light than in the presence of no light. The "lie" light also influenced participants' self-perceptions: They had less confidence in their true statements in the presence of the "lie" light than in the presence of no light.

A replication of this study supported the finding that people are more likely to believe false statements about previous behaviors in the presence of a "truth" light.[8] In addition, the data suggested that the "lie" light might cause people to be more cautious and vigilant in their responses. If people are asked to make statements in a situation associated with lying, they exercise a great deal of caution in how they interpret their statements. If people are asked to make statements in a situation associated with truth-telling, they tend to believe the truth-telling cues and are also possibly less vigilant and more vulnerable to outside suggestions. Another study has shown that people believe the statements they make in the presence of a "truth" light if they feel they made the statements of their own free will. People do not believe statements they feel forced to make in the presence of a "truth" light.[9]

Philip Zimbardo has provided a fairly detailed description of tactics used by police during interrogations.[10] If we compare what we have learned from the "truth" and "lie" light experiments with what goes on in actual police interrogations, we see some very interesting parallels. Police manuals suggest that suspects be made to feel like a "guest" of the police. The interrogation room should never resemble a jail or office of the police department. There should be no guns or other police symbols present. The interrogator should wear a conservative suit and act in an authoritative but pleasant manner. All of these tactics insure that suspects will perceive the interrogation as a truth-telling situation in which they are acting out of their own free will. In addition, if police interrogators watch the carotid artery in a suspect's neck as well as the suspect's gestures and body movements, they may be able to "help" the suspect label these reactions as signs of guilt or an impulse to confess.

An understanding of police confessions in terms of a knowledge of self-perception has led Bem to the ironic conclusion that when overt coercive tactics in interrogations are reduced, the person being interrogated becomes more susceptible to thought control through self-persuasion.[11] It is possible to beat a confession out of a person with force without getting the person to believe the confession. Under conditions of apparent free will and cues for truth-telling, a person can be induced to confess and even believe the confession. The danger of abuses resulting from police confessions has led Bem to propose that interrogations be made public or at least recorded on tamper-proof magnetic tape.

In addition to arranging cues for truth-telling, police interrogators also use subtle techniques for eliciting confessions. One approach is to encourage the suspect to confess by laying the blame on someone else. A person may admit to robbing someone who had previously "done him wrong" and "deserved it." A man accused of rape might be tempted by the interrogator to blame the woman for enticing him or acting like a prostitute. Suspects can also be scared with charges far more serious than those for which they are arrested. A fake line-up can be arranged in which the suspect is falsely identified for a far more serious crime. The suspect may then be happy to confess to the original crime rather than face trial for the more serious crime. The "Mutt and Jeff" approach is sometimes used: One of the interrogators is a bully and is excessively harsh toward the suspect. A second interrogator who has "befriended" the suspect comes to the rescue and tells the tough interrogator to leave the suspect alone. The suspect is then motivated to confess to the friendly interrogator because the bully is likely to return to harrass him again in the future. When two suspects are related to a crime they can be played off against each other by telling each of them the other has put the entire blame on him. It can also be arranged that one suspect hears faked sounds of his partner being roughed-up in the room next door and is motivated to confess in order to avoid the same treatment. A fake or real note can be written from one suspect to another saying, "I have told the truth, you should do the same." In one well-known case, two suspects confronted with what seemed to be overwhelming evidence confessed to murder in order to have the charge reduced from homicide to manslaughter. Some time later the "corpse" turned up alive! Zimbardo argues that police confessions pose a severe threat to American justice. Like Bem, he believes they should be carefully monitored. Zimbardo also feels that interrogations should be made in the presence of attorneys or recorded on videotape.[12]

Influencing Attitudes
with False Feedback

We learned in Chapters Two and Three how false feedback has been employed in studies of the self-perception of bodily responses. False feedback can also be used to learn more about how people interpret their overt behaviors. Female college students in one experiment, for example, were given the opportunity to look at a series of color slides of paintings.[13] It was arranged that participants could control the projector and look at each painting for as long as they wished. Immediately after changing each slide, participants were told by the experimenter (who was operating an electric timer) how long they had looked at the painting. The experimenter also mentioned how long most other participants had looked at the same painting. The times given to participants for their own looking durations were true. The times given for those of other participants were false, having been arranged to make participants think they had looked at the painting significantly longer than others, for an average length of time, or significantly shorter than others. A week later, participants returned to look at the paintings for a second time. The participants were also asked to rate each painting on how appealing it was to them. Before completing their ratings, participants were reminded of the false feedback they had been given about their previous viewing times. Results showed that participants gave more favorable ratings to paintings they had supposedly looked at for a longer time than other people in the study. Participants gave less favorable ratings to paintings they had supposedly looked at for a shorter time than other people in the study. Apparently, the participants interpreted their perceived slide-viewing behaviors as a a sign of how much they enjoyed the paintings.

Female college students in a similar study were interviewed about their attitudes toward various aspects of college life.[14] Halfway through the interview one group of students was falsely told that their answers to the interview questions had been longer than the answers of most other students. A second group of students was told that their answers to the interview questions had been of average length, and a third group of students was told their answers had been shorter than the answers of most other students. After completing the second half of the interview, participants were asked to evaluate the interview on how interesting it had been to them. Participants thinking their answers had been longer than those of other students rated the interview as significantly more interesting than participants who thought their answers were of average length or shorter than average length. Participants in this study apparently used their perceptions of the length of their responses as a sign of their interest in the interview.

A slightly different application of false feedback about behavior is seen in the following experiment. Participants completed a rather lengthy questionnaire about their attitudes toward various issues.[15] One week later the participants returned and were asked to fill out a more detailed opinion survey on two of the issues included in the original questionnaire. Without the participants' knowledge, their original responses to questions on one of these two issues had been altered. Participants' responses on the other issue were left the same to alleviate any possible suspicion. The experimenters wanted to see if they could alter the attitudes of the participants by making them falsely think they had agreed or disagreed with the particular item that had been altered. It was found that if participants were falsely led to believe they had agreed (or disagreed) with a question during the original testing they were more likely to agree (or disagree) with the same question a week later.

A study with male and female college students was conducted to investigate self-perceptions of gazing behavior.[16] The students were introduced to each other in opposite sex pairs and left alone for ten minutes to get to know each other. Afterward, the students were falsely told that they had been observed through a one-way mirror and that they had gazed at their partner significantly more, an average amount, or significantly less than other participants in the study. After receiving this false information, participants were given a rating form on which to evaluate their partners. The female students were most favorable toward their male partners if they thought they had gazed toward the males significantly more than other participants and least favorable when they thought they had gazed very little. Females apparently interpreted a large amount of gazing behavior as a positive reaction toward the males. Male students were most favorable toward their female partners if they thought they had not gazed toward the females very much. The experimenters concluded that males interpreted a small amount of gazing behavior as a positive reaction toward the females.

We have seen that people's awareness of their past behaviors can influence their attitudes and self-perceptions. Researchers have also shown that people's self-perceptions are influenced by judgments they receive from others. Participants in an experiment were given false information about how an experimenter had predicted their attitudes.[17] The experimenter appeared very confident in her judgment. If the experimenter appeared to believe that participants agreed with a particular issue, participants were influenced to show more agreement with the issue on a questionnaire. If the experimenter appeared to believe that participants disagreed with a particular issue, participants were influenced to show less agreement with the issue on a questionnaire. Apparently, the participants concluded that if another person is confident they hold a certain opinion, it is likely that they actually *do* hold that opinion.

Influencing Attitudes with Reinforcement

Several studies have shown that it is possible to influence people's self-perceptions by altering their behaviors with techniques of operant reinforcement. A group of investigators was successful in changing the self-perceptions of typically quiet members of a group by reinforcing their active participation in the group's discussions.[18] Male participants in one experiment were assigned to groups of four and provided with a problem to discuss. After ten minutes, the discussions were interrupted and the participants were asked to evaluate their own participation as well as the participation of others. The groups were then reconvened to discuss a second problem and the reinforcement treatment was begun. All participants had in front of them a green light and a red light. It was arranged so that participants could only see their own lights. The participants were told that psychologists were monitoring the conversations. They were instructed that whenever they were doing something positive or helpful to the group discussion their green light would go on, and whenever their behavior was in some way hampering the group discussion their red light would go on. In reality, the lights were arranged to increase the amount of talking by one of the quiet group members. Whenever he talked his green light was illuminated to reinforce him to talk more. If the other group members talked too much their red lights were turned on to get them to talk less. The experimenters were successful in getting the quiet group members to talk more. In addition, the group members who learned to talk more showed increased satisfaction with their performance in the discussion. Other members also became more favorable toward the participants whose increased participation had been reinforced.

Reinforcement lights were similarly used in an attempt to increase the gazing behavior of male college students toward a female interviewer.[9] Female students interviewed male students about their attitudes toward various contemporary issues. During the interview the male students had two of their fingers hooked up to an electronic recording device. They were told that a small green light in front of them would light up when their physiological responses favored a successful interview, and a small red light would come on when their physiological responses were not "favorable." In reality, the green light was illuminated whenever the males gazed at the interviewer. The red light was illuminated when the males looked away from the interviewer for more than six seconds. This reinforcement technique was successful in getting the males to gaze more toward the female interviewers. The males' evaluations of the interviewers, however, were not affected by this change in their behavior. This is probably because the males were not aware that their gazing behavior had changed.

In the study we read about earlier in which experimenters used false feedback about gazing to influence the attitudes of male and female college students, the amount that participants had supposedly gazed was brought to their attention. They could say to themselves, "I looked a lot (very little) at my partner. I must feel positively (negatively) toward him (her)." The males in the above study using reinforcement lights were presumably not aware of their gazing behavior so they could not make this self-interpretation. Another factor that could have prevented participants from changing their attitudes in the studies using lights to reinforce talking and gazing behaviors would be an awareness that their behaviors were being controlled by the lights rather than by themselves. Interviews with participants after both of these studies indicated that the participants were not aware of the coercive role of the lights. They attributed any changes in behavior of which they were aware to their own doing.

Influencing Attitudes by Inducing Discrepant Behaviors

Leon Festinger developed a theory of cognitive dissonance in which he proposed that people are motivated to seek consistency between their attitudes and behaviors. If people behave in a certain manner they will attempt to perceive their attitudes as consistent with their behavior. If people believe they hold certain attitudes they will attempt to behave or at least interpret their behaviors as consistent with their attitudes.[20]

In a well-known study designed to test Festinger's theory of cognitive dissonance, college students were assigned randomly to one of three different groups.[21] Students in the first group were given a long series of boring tasks and then paid $1 for telling another student the tasks were actually interesting. Students in the second group also completed the boring tasks and were then paid $20 to convince another student the tasks were interesting. Students in a third, control group completed the boring tasks but did not have to convince anyone that they were interesting. After engaging in the behavior of telling another person that some really boring tasks were interesting, the students were asked to give their personal opinions of the tasks on a rating form.

The results of the study confirm what we have learned about self-perception. The students who were paid $1 rated the boring tasks as significantly more interesting that the students who were paid $20 or the students in the control group. In terms of Festinger's theory, the students who were paid $1 for making a false statement probably experienced cognitive dissonance because they made a false statement and had no good reason for doing it. To reduce their dissonance, these students were motivated to convince themselves that the boring tasks were actually somewhat interesting. The students who were paid $20 for making the false statement were less likely to experience dissonance because they could say they did it for the money. These students were not motivated to change their attitudes toward the tasks.

We can also interpret the results of the above experiment in terms of Bem's theory of self-perception.[22] Students in the $1 group could have said to themselves, "I made a statement that the tasks were interesting. Since I only got paid $1 I couldn't have done it for the money. Maybe the tasks actually were interesting." Students in the $20 group, by contrast, most likely said to themselves, "I made a statement that the tasks were interesting. I got paid $20 for making the statement so it is obvious that I did it for the money. The tasks actually were boring." Bem's theory of self-perception differs from Festinger's theory of cognitive dissonance in that dissonance theory emphasizes internal motivations for seeking consistency whereas Bem's theory emphasizes the self-perceptions of behaviors and their external causes. Although there are conceptual differences between cognitive dissonance theory and Bem's self-perception theory, the two turn out to be very similar in practice. Both suggest that it is possible to change people's attitudes by getting them to engage in a behavior that is inconsistent or discrepant with their beliefs. If you induce people to behave in a discrepant manner by using external force or large sums of money they will not change their attitudes because they can attribute their behaviors to the force or to the money. If you can *subtly* influence people to behave in a discrepant manner they will be motivated to change their attitudes or self-perceptions.

In the remainder of this chapter we will review research studies in which people's attitudes were changed through subtle inducements to engage in discrepant behaviors. The results of these studies can be explained either in terms of Festinger's theory that people are motivated to reduce the dissonance they experience from engaging in discrepant behaviors by changing their attitudes about the meaning of these behaviors, or according to Bem's self-perception theory. Bem would argue that people who have engaged in discrepant behaviors are in a position to say to themselves, "I engaged in a behavior that is inconsistent with what I thought I believed. I wasn't forced or paid to engage in this behavior. I must have done this act because I actually believed in it."[23]

A large body of research studies has focused on the question of whether or not people's attitudes toward various issues can be changed by getting them to write essays or verbally argue for a position that is against their original beliefs. Other research studies have attempted to change people's self-perceptions by inducing them to behave in a variety of ways that are incompatible in one way or another with their prevailing beliefs.

Essays and Arguments

From what you have just learned you should not find it difficult to design an experiment for changing people's attitudes by getting them to write an essay or verbally argue in favor of an issue with which they disagree. The goal, as we have seen, is to induce people to write an essay contrary to their original beliefs without using obvious force or offering significant monetary payment. Barry Collins and Michael Hoyt reviewed the research studies using essay writing and verbal arguments to change people's attitudes and arrived at the following conclusions.[24] To successfully change a person's attitudes, you have to arrange it so the person feels personally responsible for writing the essay or giving the verbal argument and believes that this act will have specific consequences for other people. If people are induced to write essays or give arguments that will never be taken seriously, they have little reason to become personally involved. If they write an essay or give an argument against their beliefs, and know that this act will have consequences for others, they will feel responsible for their act and this feeling of responsibility will motivate them to modify their original beliefs.

To test this proposition, Collins and Hoyt conducted the following experiment. College students were asked by a fellow student (who was supposedly working for the college administration) to write an essay arguing against a policy of open visitation in undergraduate dormitories.[25] Because it was known from a previous survey that 90 percent of the students were in favor of an open visitation policy, writing an essay against this policy was likely to produce dissonance for nearly all of the participants in the study. To make it possible to measure the importance of *consequences,* half of the students were told that the college administration would be using the essays to form their dormitory visitation policy; the remaining students were led to believe that the essays would be included in a historical report but would have no influence on the administration's decision. In addition, half of the students in each of these two groups signed a statement taking personal *responsibility* for their essays. The remaining students signed a statement saying that they were not responsible for writing the essays. Finally, half of the students in these four groups were given a *payment* of $2.50 and half of the students were paid 50¢. The results of the experiment supported Collins and Hoyt's prediction. Students who showed the greatest attitude change in favor of their essays (and contrary to their original beliefs) were those who felt their essays had high *consequences*, who felt *responsible* for their essays, and who received low *payment*.

A similar study showing the effect of consequences, responsibility, and payment was modeled after the $1–$20 experiment that we read about earlier. College students were asked to convince other people that a genuinely dull task was actually interesting.[26] Half of the students were given a high *payment* of 2 hours class credit and the remaining students were given a low payment of 1/2 hour of class credit. Students in each of these two groups were divided so that half of them felt personal *responsibility* for making the false argument because they were doing it out of their own free will; the remaining students were led to feel that they were making the false statement as a requirement of the experiment. The *consequences* of the false argument were manipulated by making half of the students in the four groups think they had successfully convinced another person that the boring tasks were interesting, and leading the other half to believe that they were not successful in convincing another person that the boring tasks were interesting.

Results of the experiment supported the conclusions outlined earlier. The students who were most strongly influenced to believe that the boring tasks were actually interesting were those who received low payment, who felt responsible for giving the false argument, and who thought that their false argument had important consequences for another person. An interesting extension of this study found that people would be motivated to believe that a dull task was interesting if they had successfully given a false argument to someone they liked.[27] If people are successful in giving a false argument to someone they don't like, they do not appear to feel responsible for the consequences of their behavior and are not motivated to change their attitudes toward the dull task.

Actions That Harm Others[28]

How do we interpret an action we perform that causes harm to another person? If we are forced to perform a harmful act or do it unintentionally, it will not necessarily influence our self-perceptions. We can attribute the harmful act to the external force or to the accident. If there is no external explanation for our misdeed, we will feel personally responsible for the harm we have done and be motivated to reconcile ourselves to this responsibility.

One way to reduce feelings of responsibility for harming another person is to offer the other person some sort of compensation. This method of reducing guilt will be successful if it is possible to give sufficient but not excessive compensation. Compensation that is not sufficient will not relieve feelings of guilt because it will not restore equity for the misdeed. Compensation that is excessive will cause discomfort by making the other person indebted for it. In addition to offering compensation for a harmful act the wrongdoer could offer to punish himself. This second option is somewhat less likely because it usually involves too great a personal cost.

A number of research studies have shown that people who feel guilty about causing harm to another person will make some sort of restitution if the opportunity is available. College students were given the task of monitoring a voltage meter that was supposedly an important part of an animal experiment.[29] Half of the students were led to believe they had ruined the experiment when the meter was surreptitiously switched to read much higher than normal. These students were later significantly more likely to donate money to a summer research fund than students who had not "ruined" the experiment. College students in a second study were made to feel guilty because they had upset a pile of supposedly carefully arranged computer cards and ruined someone's thesis.[30] These students were later significantly more willing to assist with another experiment than students who had not knocked over the cards. Participants in three other experiments were made to feel guilty because they had supposedly harmed another person by giving electric shocks or by failing at their half of a cooperative task.[31] These guilty participants were later significantly more willing to volunteer to help with a different experiment, to spare a person the discomfort of electric shock by taking it themselves, or to volunteer to donate blood. Women in a shopping center were approached by a male experimenter who handed them a camera and asked them to take his picture.[32] For half of the women the camera was rigged to make them think they had caused it to break. The remaining women also found that the camera was broken but were not led to believe that it was their fault. Shortly after this incident the women were confronted with a second female experimenter who was carrying a broken grocery bag from which a few items had "accidently" fallen. Results of this study showed that 54 percent of the women who were "guilty" of breaking the camera informed the female experimenter that she was losing some of her groceries. In contrast, only 15 percent of the "not guilty" women were willing to call the broken grocery bag to the female experimenter's attention.

An interesting finding that emerges from these studies of guilt is that participants are most likely to make restitution for the harm they have done if they do not have to come face-to-face with the victim.[33] People are usually quite motivated to reduce their guilt by agreeing to help someone who is unrelated to the person they originally harmed, but if the victim seeks restitution in person they are likely to feel uncomfortable because the victim is using their guilt to his or her advantage.

Many times there is no opportunity for reducing the guilt from harming someone by helping an unrelated person in need. If an appropriate method for offering compensation does not exist, people are motivated to search for other ways to alleviate their guilt. One thing they might do is derogate the person they have harmed. Participants in an experiment were induced with either great pressure or little pressure to give an unfavorable evaluation to another person.[34] Participants who were greatly pressured to give the negative evaluation presumably did not experience responsibility for their actions because they could attribute their misdeed to the external pressure. Participants who gave the unfavorable evaluation with only subtle pressure from the experimenter were in a position to feel personal responsibility for their negative act. These participants tended to derogate the person they had harmed by convincing themselves they really didn't like him. This derogation was more likely to occur if the participants believed they would not see the person in the future and therefore would not have to explain why they had made the unfavorable evaluation.

A study of juvenile delinquents found that the delinquents commonly defended their misdeeds against people by labeling their victims as bums who deserved what they got.[35] William Ryan has described the use of derogation on a broader scale in his book *Blaming the Victim.* Ryan points out how American society tends to "explain" the poor school performance of underprivileged children by blaming the children for lack of interest and motivation. Minority people are often blamed for their disadvantages because they lack ambition or other personal qualities. People on welfare are blamed for being unwilling to work. By blaming the victims in our society for their plight, we protect ourselves from admitting weaknesses in our government or social policies.[36] We may also be motivated to blame victims because most of us like to believe that we live in a just world where deserving people are rewarded and undeserving people are punished. If we see people suffering through no fault of their own, we can either admit that the world is not such a just place after all or convince ourselves that the people actually do deserve to suffer.[37]

Another way people can reduce the responsibility they feel from harming another person is to convince themselves that the harm was only minor. Participants in an experiment were induced to deliver electric shocks to another person.[38] Half of the participants were led to believe they had chosen to give the shocks. The remaining participants felt they were giving the shocks because the experimenter told them to do so. The participants who felt they had chosen to give the shocks judged the shocks to be less painful than participants who felt they had been forced to give the shocks. The tendency to underestimate the painfulness of the shocks occurred primarily when the "victim" was a male. Participants apparently could not convince themselves that an electric shock would not be painful to a woman. When the victim was a female, the participants reduced their guilt for giving the shocks by convincing themselves that they were forced to do it by the experimenter.

A third way to reduce the discomfort produced by causing harm to another person is to deny responsibility for our actions. A good example of this type of altered self-perception is found in war criminals who explain their behavior by saying they were "only following orders." The tendency to deny responsibility for harming others was shown in an experiment where participants had to choose between two available tasks.[39] The participants knew that one task required them to give electric shocks to another person whereas the other task allowed them to give pleasant sensations to another person. The problem for the participants was that they had to gamble in their choice of tasks because they did not know which was the pleasant task and which was the unpleasant task. Participants in one group were provided with a rather easy means of identifying the pleasant and unpleasant tasks; all they had to do was ask an experimenter who was in a different room in the same building. Participants in a second group could find out how to identify the tasks only by walking to another building many blocks away.

As it turned out, none of the participants in the study took the trouble to identify the pleasant and unpleasant tasks. The decision not to seek further information about the tasks resulted partly from the inconvenience involved and partly from subtle pressures applied by the person conducting the experiment. However, it was arranged that all the participants would attribute their decision not to seek more information about the tasks to their own free choice. The participants were then led to believe that the task they chose was the one requiring them to deliver electric shocks. How much responsibility were the participants willing to accept for the fact that they would have to shock another person? Participants who had rejected a very easy opportunity for identifying the tasks might experience considerable discomfort. With only a small effort they could have avoided giving shocks to another person. Participants who could only identify the tasks with considerable effort and inconvenience probably would not experience as much discomfort. They could have avoided giving shocks to another person only at a relatively great expense to themselves.

The results of the experiment supported this interpretation. Participants who could have easily identified the tasks considered themselves significantly less personally responsible for having to shock another person than participants who could have identified the tasks only with great difficulty. Participants in the first group were motivated to reduce their guilt for not making the small effort to avoid the unpleasant task by convincing themselves that they were not responsible for their actions.

It is easier to deny responsibility for harming others when we have acted as part of a group rather than alone. College students in an experiment were asked individually or in groups of three to give advice to another person on how to perform some problem-solving tasks.[40] Half of the students were led to believe their advice had been useful and that they had helped the other person win some money. These students took responsibility for their helpful advice and evaluated the other person in a favorable manner. The remaining students were led to believe their advice had been harmful and had caused the other person to lose money. How did the students interpret their actions when they thought their advice had been harmful to the other person?

Students who were in groups tended to deny responsibility for the harmful advice. This was possible because they could easily convince themselves that the advice had also come from the other two group members. Students who had individually given harmful advice could not deny responsibility for the harm by attributing it to others. They were more likely than other participants in the experiment to convince themselves that the person suffering the harm had not really followed their advice and that his losses weren't really all that bad. All of the students who thought their advice had been harmful to another person tended to derogate that person by evaluating him negatively on a rating form.

It was pointed out earlier that people usually rely on derogation, underestimation of suffering, and denial of responsibility to reduce the discomfort they feel from causing harm if there are no satisfactory means available for compensating the victim. They are more likely to use the above techniques if they have limited contact with the victim. It is much harder for people to warp their perceptions if they are forced to be in contact with the victim for a relatively long period of time.

With this understanding, it should not be surprising that the victims of our society are often obliged to live in separate neighborhoods and attend separate schools.

A final way in which discomfort from harming another person can be reduced is if the victim takes definite action. The victim could forgive the wrong-doer. Alternately, the victim could retaliate against the person who harmed him. More likely than the first alternative and less frightening than the second is the third alternative of intervention by an outside agency. In our society we have social welfare agencies to restore equity between the "victims" and the "harm-doers." People are more likely to reduce their derogation of a victim if they give aid to the victim out of their own choice. If they feel forced to give aid to a person they have victimized, they do not necessarily reduce their derogation.[41] The challenge for the victims of our society is to get us to give them aid with the feeling that we are doing it of our own free will.

Other Discrepant Behaviors

A number of researchers have attempted to change people's attitudes by getting them to engage in discrepant behaviors requiring greater personal commitment than giving arguments or writing essays. In one experiment, for example, female college students were randomly exposed to different severities of initiation to gain admission into a discussion group.[42] Severe initiation consisted in reading highly embarrassing material in front of other people. The embarrassing material included a number of obscene words and vivid descriptions of sexual activity from contemporary novels. Participants who received a mild initiation only had to read publicly a list of sex-related words that were not obscene. Participants in a third group did not undergo an initiation as a requirement for joining the discussion group. After performing their respective rites of initiation, participants listened to a tape recording of a "typical" discussion taking place in the group they were supposedly going to join. The tape-recorded discussion was arranged to be as dull and banal as possible. The voices on the tape were dry and the recorded material was full of contradictions, unfinished sentences, and long pauses. After hearing the tape recording showing their discussion group to be worthless and uninteresting, the participants were asked to give their impressions of the discussion group on a rating form.

As you would expect, participants who had undergone a severe initiation were in a state of dissonance because they had been induced to engage in an unfavorable behavior for no good reason. They were motivated to explain their willingness to undergo the initiation by convincing themselves that their discussion group was not really all that bad. Compared with participants who underwent mild initiation or no initiation, they rated the discussion groups as being significantly more interesting and favorable.

How can you change a person's attitudes to become more favorable toward a certain food? The trick is to get the person to eat the food thinking he or she made the choice to do so. A group of eighth grade children were offered a prize of a record or movie ticket if they would agree to eat either a small amount or large amount of a vegetable they intensely disliked.[43] Children in the first group committed themselves to eat one dish of the vegetable. Children in the second group committed themselves to eat four dishes of the vegetable during the course of several weeks. The children were then asked to state how much they liked the vegetables on a rating form. Results showed that children who had committed themselves to eat a large amount of the disliked vegetable rated it more favorably than children who had committed themselves to eat only a small amount of the vegetable. This experiment was probably successful because the prize for eating the vegetables was subtle and sufficiently separated from the children's commitments to eat the vegetables. The children therefore could not say they had agreed to eat the disliked vegetable solely to win the prize. They were instead motivated to explain their commitment by increasing their positive attitude toward the vegetable.

College students were led to believe that as part of an experiment they would be eating a dead worm.[44] It was emphasized that the students were volunteers who felt free to terminate the experiment whenever they wished. This was done so that the students would perceive that they acted of their own free will in the experiment. After being given the negative expectation that they were to eat the worm, one group of students was given two choices. They could actually eat the worm or they could instead choose to participate in a simple study of perception. Earlier research had shown that when college students with no previous expectations are given the choice of either eating a worm or doing the study of perception, they *all* choose the study of perception. In this experiment, more than three-fourths of the students who at first believed they would have to eat a worm later chose to eat the worm! A second group of students in this experiment, who believed they would have to eat the worm, were allowed to choose between giving themselves electric shock or doing the study of perception. Half of these students chose to give themselves electric shock! Why did the students in this experiment choose to suffer when they didn't have to?

After believing they would eat the worm ("of their own free will"), the students changed their self-perceptions in one of three ways. Some of the students came to see themselves as heroes or martyrs who were willing to endure discomfort for the good of science. Other students convinced themselves that eating a worm really wasn't all that bad. A third group of students changed their self-perceptions to believe that the discomfort of eating the worm or giving themselves electric shock was something they deserved. The reaction of this last group of students is interesting because it is similar to the self-depreciation that is characteristic of people suffering from depression. The authors of the experiment point out that it is not uncommon for people suffering from terminal illnesses or other misfortunes to "explain" their suffering by concluding that they must have done something wrong to deserve it. The authors argue that changes in self-perception may be an adaptive way of dealing with suffering that is *inevitable.* If changes in self-perception lead to suffering that could otherwise be *avoided,* they are probably in the long run maladaptive.

A group of army reservists was induced by their drill sergeant to eat fried grasshoppers.[45] The drill sergeant of some of the reservists was friendly and courteous. The drill sergeant of other reservists was formal, cool, and unfriendly. Which group of reservists became more favorable toward eating grasshoppers? Reservists in the first group could say to themselves, "I ate some grasshoppers. I didn't really like the idea, but the drill sergeant was nice about it. I did it because he said it was a good thing to do." Reservists in the second group were in a position to say to themselves, "I ate some grasshoppers. The drill sergeant was really nasty about it. I would not have eaten the grasshoppers for his sake, so I must not have thought they were really all that bad." Of the reservists who ate the grasshoppers, those with the negative drill sergeant rated the idea of eating grasshoppers significantly more favorably than those with the positive drill sergeant.

One problem in this study was that half of the reservists with the negative drill sergeant refused to eat the grasshoppers and therefore did not change their attitudes. A third group of reservists in the experiment was offered the grasshoppers with neither positive nor negative pressure from their drill sergeant. Virtually all of these reservists ate the grasshoppers out of curiosity. These reservists changed their attitudes to become more favorable toward the grasshoppers because they were in a position to say to themselves, "I ate some grasshoppers. No one influenced me to do it. They really must not be all that bad."

The lesson from this experiment is that you can cause people to change their attitudes if you use a negative persuader to influence them to perform an undesirable behavior because the people will attribute the undesirable behavior to their own free choice. This approach is limited by the fact that many people exposed to a negative persuader will refuse to engage in the undesirable behavior in the first place.

People who refuse to follow an experimenter's request are likely to change their attitudes in the *opposite* direction: "I refused to do what was asked. I must *really* not believe in it."[46] To successfully change people's attitudes with discrepant behaviors you have to use sufficient pressure to get them to perform the behaviors, but not so much pressure that they will feel forced.

Making Alternative Choices

Another approach to changing attitudes by inducing discrepant behaviors is to offer people a choice between two or more equally attractive alternatives. If they have to decide between equally attractive alternatives, they will have to explain (to themselves) the reason for their choice. This self-explanation will be reasonable if they convince themselves that the alternative they chose is more favorable than the alternative they rejected.

Participants in a study were asked to rate the desirability of eight manufactured articles including a toaster, a fluorescent desk lamp, a stop watch, and a portable radio.[47] After rating the articles the participants were allowed to choose one of two specified articles to keep as a gift. The two articles offered as choices were ones that the participants had rated as equally desirable. After making their choices, participants were asked to rate the eight articles a second time. The participants tended to become more favorable toward the chosen article and less favorable toward the rejected article.

Grade school children in a similar study were asked to rate their liking for 16 toys.[48] The children were then allowed to choose one of the toys as a gift. When they rated the toys for the second time, the children increased their liking for the chosen toy and decreased their liking for the rejected toys.

Some Conclusions
About Influencing Attitudes

The general strategy for influencing people to hold certain attitudes is to get them to behave in ways that are consistent with these attitudes. This strategy will be most successful if the people believe they have chosen to behave that way and if they are aware of their behaviors and feel they will be of some consequence.

The technique of influencing a person's self-perceptions with environmental cues satisfies the above requirements by focusing on behaviors that are already taking place. The person is aware of these behaviors and does not feel that they were a result of external forces. Because this technique deals with ongoing behaviors, it cannot influence self-perceptions related to behaviors that have not yet taken place.

False feedback operates to make people highly aware of their ostensible behaviors. There are no discernible external reasons for these "behaviors," and therefore people attribute them to their own choice. False feedback techniques are limited by problems of credibility. There are constraints on the kinds of behaviors one can convince people they have performed. We learned in Chapter Three that when people are given false feedback about their bodily states they engage in testing behaviors to find out if these supposed bodily states are actually true. The same thing is likely to happen with false feedback about behaviors. People are more prone to believe false feedback about behaviors that they cannot disprove. There was no easy way for participants in the studies we read about to determine the true time that other people had looked at paintings or the true length of their answers to the interview questions. Participants probably believed the false feedback about their gazing behaviors because the amount that people gaze at others is something about which they are not generally aware. An experiment attempting to give participants false feedback about their interpersonal distance was not successful because the participants could not be convinced to believe false feedback about the relative distance they were sitting from each other.[49] Research has shown that false feedback about bodily states is most likely to influence people when the self-perceptions involved have minor consequences. When the false feedback about bodily states implies consequences that are important, people will be motivated to verify the false feedback before they alter their self-perceptions.[50] The same generally holds true for false feedback about behavior. It would be difficult for false feedback about behavior to result in long-term changes in self-perception because people are continually testing their beliefs with feedback from the outside world.

Reinforcement techniques hold more promise than false feedback for long-term changes in self-perception if the newly reinforced behaviors can be maintained. Two limitations of reinforcement techniques are if people are not aware of their newly reinforced behaviors and if they can attribute these behaviors to the reinforcement rather than to themselves.

It is possible to influence people to change their attitudes by getting them to act in a way that is discrepant with those attitudes, if the inducements for engaging in these behaviors are sufficiently subtle. The people who participated in the studies reviewed in this chapter were in a position to perceive that their discrepant acts resulted from their own choice and therefore reflected personal attitudes. The strategy of changing people's attitudes by subtly influencing their actions is not limited to the inducement of behaviors that are discrepant. In Chapter Five we will use our knowledge of how people perceive themselves through their actions as a basis for learning methods of changing attitudes by influencing behaviors in a wide variety of situations.

FIVE

Self-Perception
and Attitude Change

Our examination of various techniques for changing people's attitudes has revealed that the success of these methods depends on the prototypical strategy of influencing people to behave in a way that is consistent with the attitudes to be instilled. For this approach to work, the people being induced to change their attitudes must not only attribute their new behaviors to their own free will rather than to external forces, they must also feel responsible for them and believe that the behaviors have meaningful consequences. Festinger's theory of cognitive dissonance suggests that people change their attitudes to correspond with newly acquired behaviors in order to reduce dissonance. Bem's theory of self-perception argues that people who behave in a new way consider their new behaviors to be external signs of their beliefs. Festinger's theory has limitations of ambiguity because it does not provide specific rules about how cognitive dissonance is instilled and how it is reduced.[1] In addition, it appears possible to change people's attitudes by getting them to engage in behaviors that are not necessarily discrepant or "dissonance producing." Bem's theory studies functional relationships between environmental variables, behaviors, and attitudes and does not grapple with inferred inner motives.

Because of our interest in self-perception we will focus our discussion on the theory proposed by Bem. Our purpose in this chapter will be to learn how people change their attitudes after being influenced to engage in behaviors they can attribute to themselves. The research we will analyze ranges from the laboratory study of specific responses (such as interpersonal attraction, the perception of pain, and compliance) to the investigation of large-scale behaviors (such as racial prejudice and brainwashing) occurring in the outside world.

Subtle Manipulations of Behavior

Liking Other People

How can you get someone else to like you? Theoretically, it is simple. You influence the person to be nice to you while making the person feel he or she acted of his or her own free will. In each of the following experiments, the experimenter was able to influence the behavior of participants while making them believe they were acting out of their own choice.

Participants in one experiment were given the task of testing other people on a simple learning task.[2] The participants were instructed to act positively toward half of the people, giving compliments for their performance, and to act negatively toward the remaining people as they worked on the tasks, criticizing them for their performance. After interacting with the people in the experiment, the participants were asked to state how much they liked them on a rating scale. Results of the experiment showed that participants were significantly more favorable toward the people they had treated in a positive manner. The participants had apparently been influenced to say to themselves, "I behaved in a kind (harsh) manner toward that person. I must like (dislike) him."

Male participants in a second experiment performed a task in which they earned an average of two dollars.[3] After the study was over, the experimenter asked one group of participants if they would be willing to return the money they had earned because he had run out of funds and needed the money to continue the experiment. The experimenter explained that he couldn't force the participants to return the money, but hoped they would return it as a personal favor.

As it turned out, almost all of the participants were willing to return the money to the experimenter. Because a few participants did not return the money, it can be assumed that the participants who did return the money felt they were acting out of their own free choice. A second group of participants was not asked to return the money they had earned. After this treatment, a person who was supposedly unrelated to the experiment asked the participants to evaluate the experimenter. As you would expect, the participants who were asked to do a favor for the experimenter (and did it) liked him significantly more than the participants who were not asked to do the favor.

In Chapter Four we read about several studies showing how people will react negatively toward someone they have harmed. Participants in a third experiment were given the task to deliver electric shocks to another person.[4] Participants in one group were made to feel that they had little choice in the matter. Participants in a second group were told that their participation in the experiment was completely up to them, that they had no obligation toward the experimenter, and that they could leave any time they wished. These participants were instructed that they would be given full responsibility for remaining in the experiment and delivering the shocks. Half of the participants in the two above groups were given false results from a personality test that were positive and made them feel like strong and independent people. The remaining participants in the two above groups were given false results from a personality test that were negative and showed them to be weak and rather dependent people.

After delivering the electric shocks to the other person in the experiment, the participants were asked to evaluate him on a rating form. Participants who felt they had shocked the person out of their own free choice and who saw themselves as strong and independent people were most likely to rate the person they had shocked very negatively. They were in a position to interpret their behavior as a sign of their own negative feelings. The remaining participants could explain their behavior of shocking the other person by attributing it to the demands of the experimenter or to the weakness they had been led to see in their own personality.

Perceiving Pain

Researchers have used subtle manipulations of behavior to show how people's attitudes toward painful or aversive stimuli can be influenced. Male participants in an experiment were given a series of 2-second electric shocks.[5] The shocks were strong enough to cause some discomfort without being harmful. Each participant was provided with a button that he could press to turn off the shocks whenever he desired. It was arranged that during some of the shocks a light of one color would be illuminated and during other shocks a different colored light would be illuminated. The participants had been instructed that when the first light was on they should immediately press the button to turn off the shock. When the second light was on, the participants were encouraged to refrain from pressing the button and to endure the shock. The participants rated each shock on a rating form in terms of how uncomfortable it was to them. Even thought there was no overall difference between the shocks, participants rated the shocks they had escaped as significantly more uncomfortable than the shocks they had endured. The participants were influenced to use their behavior in escaping or enduring the shocks as an indication of how uncomfortable the shocks had been.

The success of the above experiment depended on the subtle manipulation of the participants' behavior of escaping or enduring the shocks. The participants were instructed to respond to the differently colored lights in a manner that assured them they were actually behaving out of their own free will. To demonstrate the importance of influencing people's behavior in a subtle manner, the following experiment was conducted.[6] Participants were placed in a situation similar to that of the participants in the previous experiment. Participants in one group were told that when one of two different lights came on, they would be *required* to either escape or endure a rather uncomfortable loud noise. Participants in a second group were told that it would be preferable for them to escape the noise with one light and endure the noise with the other light, but that they were free to make their *own choice* in determining their final reactions. Because the participants had no reason not to follow the experimenter's suggestions, they ultimately complied by enduring the noise with one light and escaping the noise with the other light. However, only participants in the "free choice" group were influenced to label the noise they had escaped as more uncomfortable than the noise they had endured. Participants in the "requirement" group were in a position to say to themselves, "I endured the noise some of the time and escaped it other times because the experimenter required me to do it. My own feelings toward the noise had nothing to do with how I reacted." Because participants in the "requirement" group felt forced to endure certain blasts of noise, they ended up rating these as being even more uncomfortable than the noise blasts they were required to escape.

A third study of pain perception was successful in subtly influencing participants' behaviors and consequent reactions to pain by having them engage in role playing.[7] The participants in the experiment, who were going to be tested for their reactions to electric shock, were divided into three groups. One group was instructed to act very upset about their experience of being shocked. The participants were asked to behave as if they were genuinely nervous about the shocks and to act as if the shocks were very painful. It was made clear that the participants should not be inhibited, but rather act out any negative reactions they felt toward the electric shocks. A second group of participants was instructed to act calm and relaxed about their experience of being shocked. They were encouraged to smile, relax themselves, and behave as if the shocks were not at all disturbing to them. Participants in a third control group were given no instructions about role playing and told to act in whatever manner they felt most suitable.

After this experience of behaving in different manners in the face of electric shock, the participants were tested by a second experimenter who was supposedly unrelated to the first part of the experiment. This second experimenter tested the participants' reactions to a second series of electric shocks with no instructions about how they should behave. The experimenters wanted to see if the participants' experience of watching themselves react in a certain manner during the first part of the experiment would influence their self-perceptions of tolerance for electric shocks in the second part. The results supported the experimenters' expectations. Participants who had previously acted as if they were upset by the experience of being shocked showed less tolerance for the second series of shocks than participants in the control group. Participants who had previously acted as if they were not at all upset by the experience of being shocked showed more tolerance for the second series of shocks than participants in the control group.

Another interesting finding in this experiment showed that there was a significant relationship between participants' awareness of how they had acted during the role playing session and their reactions to the final series of shocks. People are most likely to change their attitudes if they clearly recognize the behaviors they are role playing and probably also if they attribute their role playing to their own choice rather than to external forces.

Male and female college students in a similar experiment were exposed to a series of electric shocks with the instructions that they should use their facial expressions to convince an observer watching them through a one-way mirror that some of the shocks were very painful and other shocks were very mild.[8] The actual severity of the "painful" and "mild" shocks was always equal. Results showed that the college students were not only successful in convincing the observers that the shocks were either painful or mild, but also successful in convincing themselves. When the students pretended that the shocks were extremely painful, their physiological arousal (measured by skin conductance) was significantly higher than when they acted as if the shocks were very mild. In addition, the students evaluated the supposedly painful shocks as being more uncomfortable than the supposedly mild shocks.

The authors of this study felt that Bem's theory of self-perception could not fully account for these results because the college students had received direct external instructions to act as if the shocks were mild or painful. The students could therefore attribute their facial expressions to the instructions of the experimenter rather than to their own choice. Consequently, the researchers concluded that there is a direct physiological link between facial expressions and subjective feelings. Research studies have not yet ascertained how much of the relationship between facial expressions and emotions is caused by this possible physiological link and how much results from self-perceptions of facial behaviors. We do know, however, that the influence of facial expressions on emotions is often quite strong.

Perceiving Emotions

Anna, the schoolteacher in "The King and I," advises that to conquer fear it is often helpful to "whistle a happy tune." Many times during your life you have probably been given the encouragement, "Smile! It will make you feel better." Let me offer you that challenge. Make yourself smile. I'll bet you will have a momentary good feeling.

Male college students were told that they were participating in an experiment concerned with the activity of facial muscles under various conditions of perception.[9] Small electrodes from a recording instrument were attached to various parts of each participant's face. The experiment consisted of getting participants to contract certain facial muscles and relax other facial muscles so that sometimes they were smiling and sometimes they were frowning. While they were effecting these various smiling and frowning expressions, the participants were asked to evaluate their reactions to a series of pictures or cartoons.

The experimenter's chief interest was to see if the participants' reactions to the pictures and cartoons would have anything to do with their facial expressions. The only purpose of the electronic recording equipment was to provide an excuse for getting participants to smile or frown. The experimenter felt that if he simply asked participants to smile or frown they would interpret their behaviors as a response to his request rather than as an indication of their true feelings. By getting the participants to smile or frown in a very subtle manner, the experimenter hoped that he could influence their perceived emotions.

The attempt of the experimenter was successful. Participants who looked at the pictures while they were smiling saw themselves as happy and elated. Participants who looked at the pictures while they were frowning saw themselves as aggressive. In addition, when participants were smiling they rated the cartoons as significantly more humorous and significantly less aggressive than when they were frowning. The reaction of one participant in the experiment shows the power of facial expressions in influencing our emotions:

> When my jaw was clenched and my brows were down, I tried not to be
> angry but it just fit the position. I'm not in any angry mood but I found

my thoughts wandering to things that made me angry, which is sort of silly, I guess. I knew I was in an experiment and knew I had no reason to feel that way, but I just lost control.[10]

A somewhat less complicated method of influencing expressive behaviors was carried out in an experiment where high school students were shown segments from slapstick movies by Abbott and Costello and W. C. Fields.[11] Results showed that both boys and girls smiled and laughed more when canned laughter was added to the soundtrack of the films. The increased laughter stimulated by the canned laughter on the soundtrack led girls to rate the movies as funnier. Boys who were influenced to laugh by the canned laughter did not rate the movies as funnier. This was possibly because boys felt their laughter was part of being in and going along with the experiment rather than a sign of their specific appreciation for the movies.

A study with college students found similar results.[12] Male and female college students were exposed to a series of cartoons and asked to rate the cartoons on how funny they were. Half of the cartoons were accompanied by canned laughter and half of them were not. It turned out that the canned laughter was successful in getting both the male and female students to laugh and smile more. However, only the female students showed a relationship between the amount they smiled and laughed and their ratings of funniness in the cartoons. The authors of this experiment suggested that males might be less likely than females to use their expressive behaviors as signs of their attitudes.

Forbidden Fruits Versus Sour Grapes

Sometimes people who are prohibited from engaging in a certain activity have the "forbidden fruit" reaction and come to view the activity as more desirable. On other occasions they react in a "sour grapes" fashion and come to perceive the activity as less desirable. One factor determining which of these two reactions occurs is the explanation people give themselves for why they did not engage in the behavior in the first place. If we refrain from engaging in a prohibited activity "of our own volition" we can easily take the sour grapes reaction and convince ourselves the activity wasn't all that desirable anyway. If we refrain from engaging in the prohibited activity because of external threats of punishment, we may still see the activity as very desirable and react to it as a forbidden fruit.

Preschool girls and boys were left alone in a room for ten minutes with a number of toys.[13] Before leaving each child, a male adult pointed at one toy which the child liked and said that he did not want the child to play with it. The children were told that they could play with any of the toys except the one forbidden by the adult. Half of the children were given a mild threat from the adult who said that he would be annoyed if they didn't follow his request. The remaining children were given a severe threat. The adult said that he would be very angry if they played with the toy and that he would send them home and never invite them back again.

After their ten-minute experience with the toys, the children were tested for how much they liked the toy that had been forbidden. It had been determined by secret observation through a one-way mirror that none of the children had actually played with the forbidden toy. Children in the mild threat group became significantly more unfavorable toward the forbidden toy than children in the severe threat group. They were in a position to convince themselves that they hadn't played with the toy because it wasn't attractive to them. Children in the severe threat group did not devalue the toy so much because they could explain their reluctance to play with it as coming from fear of punishment by the adult.

A number of research studies using the same method of forbidding children from playing with an attractive toy have led to the following conclusions about the relative likelihood of forbidden fruit versus sour grapes reactions.[14] Children in one experiment were made more aware of their behaviors of not playing with the forbidden toy by a janitor who "accidently" came into the room while they were alone with the toys. The janitor pointed to the forbidden toy and asked the children why they were not playing with it. Children in a second experiment were "accidently" interrupted by an adult who picked up the forbidden toy in a way that would make the children aware that they had not been playing with it. In both experiments the children under conditions of mild threat were even more likely to devalue the forbidden toy when their attention toward the toy and their awareness of not playing with it had been increased. Children under conditions of severe threat saw the forbidden toy as increasingly desirable after their attention had been drawn to the toy and their awareness of avoiding it had increased.

In a third experiment, children were distracted from the forbidden toy with the opportunity to play with a toy that was very similar.[15] These children did not devalue the forbidden toy under mild threat because their attention to the forbidden toy and their awareness of not playing with it had been very much decreased. The above studies reinforce our general conclusion that people are most likely to use their behaviors as indications of attitudes if their awareness of the behaviors and the circumstances that control them is high.

A second conclusion reinforced by forbidden-toy research is that people are most likely to interpret their behaviors as a sign of their attitudes if they believe they have acted of their own volition. Children in a forbidden toy experiment were told that all of the children participating before them had followed the adult's wishes and not played with the forbidden toy.[16] Half of the children were given this information before they were left alone in the room with the forbidden toy. The remaining children were given this information after they themselves had refrained from playing with the forbidden toy. Results of the experiment showed that the first group of children did not devalue the toy. These children were less likely to view their behavior of not playing with the toy as coming from their own volition because they knew that all of the other children had done exactly the same thing. Children in the second group had already made the choice not to play with the forbidden toy. Finding out later that other children had behaved in the same manner did not prohibit them from viewing their actions as self-motivated. When they had resisted playing with the forbidden toy under conditions of mild threat they devalued the toy in the same way as children in the previous forbidden toy studies.

The self-perceptions made by children of their behaviors in forbidden-toy situations can be very durable. Children in an experiment were influenced not to play with a toy by an adult who gave either a mild or a severe threat.[17] Three weeks later the children participated in a study with a different adult; they played a game in which they could win a prize. The game was set up so that the children could only get enough points to win a prize if they falsified their scores. The experimenters were interested in seeing whether or not children would cheat if they were given the temptation and opportunity to do so. The children who had previously resisted temptation under conditions of mild threat falsified their scores in the game significantly less than children who had previously resisted temptation under severe threat. The children who had previously refrained from playing with a forbidden toy because of a mild threat could attribute their behavior to their own free choice. They were in a position to perceive themselves as people who can resist temptation. We have learned this lesson before. To change people's self-perceptions, and their future behaviors stemming from these self-perceptions, it is necessary to influence them to attribute their behaviors to their own choice rather than to external forces.

Providing Labels

In addition to manipulating people's behaviors in a subtle manner, researchers have attempted to change people's attitudes by labeling their actions in a way that would modify their self-perceptions. Women experimenters went to 153 homes in working and middle-class neighborhoods and asked adults who answered the door if they would be willing to contribute to the Heart Association.[18] Approximately half of the 99 adults who were willing to make a contribution were told by the experimenter, "You are a generous person. I wish more of the people I met were as charitable as you." The remaining adults who made a contribution were not given this label. Similarly, approximately half of the 54 adults who did not make a contribution were told by the experimenter, "Let me give you one of our health leaflets anyway. We've been giving them to everyone, even people like you who are uncharitable and don't normally give to these causes." The remaining adults who did not contribute were not provided with the above label.

Between one and two weeks after the labeling procedure, the above 153 adults were contacted by a male experimenter who was collecting donations for Multiple Sclerosis. The question was whether the labels previously given to the people would have any effect on their behaviors in a subsequent and supposedly unrelated situation. For the people who had previously been labeled as charitable, the results were significant. Previous donors in the labeled group gave significantly more money to the Multiple Sclerosis charity than previous donors who had not been labeled. Previous non-donors who had been labeled as uncharitable gave less money to the Multiple Sclerosis charity than previous non-donors with no label, but the difference was not statistically significant.

The authors of the study hypothesized that charitable labels might have had a greater effect on Multiple Sclerosis donations than uncharitable labels because the nondonors gave so little money in the first place that it was hard for a label to influence them to give even less. It is also possible that the uncharitable label made some of the non-donors feel guilty and they might have been motivated to give a bit more money the next time. Another important observation from this study was that nonlabeled people were not consistent in their behavior of contributing to the different charities. Their willingness to contribute to the first charity had no relationship to their willingness to contribute to the second charity. For labeled adults the results were different. There was a strong relationship between their contributions to the first and second charities. It is possible to conclude that people are generally not very aware of how they act and therefore don't often form conclusions about themselves that would influence them to behave in a consistent manner, but labeling or other methods of making people aware of their behaviors can increase the consistency of their behaviors. This issue will be elaborated in Chapter Nine.

Researchers carried out another attempt at influencing self-perceptions with labeling by telling two groups of participants in an experiment that they were "doers."[19] The participants were given false results from a personality test telling them that they were analytical, active, and independent. The participants were also told that they were the kind of people whose attitudes would lead them to act independently of others. Participants in the first group were told that they had been chosen to be in the experiment specifically because of their "doer" personality. Participants in the second group were led to believe that their "doer" personality had nothing to do with their participation in the experiment. A third group of participants did not receive the false personality feedback.

Measuring how willing the participants would be to distribute leaflets in support of an issue with which they were sympathetic was one step in the experiment. A person supposedly unrelated to the experimenter who had given the false personality feedback made this measurement so that participants would not become suspicious about any possible connection. Results showed that participants who felt chosen for the experiment because they had a "doer" personality were significantly more willing to distribute leaflets than participants in the other two groups. This experiment showed that simply labeling participants as "doers" was not sufficient to change their later behavior. Their awareness of the label had to be strengthened by making it an integral part of their involvement in the experiment.

People who work with delinquent children are well aware that continually telling children they are bad reinforces undesirable behaviors. Making children feel they are good, on the other hand, is often likely to increase desirable behaviors. This principle, of course, is not limited to children or to desirable and undesirable behaviors. We have all seen it operate in our own experiences. The following studies provide an interesting illustration.

The first study involved fifth-grade children in a public school.[20] The experimenters were interested in getting the children to reduce their littering behavior. One group of children was exposed to arguments of persuasion. During the course of eight days the teacher explained to the children that garbage and litter looked terrible, drew flies, and presented a danger to health. Antilittering posters were placed in the classroom and the school principal made a special visit to point out how messy the room was and to remind the children about the importance of being neat and orderly. A note left on the board by the janitor reminded the children to pick up papers off the floor.

A second group of children was exposed to a labeling treatment. During the course of eight days the teacher commented to the children that they were generally neat people and that they would not litter like some of the other students in the school. When the principal visited the classroom he commented on how neat it was and that he had noticed certain students cleaning up after themselves. A note left on the board by the janitor said that the room was easy for him to clean.

Several weeks after the above treatments a number of measures of littering behavior were taken. The children were not aware that their littering behavior was being measured and were therefore under no direct pressure to alter their behavior. Results showed that children in the labeled group were significantly more likely to clean up after themselves and appropriately discard litter than children in the persuasion group. Children in the persuasion group did not litter any less than other children in the school who had not been part of the experiment.

In the second study researchers sought to influence mathematics performance of second-grade children.[21] One group of children was persuaded to work hard and to do well in arithmetic. The teacher gave them the following kinds of comments:

You should be a good arithmetic student.

You should spend more time on arithmetic.

You should get good grades in arithmetic.

You should work harder in arithmetic.[22]

A second group of students was provided with labels for success in arithmetic. The teacher gave them the following kinds of comments:

You are a very good arithmetic student.

You really work hard in arithmetic.

You seem to know your arithmetic assignments well.

You're trying more in arithmetic.[23]

The results of this experiment were fairly powerful. Children in the labeled group performed significantly better on mathematics tests that were given in the weeks following their treatment than children in the persuasion group.

At this point we can see two reasons why emphasizing people's positive self-perceptions can be more effective in changing their behaviors than persuading (or nagging) them or providing them with negative labels. First of all, continually emphasizing the negative behaviors of people may influence them to label themselves in a negative manner and then behave in a way that is consistent with this negative self-perception. In the second place, if people do change their behavior as a result of persuasion, the new behavior is not likely to be long-lasting because it is attributable to persuasion rather than to free choice.

In Chapter Four we learned how environmental cues can influence people's responses during police interrogations. The following study shows that self-labeling can influence people's responses to questions about how they interpret their behaviors.[24] College students were given a series of questions about their participation in a certain course. For one group of students the questions were worded to emphasize external or extrinsic reasons for their actions in the course. They were asked to complete sentences such as:

> Generally I raise my hand *in order to* . . .
>
> I generally attend lectures *in order to* . . .
>
> I generally discuss topics with my friends *in order to* . . .
>
> I generally raise questions in class *in order to* . . .[25]

Students in the second group were asked to respond to the same questions worded in a way to emphasize internal or intrinsic reasons for their activities in the class. In all of the above questions, the words "in order to" were changed to "because I."

After answering the questions emphasizing extrinsic or intrinsic reasons for their actions, the students were asked a second series of questions that measured how much they felt they were influenced by the grade in the course and how much they were influenced by other factors such as their own personal interest. Results showed that students who had been influenced to label their activities in the course as extrinsically motivated were more likely to perceive they took the course to get a good grade. Students who had been influenced to label their activities in the course as intrinsically motivated were more likely to perceive their participation in the course as directed toward their own personal interest.

In addition to showing the effects of labeling behaviors as extrinsically or intrinsically motivated, this study points out how the simple wording of questionnaires can influence people's responses. Public opinion pollsters are well aware of the importance of wording their questions in the appropriate manner to "discover" the conclusions desired by their clients.

The Foot-in-the-Door Technique

How can you influence an originally negative person to like you better? It may occur to you to do something nice for the person. The problem with this approach is that it might make the person uncomfortable because now he or she owes you something. An alternative approach is to get the other person to do you a favor. Ben Franklin gave the following account of how this can be accomplished:

I therefore did not like the opposition of this new member who was a gentleman of fortune and education with talents that were likely to give him great influence in the House which, indeed, afterward, happened. I did not, however, aim at gaining his favor by paying any servile respect to him, but, after some time, took this other method.

Having heard that he had in his library a certain very scarce and curious book, I wrote a note to him, expressing my desire of perusing that book and requesting that he would do me the favor of lending it to me for a few days.

He sent it immediately ... and I returned it in about a week with another note expressing strongly my sense of the favor.

When we next met in the House, he spoke to me (which he had never done before) and with great civility; and he ever afterward manifested a readiness to serve me on all occasions, so that we became great friends and our friendship continued to his death.[26]

The strategy of getting people to do a small favor so they will later be more likely to do a large favor is called the foot-in-the-door technique. A male experimenter telephoned 156 housewives in a California suburb and asked if they would be willing to answer some questions about different brands of household soaps with which they were familiar.[27] Three days later, the housewives were called again and asked if they would be willing to have five men come to their homes to make a survey of the products they used. The survey would supposedly take about two hours and involve the men going through the cupboards and making a list of household goods that were present.

The experimenter was interested in seeing if women who had been asked to do the first small favor would be more willing to agree to the second larger favor. The results were significant. Fifty-three percent of the housewives who had previously been asked to answer the questions over the phone were willing to have the men come to their homes. A second group of housewives was asked to allow the men to come to their homes without previously being asked to answer questions over the phone. Only 22 percent of these women agreed to have the men come to their house.

To find out if the foot-in-the-door technique could successfully influence people's behaviors by changing their self-perceptions, a second experiment was conducted.[28] Male and female experimenters went to 127 homes and asked the residents to do a small favor. Half of the residents were given a small ecology sticker or a small safe-driving sticker with the request that they place it in a window or in their car. The remaining residents were asked to sign a petition advocating legislation for safe driving or for ecology. Two weeks later, a different experimenter came to the houses and asked the residents to put a large sign in their front yard reading, "Drive Carefully."

Again, the results were significant. Only 17 percent of the residents who had not previously been asked to do a small favor agreed to put the large sign in their yard. In contrast, 55 percent of the residents who had originally been asked to do one of the small favors were willing to have the large sign placed in their yard.

This experiment is especially interesting because it showed that people who were asked to do a small favor were later more willing to agree to do a large favor even if the later request was made by a *different* person for a *different* issue. If people are more willing to agree to a larger request when they have previously performed an *unrelated* small request, it is not likely that they are willing because the first request made them feel obligated. The foot-in-the-door technique probably works in this case by influencing a change in the person's self-perception. The authors of the study provide the following explanation:

> What may occur is a change in the person's feelings about getting involved or about taking action. Once he has agreed to a request, his attitude may change. He may become, in his own eyes, the kind of person who does this sort of thing, who agrees to requests made by strangers, who takes action on things he believes in, who cooperates with good causes.[29]

The foot-in-the-door technique has been found to increase people's compliance in a number of different situations. One investigator found that pedestrians were more likely to give a dime to experimenters if the experimenters first asked them what time it was. In a second experiment, the same investigator asked college students to write letters encouraging high school students to attend college.[30] These students were later more likely to volunteer to work on a university publicity campaign than students who had not been exposed to the letter writing request. A different group of investigators reported that people were significantly more likely to donate money to the Cancer Society if they had been asked earlier to wear a Cancer Society pin.[31]

If people are more likely to agree with a request when they have complied with a previous request, they should be less likely to agree with a request when they have not complied with a previous request. Residents in a Minneapolis suburb were contacted by telephone and asked if they would be willing to answer a series of questions.[32] Half of the residents were placed in a "small request" group and told that they would be given 8 questions. The remaining residents were placed in a "large request" group and told that they would be given 50 questions. Not surprisingly, most of the residents in the small request group agreed to comply with the request and most of the residents in the large request group did not.

Two days later, all of the residents were telephoned by a different experimenter and asked if they would be willing to answer 30 questions for an entirely different survey. Results showed that over 50 percent of the residents who had previously been asked to do the small favor were willing to comply with the second favor. In contrast, only 22 percent of the residents who had previously been asked to comply with the large favor were willing to comply with the second favor. Of the residents who were only asked to comply with the later favor, 33 percent of them agreed to do so.

This experiment relates to our study of self-perception in the following way. Residents in the small request group were in a position to see themselves as compliers (and were more likely to agree with the second request) because they had been induced to comply with the first request. Residents in the large request group were in a position to see themselves as noncompliers (and were less likely to agree with the second request) because they had been influenced not to comply with the first request.

At this point, we have the notion that if people are asked to agree to a large initial request, they are likely to refuse and then be less willing to agree to fulfill a second more moderate request. In some situations, however, the foot-in-the-door technique works in a different way. Let's say that someone asks us to do a large favor and we refuse. The same person then asks us to do a smaller favor. We might agree to do the smaller favor to bargain our way out of the situation. The person has made a concession by first asking for a large favor and then agreeing to settle for our compliance with a smaller favor.[33]

We can combine our understanding of self-perception with the above strategy of bargaining to reach the following conclusions. If a request for a large favor is immediately followed by a request for a smaller favor, people are likely to comply with the lesser request because they feel that the person asking the favor has made a concession. If the time period between the two requests is short, they will probably focus on the contrast between the two requests and feel that the second request is somewhat of a bargain. If asked for a large favor and then asked for a smaller one at a later time, people are likely to refuse to comply with the lesser request because if they have time to consider their behavior of refusing the large favor they might well perceive themselves as people who don't usually comply. People who are first asked a small favor are more likely to comply with a larger favor whether there is a delay between the two requests or not. Most people will agree to satisfy a small request and thereby perceive themselves as complying people.[34]

As we have seen, the foot-in-the-door technique is most successful in changing people's self-perceptions if they feel they are performing the first small request of their own free will. Women walking alone out of a department store were approached by a male experimenter who was carrying five bulky grocery bags in a very awkward manner.[35] The male experimenter asked the women if they would watch his bags for a moment while he went back into the store. Women in one group were told by the experimenter that he had just lost his wallet, which contained "a lot of money." Women in a second group were told by the experimenter that he had dropped a dollar bill in the store. All of the women were willing to comply with the experimenter's request. The experimenter then went into the store for one minute and returned with a smile on his face reporting that he had found the item he had purportedly lost. As the women went on their way they were encountered by a female experimenter walking in front of them who "accidentally" dropped a small package. The experimenters were interested in seeing which women would be most likely to pick up and return the package.

All of the women had been exposed to a foot-in-the-door treatment because they had agreed to assist the male experimenter by watching his bags. However, half of the women were provided a strong external reason for assisting the male experimenter. Having been told that he had lost his wallet, these women could easily attribute their inconvenience of watching the bags to his far greater inconvenience of losing a wallet. By contrast, the remaining women did not have a good external reason for assisting the male experimenter. The loss of a dollar bill was probably no more inconvenient to the experimenter than the effort of watching the bags was to the women. Therefore women in this group could perceive their behavior of watching the bags as a sign that they were generally helpful people.

The results of the experiment supported this reasoning. Women who had watched the male experimenter's bags so that he could ostensibly retrieve a dollar bill were significantly more likely to assist the female experimenter who had dropped the package than women who had previously watched the male experimenter's bags so that he could purportedly retrieve his wallet.

Another study showing the importance of how people perceive their responses to an initial foot-in-the-door request was carried out in the following way.[36] Residents of a rather conservative middle-class community in Pennsylvania were telephoned and asked if they would be willing to talk to an interviewer who would come to their house for five to ten minutes. The residents who agreed to speak with an interviewer were divided into three groups. One group of residents was interviewed by a hippie-looking student who wore blue jeans and had a beard and exceptionally long hair. A second group of residents was interviewed by a conventionally dressed student who wore a tie and jacket and was clean shaven with short hair. The third group of residents was not approached by an interviewer and served as a control group.

The interviewers rang at each resident's door, introduced themselves, and waited for the residents to invite them inside. The interviewers then gave a brief argument in favor of income taxes over sales taxes, thanked the residents for their time, and departed. This sequence of events was followed in a rehearsed fashion in order to make all of the interactions between the residents and the interviewers as consistent as possible. Several days later the residents were visited by a well-dressed experimenter who supposedly had no connection with the previous interviewer. The experimenter asked the residents to fill out a brief questionnaire measuring their attitudes toward income taxes versus sales taxes. Results showed that residents who had been interviewed by the hippie-looking student were significantly more favorable toward income taxes than residents who had been interviewed by the conventionally dressed student. Residents who were interviewed by the conventionally dressed student were no more favorable toward income taxes than residents who had not been interviewed at all.

Why should a pro–income tax argument given by a hippie influence residents more than a pro–income tax argument given by a straight student? The authors of the experiment propose the following explanation. If the assumption that the residents were generally conservative and not favorable toward hippies is correct, the residents interviewed by the long-haired student might have said to themselves, "I was willing to allow a 'hippie freak' into my house and I even listened to his arguments. Since I am usually not willing to relate to this kind of people, he must have had something very worthwhile to say." Residents who were interviewed by the conventional student could have said to themselves, "I was willing to allow the student into my house because he was clean and neatly dressed. There is no reason why I should agree with what he had to say." It may have occurred to you that the real reason why the residents allowed the interviewers into their homes is because they had been subtly influenced to commit themselves to the interviews by the original phone call. Nonetheless, the experimenters were successful in changing the residents' attitudes by getting them to perceive their behaviors in terms of the type of interviewer they had "allowed" into their house.

Changing Folkways with Stateways

In his book *Folkways*, William Graham Sumner argues that people's actions are primarily determined by folkways that have been handed down from the earliest human cultures.[37] Because Sumner believed that folkways are unconscious and instinctual he did not think they can be easily changed by human laws or decisions. It was Sumner's argument, "stateways cannot change folkways," that influenced the United States Supreme Court in 1896 to rule against federal requirements for integration. The basis for the decision was that because people's racial attitudes are based on folkways, a change in law would have no power to alter them. In 1954 the Supreme Court ruled that segregation was unconstitutional. This reversal of a Supreme Court decision is noteworthy because it illustrates how much our legal system is based on assumptions about human attitudes and behaviors. It also relates to our present discussion by suggesting that people's attitudes can be modified through behavioral changes resulting from societal influences.[38] Let us look at some examples of how this can happen.

In 1942, only 30 percent of the whites throughout the United States stated that they were in favor of school integration.[39] In 1956, two years after the Supreme Court decision, this figure had changed to 49 percent. By 1963, 63 percent of white Americans stated that they were in favor of school integration. The number of whites in the southern states accepting the idea of school integration rose from 2 percent in 1942, to 14 percent in 1956, to 32 percent in 1963.

In 1942, 35 percent of whites throughout the United States approved of residential integration. By 1956 this figure had risen to 51 percent. In 1963, 63 percent of whites throughout the United States were in favor of residential integration. The percentage of southern whites who accepted integrated neighborhoods changed from 12 percent in 1942, to 38 percent in 1956, to 51 percent in 1963. Similar changes occurred in attitudes toward public transportation. In 1942, 44 percent of whites across the United States approved of integrated public transportation. By 1956, this figure had changed to 60 percent. In 1963, 78 percent of whites throughout the United States approved of integrated public transportation. The percentage of southern whites accepting integrated public transportation changed from 4 percent in 1942, to 27 percent in 1956, to 51 percent in 1963. Although there are probably many reasons for these changes in racial attitudes, one possible factor is the alteration of behaviors and lifestyles resulting from the 1954 Supreme Court decision.

Other research studies have also shown that changes in behavior resulting from integration can lead to changes in racial attitudes. One study conducted in 1950 found that whites were no less likely to shop from black sales clerks than from white sales clerks.[40] Even though some of the whites in this study expressed prejudiced attitudes in other areas, their experience of shopping from black sales clerks led them to view black sales clerks and white sales clerks as equally competent. A second study conducted in 1952 compared the beliefs on equality of white clerical workers who had been working in integrated offices with the beliefs of white clerical workers who had never worked in integrated offices.[41] The white workers who had worked with black workers agreed significantly more with the notion that blacks and whites should be given equal work status. A 1948 study of university students and government employees found that whites who had experienced contact with blacks were significantly more favorable toward blacks than whites who had no previous experience with blacks.[42]

Research comparing whites who have lived in integrated housing with whites who have not experienced integrated housing has uncovered the following data. One group of investigators reported that only 3 percent of white housewives in segregated housing projects knew any black housewives by first name.[43] In integrated housing projects between 49 and 77 percent of white housewives reported that they knew black housewives by first name. In segregated housing projects only 1–4 percent of the white housewives reported that they shared activities such as shopping and baby sitting with black housewives. In integrated housing projects between 39 and 72 percent of white housewives reported sharing these activities with blacks. A second group of investigators found that 45 percent of whites who had previously lived or worked with blacks were in favor of interracial housing whereas only 16 percent of whites with no previous interactions with blacks favored interracial housing.[44] Two other studies have also revealed that blacks as well as whites who live in integrated neighborhoods have more interaction with and are more favorable toward people of different races than blacks and whites who live in segregated neighborhoods.[45]

During World War II a number of previously all-white infantry companies were integrated with black soldiers. Shortly after the end of the war in Europe, a survey was taken to see what changes had occurred in the racial attitudes of white soldiers as a result of this experience.[46] When white soldiers who had been in integrated companies were asked if they were favorable toward having white and black platoons in the same company, 60 percent of them said they would prefer it or just as soon have it as any other setup. Only 11 percent of white soldiers who did not have the experience of integrated companies said they would prefer or be satisfied with black and white platoons in the same company. When white soldiers in integrated companies were asked if their attitudes toward blacks had changed as a result of their experience, 77 percent of them reported that they had become more favorable. A platoon sergeant from South Carolina made the following comment:

> When I heard about it I said I'd be dammed if I'd wear the same shoulder patch they did. After the first day when we saw how they fought, I changed my mind. They're just like any of the other boys to us.[47]

The above summary of research on integration is related to our study of attitude change because it suggests that people can be influenced to make the self-perception, "I am willing to interact with people of a different race. They must not be all that bad." Research on integration does not provide as strict a test of Bem's theory of self-perception and attitude change as other research we have considered because it is not as well controlled. Besides holding different opinions on integration, people who have and have not experienced interracial contact differ in other ways that might influence their racial attitudes. Moreover, in addition to observing their own behaviors, people in interracial situations learn to reduce some of the negative stereotypes they have held for other racial groups.

The results of studies on integration are not as powerful as they might first appear for the following reason. In many cases researchers found that whites were willing to accept blacks within a particular context of integration but this acceptance did not generalize to other situations. White sales clerks in integrated stores, for instance, were willing to work on an equal status with blacks but they were not necessarily willing to live in the same neighborhood. Similarly, white soldiers were willing to fight side by side with black soldiers, but they were not necessarily willing to socialize with black soldiers. A study of white coal miners showed that they worked with blacks in the mines, but once outside the mines they lived in segregated neighborhoods.[48]

The finding that people are inclined to alter their racial attitudes to fit specific contexts of behavior suggests that the effect of partial integration may be limited, but the finding does not necessarily contradict Bem's theory of attitudes. If integration can influence people to treat others "equally" in some but not all situations, this means it causes them to change the way they label their attitudes in some situations. To achieve the ultimate goal of a totally integrated society, it will be necessary to get people to engage in positive interracial behaviors in all areas of their lives. Although this goal has not been attained in our society, several studies have been carried out specifically to reduce the prejudice of the participants.

In the early 1960s a group of highly prejudiced white female students in the South was recruited to work part-time on a management training project.[49] The female students were told that they would be working for two hours a day on a group project the government was testing to learn how to train people to work together. The project consisted in a management game in which the participants worked in teams of three and shared the responsibilities of operating an imaginary railroad. When the female students arrived to participate in the project they were assigned to work with two other females who were actually confederates of the experimenter. One of these females was white and the other was black. The purpose of the study was to see if any attitude changes would occur in the participants as a result of their experience of working in an integrated setting.

At the outset of the study there was some doubt whether or not the white participants would be willing to work on the task with a black person. The white females had said they would be unwilling to admit blacks to any clubs with which they were affiliated. In addition, the participants had said that if their boss began hiring many blacks they would not like it at all and would want to quit. As it turned out, the female participants did end up spending 20 days working with the black and white confederates. The study employed black and white confederates rather than random black and white females because the experimenter felt that it was important for the black and white partners to be well trained in serving as positive models. The management game required the three females to sit at a table together and make decisions on the basis of equal status. It was also arranged that food would be delivered to the three females during their lunch break. To appreciate this study, you must understand that when it was conducted it was most unusual for Southern blacks and whites to eat together or work under conditions of equal status.

During the course of the study some interesting changes took place. When the white participants were first introduced to their black and white partners they typically directed all of their comments to the white partner and virtually ignored the black partner. By the end of their experience the participants' interactions with the black and white partners were almost equal. On one occasion, a white participant asked the black partner at lunch if she could eat her leftover blackberry pie. Another white participant hitched a ride downtown with a black confederate because it would save her the bus fare. If the whites had been asked before the study if they would engage in such activities they most surely would have thought the person asking the question was crazy or making a joke. On the basis of responses correlated with attitude scales, investigators concluded that about 35 percent of the white females had become more favorable toward blacks as a result of their experience. The whites who became more favorable toward blacks were those who had had positive attitudes toward other people as well as toward themselves.

During the 1970s researchers conducted a study of children from low-income families who were attending an interracial summer camp.[50] To measure the effects of interracial experience a comparison was made between children experiencing their first night of camp with children who had been in the interracial camp for five days. The results of this study showed that children with five days of interracial experience were more likely to choose children from other races as friends than children who were spending their first night in the camp. Children with five days of interracial experience were also more likely to be influenced by and imitate adults of other races than children who had not yet had any interracial contact. This second finding is important because it shows that children who had the experience of interacting with children of different races also became more favorable toward adults of different races with whom they had had no previous contact.

From what we have learned about the self-perception of attitudes we would not expect that integration would always lead to more favorable attitudes between members of different ethnic groups. If people find themselves acting in negative ways in interracial contexts their attitudes toward members of other ethnic groups might become even more unfavorable. A review of research on intergroup contact suggests that integration is most likely to lead to positive attitudes if the different ethnic groups interacting share equal status and a feeling of intimacy or common goals, and there are social norms operating to reinforce non-prejudiced attitudes.[51]

People acting on the above suggestions for successfully promoting positive behaviors in an interracial context will satisfy one of the requirements of our theory of attitudinal change: behaving in a new way. The second requirement is to influence people to believe they are engaging in these positive interracial behaviors of their own choice. It is true that people may attribute their immediate change in behavior after a change in law to the law (and its consequences) rather than to their own choice. Over time, however, people continue to engage in the new behaviors and forget that it was a law that originally influenced them to act this way. Our knowledge of self-perception tells us that stateways can change folkways if the stateways promote desired rather than undesired behaviors and if, with time, people come to see these desired behaviors a matter of habit and free choice.[52] Although our society has a long way to go to achieve total integration, it is encouraging that the 1954 Supreme Court decision is consistent with research in self-perception.

Brainwashing

Bruno Bettelheim was a prisoner in two German concentration camps, at Dachau and at Buchenwald.[53] To protect himself from personal disintegration he attempted to look at his experience as a case study. He convinced himself that the horrible events were not happening to "him as a subject," but only to "him as an object." By looking at the events in the concentration camps from the point of view of an observer rather than a participant, Bettelheim was able to maintain his feeling of personal identity.

Bettelheim describes the initial shock felt by the prisoners when they were arrested and brought to a camp. Some of the prisoners explained their situation by convincing themselves that they were important people who were dangerous to the Nazis and were arrested for that reason. Other prisoners felt that they were arrested by "mistake" and that they would soon be released. Another group of prisoners felt guilty that they had allowed the Nazis to take power and convinced themselves that after liberation they would make up for their previous lack of assertiveness. After experiencing severe physical suffering and observing death all around them, the prisoners eventually became apathetic and indifferent.

The main goal of the Nazis was to produce a childlike dependency in their prisoners. To this end, they regulated every aspect of the prisoners' lives from the outside. Personal functions such as eating, washing, and elimination were possible only with the permission of the guards, and prisoners had to address one another in German terms typically reserved for children. They were also forced to do meaningless labor and subjected to arbitrary punishment.

A common reaction of prisoners in the concentration camps was to identify with and imitate the guards. They attempted to sew and mend their uniforms to resemble Gestapo uniforms and copied the guards' mannerisms and leisure-time activities. Some prisoners went as far as adopting and enforcing rules that were originally handed down by the guards on a whim. The Nazis were generally successful in making concentration camps prisoners completely dependent on the will of the guards. From what we know about self-perception it is apparent that the Nazis could maintain full control over the behaviors of the prisoners as long as the prisoners were in the concentration camps. There is little reason to believe that the behaviors adopted for survival in the concentration camps would continue once the prisoners reentered a "normal" environment.

During the Korean War, Americans who were captured by the Chinese Communists were exposed to a very different kind of treatment.[54] American prisoners reported that their Chinese captors greeted them with outstretched hands, saying, "Congratulations! You've been liberated." The prisoners were told that because the United Nations forces had entered the war illegally they were war criminals and could legally be shot. However, since it was their leaders rather than they who were at fault, the Chinese captors were happy to welcome them and help them learn the "truth" about the war.

During their marches to the POW camps, the prisoners experienced severe conditions, with little food and shelter and general physical exhaustion. These conditions were attributed by the Chinese to the hardships resulting from the bombings by United Nations troops. The Chinese captors were never "intentionally" harsh, and in their manner and words they were solicitous and sympathetic. The Chinese maintained total control over the prisoners and prevented the development of group feeling by prohibiting group meetings and rewarding the prisoners for monitoring each other's behaviors. Prisoners were exposed only to communist news media, their mail from home was censored, and their personal contact with the outside world was restricted.

The "teaching" and "relearning" that went on in the POW camps consisted of lectures, group discussions, and testimonials. The prisoners were induced to engage in self-criticism and to confess their "wrongdoings" publicly. The self-criticisms and confessions were arranged to begin on an innocuous, trivial level. When the prisoners began to perceive these behaviors as more or less natural, they were induced to build up to confessions on more substantive issues. An attempt was made to insure that the prisoners would actually participate in this process. It was not satisfactory for prisoners to simply observe others engage in these activities.

It is apparent that the Chinese made use of principles for inducing changes in attitude that are very similar to those we have examined in our study of self-perception. There are also interesting parallels between the confessions in the POW camps and the police confessions about which we read in Chapter Four: the attempt of the Chinese to act as "friends" rather than "captors" and to induce desired behaviors from prisoners not by "force" but by "encouraging" the prisoners to engage in "active learning." How successful was this attempt at changing prisoners' attitudes?

A study of over 3,000 repatriated POWS concluded that approximately 15 percent had been successfully induced to make confessions during their period of imprisonment.[55] The two most important factors contributing to the confessions of these prisoners were that they had been imprisoned for a long period of time and that they had been given rewards for their collaboration. It was common practice for the Chinese to provide cooperative prisoners with rewards including more food, better living conditions, and luxury items such as cigarettes, combs, soap, and candy. However, it is interesting for our study of self-perception that there was very little correlation between the degree to which prisoners collaborated in making confessions and the degree to which they actually changed their attitudes.

Our knowledge of self-perception enables us to understand why the Chinese Communist attempt at changing prisoners' attitudes met with only limited success. The primary reason that some prisoners made false confessions was to gain certain rewards in the face of severe privation. There is no evidence of anything magical or mystical about such a reaction.[56] As we know, inducing people to make confessions will not necessarily change their attitudes. For one thing, the external forces for collaboration were not particularly subtle. Even though the Chinese behaved like friends rather than captors, it was quite clear to the prisoners that their lives were under Chinese control. A second factor limiting the extent of attitude change was the fact that when the prisoners were repatriated they found themselves in a new environment with totally different demands on their behaviors. By observing their behaviors after their return to the United States, the repatriated prisoners were influenced to infer for themselves an entirely different set of beliefs. A third factor limiting the extent of the change in attitudes was the ability of prisoners to discount their behaviors of making confessions at the time they were making them. The prisoners often took advantage of American slang and idiom to emphasize wrong parts of sentences or to insert words and phrases to make their confessions come across to other prisoners as a joke on the Chinese. On one occasion a number of prisoners made fun by playing baseball with a basketball and telling the Chinese that this was how the game was actually played. On another occasion prisoners in a group photograph made fun by "giving the finger."[57]

In concluding our discussion of brainwashing it is worthwhile to reemphasize that most people underestimate the importance of environmental factors in determining behavior. Any human being can be induced to make confessions under sufficiently severe conditions. This confession does not reflect a change in the person's inner attitude. It is purely a function of external forces in the environment. In sum, it is most likely that a person who makes a confession under force is not manifesting a change in attitude. If we prosecute people for making confessions we are not prosecuting them for changing their beliefs to an opposing point of view; we are prosecuting them for engaging in a behavior that will presumably save their lives. When we idolize people who refrain from making confessions we are not valuing their refusal to change their patriotic beliefs but rather their determination not to make certain statements under external conditions of threat.[58]

Some Conclusions About Strategies for Changing People's Attitudes

In relating our study of self-perception to techniques for changing people's attitudes we have analyzed at one extreme experiments designed to influence changes in behaviors in very subtle ways and at the other extreme the incredible changes in people's lives that were perpetrated by the Nazis. We have seen that people can be influenced to change their attitudes if they are induced to alter their actions by subtle persuasion or by means of a small initial request. People also change their attitudes when they are provided with alternative ways for interpreting or labeling their on-going behaviors. Facial expressions might influence the self-perception of emotions because of a possible physiological link between facial expressions and subjective experience. Stateways can change folkways if they lead to positive behaviors because with time the feeling of being forced by the law becomes attenuated. Concentration camps and POW camps teach us more about the human potential for brutality than about methods for changing attitudes. The people who survived these experiences would probably appreciate the strategies we learned in Chapter Three for positive self-labeling and the techniques we will discuss in Chapter Eight for achieving self-control.

SIX

Personal Control
and Motivation

In Chapters Four and Five we discovered that people make judgments about their attitudes by observing their behaviors and the apparent causes of those behaviors. Behaviors attributed to free choice are generally perceived as reflecting attitudes and beliefs. Behaviors attributed to rewards, inducements, and pressures from others are usually perceived as a product of these external forces rather than as a sign of personal attitudes or beliefs. Now that we have reviewed research showing how people's attitudes can be changed by inducing them to engage in behaviors attributable to their own free choice, we are ready to examine in greater detail the conditions under which people learn to attribute their behaviors to themselves rather than to forces in the outside environment. This chapter will begin by comparing people who view the events in their lives as primarily under internal control with people who view them as primarily under external control. Later in the chapter we will see that most people have a tendency to feel a false sense of control over random outcomes occurring in gambling and games of chance. Finally, we will analyze research showing the conditions under which internal attributions of behavior can be "undermined" with external inducements or rewards, and consider suggestions for deriving the maximum benefit from external incentives in educational and work environments.

Self-Perception of Internal
Versus External Control

If someone asked you what causes unhappiness, on which of the following two arguments would you base your response?

a. Many of the unhappy things in people's lives are partly due to bad luck.

b. People's misfortunes result from the mistakes they make.

Which of the following two arguments is most closely related to your beliefs about why people like you?

a. No matter how hard you try some people just don't like you.

b. People who can't get others to like them don't understand how to get along with others.

Which one of the following two arguments sums up your philosophy of success?

a. Getting a good job depends mainly on being in the right place at the right time.

b. Becoming a success is a matter of hard work, luck has nothing to do with it.[2]

If you agreed with the first argument presented for each of the above issues, chances are that you view events in your life as largely determined by forces beyond your control. If you chose the second argument for each question, you are probably more inclined to believe that your own actions determine most of the events in your life. The notion that people's behaviors reflect their belief in external or internal control was developed by Julian Rotter.[3] The above questions are part of a 23-item scale constructed by Rotter to measure whether people believe primarily in external or internal control. People who believe in external control are inclined to explain the events in their lives as the result of external forces in society. Because the actions of society are unpredictable, they consider whatever happens in their life as primarily a matter of luck or chance. People who believe in internal control perceive many of the events in their lives as being contingent upon their own behaviors. They do not consider what happens to them purely a matter of luck or chance because they think they can influence their own actions.

A good deal of research has been conducted on people's perceptions of external versus internal control. In my discussion of this research I will refer to people who believe primarily in external control as "external people" or "externals," and to people who believe primarily in internal control as "internal people" or "internals." The distinction between externals and internals is made on the basis of responses to questions such as the ones on Rotter's scale. People's perceptions of the relative influence of external and internal forces in their lives evolve as a result of their experiences and individual development. The self-perception of external versus internal control is a way of looking at the world and has nothing to do with intrinsic or genetic differences between people.

Consequences of Internal and External Control

The degree to which people perceive events as being internally or externally controlled affects many aspects of their lives: personal effectiveness, social interaction, academic and intellectual achievement, and personal adjustment.

Acquiring Information for Personal Decisions

Because internal people believe they can control events in their lives, we would expect them to be more motivated than external people in seeking and effectively using information for making personal decisions. Research with hospital patients has shown that internals seek more information from physicians and nurses and are more knowledgeable about their condition than externals.[4] Internal prisoners were shown to be more familiar with the rules and regulations of the prison and to have more information about opportunities for parole than external prisoners.[5] External and internal college students in a computer simulation study were given information to be used in choices of marriage partners.[6] Internal students used this information much more effectively than external students.

College students participating in a study were given false results from a personality test which made it appear that they had many personality weaknesses.[7] After receiving this negative information, internal students were significantly more willing than external students to take action to correct the perceived weaknesses.

Personal Effectiveness

Research studies have shown that internals are more successful than externals at problem-solving tasks, especially if the tasks depend on cues or rules not made explicit by the experimenter.[8] Apparently internals are more effective than externals at bringing personal observations and experience to bear on the problem-solving tasks. Externals restrict themselves to cues that are provided from the outside. Other studies have shown that internals are more effective than externals in changing other people's attitudes and in influencing other people to judge them in a favorable manner.[9]

Externals and internals attempted to persuade other people of the same sex to take a certain point of view.[10] Internals rated the other people favorably if they were willing to yield to their arguments and unfavorably if they resisted and did not yield to their arguments. Internals apparently had enough confidence in their sense of control to give favorable ratings to people who yielded and unfavorable ratings to people who resisted. Externals gave more favorable evaluations to people who resisted and less favorable evaluations to people who yielded. Because externals did not expect to be personally effective in changing people's attitudes, they apparently thought less of people who were willing to yield.

Skill Versus Luck

Internals are more likely than externals to view their performance on tasks as a function of skill rather than luck.[11] There is some evidence that internals prefer to work on tasks based on skill whereas externals prefer to work on tasks based on luck. Internals also spend more time and effort than externals on tasks that are based on skill whereas externals become more personally involved than internals in tasks based on luck.

Conformity and Attitude Change

Because internals believe in personal control, they are less susceptible than externals to social influence. Externals are more likely to be affected by outer sources of approval and disapproval. Internals and externals were put in groups where they had to make judgments that were contradicted by other group members.[12] When the participants were required to bet money about the correctness of their judgments, internals were significantly more inclined than externals to stick with their own beliefs rather than yield to the contradictory views of the group. Other studies have shown that externals are more likely than internals to change their verbal responses to gain social approval from others.[13] Some internals have actively resisted other people's attempts to influence their behaviors.

Internals and externals were exposed to a persuasive argument by a communicator of either high or low prestige.[14] The externals were significantly more influenced than internals by the "high prestige" communicator. In addition, the externals gave more credance to the argument given by the high rather than low prestige communicator. The prestige of the communicator did not influence the judgments of the internals. A similar study found that externals would accept arguments from a person of high prestige even when the prestige of the person had no relevance to the argument.[15] Internals paid attention to the prestige of the person only when it was specifically relevant to the argument. Research has also shown that externals are more willing than internals to accept evaluations of their performance and their personality.[16]

One interesting study found that it was possible to change the attitudes of internals by subtly inducing them to write an essay.[17] Because internals believe they can control their behaviors, they were apparently willing to use the essays they had written as a sign of their attitudes.

Self-Control

The belief of internals that they can control events in their lives appears to increase their efforts at self-control. Studies have revealed that internals smoke less than externals, are more successful than externals at quitting smoking, and are more likely than externals to make active use of birth control techniques.[18]

Social Activism

We would expect internals to believe more than externals that their actions can have some effect on the outside world. A number of research studies have found internals to be more involved than externals with political and social activism. Other research studies have found no difference between internals and externals in political and social activism.[19] One reason for this apparent discrepancy is that expectancies for effectiveness in political and social causes are often based on factors in society that are beyond personal control. The degree to which people feel control over their own lives does not always correspond with their feelings of control over political and social events in the outside world.

Performance and Achievement

People are more likely to work hard on something if they believe there is a possibility they will succeed. Why should they expend effort on a task if the outcome of the task is completely beyond their control? Most people base the decision of whether or not to attempt a particular task partly on a realistic appraisal of their abilities and the specific nature of the task, and partly on subjective perceptions of internal versus external control over the outcomes of their efforts. A much discussed issue in education centers on the fact that some students do not perform as well as others because they believe their success or failure is determined more by luck or the whims of the instructor than by their own efforts. I will discuss the implications of this issue later in this chapter and also in Chapter Seven. Research has shown that there is a relationship between feelings of internal control and academic achievement. Studies with elementary, high school, and college students have found a positive correlation between belief in internal control and measures of grades and scores on a wide variety of achievement tests.[20]

Two factors that help internals achieve more than externals are less negative reactions to failure and greater ability to delay gratification. Externals who are asked why they succeeded or failed at a certain task are likely to mention luck, the nature of the task, or other forces beyond their control. Internals are more likely to attribute success or failure to their own efforts. Internals are also more likely than externals to show an adaptive response of increasing their goals after success and decreasing their goals slightly after failure. Externals are not reinforced by success to attempt higher goals. Because they ascribe the success to outside forces, they do not derive personal satisfaction from it. Externals also perceive failure as beyond their control and often choose unrealistic goals. Failure at these unrealistic tasks then reinforces their view that they had no control over their success or failure in the first place.

Development of competence requires the ability to delay immediate gratification. People who seek immediate rewards for small efforts are less likely to sustain efforts to achieve long-term rewards. Delay of immediate gratification is especially difficult because immediate rewards such as going to the movies, buying new clothes or a car, or getting married are much more tangible than a delayed reward of indefinable personal satisfaction which may take several years to achieve. Research has shown a fairly consistent relationship between belief in internal control and the ability to delay gratification.[21]

Personal Adjustment

Externals are generally more anxious than internals. This is probably because externals experience fears of failure and rejection as a result of their lack of perceived control over the environment. Psychologists have discovered a relation between externality and maladjustment, depression, and schizophrenia. Because externals accept events in their lives as beyond their control, they often show greater acceptance of outside threats and of negative information about themselves. The acceptance of negative events may be adaptive when there is no *realistic* possibility for exerting some kind of control over the situation (see Chapter Three). However, it is not adaptive to accept negative events as inevitable when opportunities for personal control do exist.[22]

Antecedents of Orientations Toward Internal Versus External Control

It is not possible to study the exact causes of beliefs in internal or external control. That would require rearing children from birth in specifically different manners. Nonetheless, by comparing the early experiences of internals and externals we can gain some insight into the antecedents of their orientations toward control.

Family Experiences

Internals appear to have parents who are warmer and more accepting than the parents of externals. Parents of internals are more likely to encourage their children to set goals and make their own decisions. Internals also have parents who are more consistent in the way they treat and discipline their children than the parents of externals. It is possible that children who are exposed to a consistent environment in the home are more likely to learn to associate their behaviors with predictable consequences in the outside world. First-born children are somewhat more likely to be internals than later-born children because they are often given more personal responsibility.[23] External female college students reported more stressful events in early childhood over which they had no control, such as divorce, sickness, or death in the family.[24]

Social Experiences

Lower-class and minority Americans are generally more external than Americans in more privileged positions. It is probably realistic for underprivileged Americans to believe in external control because they actually *are* denied power and influence in American society. Because externality causes other undesirable consequences, this process results in an unfortunate vicious circle. Underprivileged people are in danger of becoming more underprivileged because their original realistic perceptions of externality interfere with future motivation to overcome obstacles in their lives.[25]

Changing Beliefs in Internal
Versus External Control

To believe in internal control, people must experience situations in which their personal actions produce desired consequences. A number of different psychologists have developed programs for teaching children and adults to increase their self-perceptions of internal control.[26] Placed in controlled learning situations, participants in these programs are taught to set realistic goals and to take personal responsibility for their actions. As part of their training, participants discuss things that have happened in their lives and learn to ask questions such as, Did I *allow* that to happen to me? and What could *I* have done about it? Participants in these training sessions also talk about their goals in life and help each other devise strategies for achieving these goals. They are encouraged to view events in their lives as being less under external control and more under personal control. Participants encourage each other to have more confidence in themselves. Such training programs have generally been successful in influencing people to have greater feelings of internal control.

Important experiences in life can influence people's feelings of external versus internal control. After their disappointment at the 1968 Democratic National Convention, supporters of Eugene McCarthy believed more in external control.[27] Male college students whose draft status was made more desirable by the Selective Service lottery became more external than students whose draft status was not influenced by the lottery.[28] Students who received very negative feedback on an examination became significantly more external (at least for the moment) than students who did not receive the negative evaluations.[29]

There is evidence that college students in the United States have become increasingly external during the last ten years. This shift toward externality might be due to events such as Vietnam, Watergate, and the decrease in job opportunities which have made college students feel less control over their lives and the world around them.[30]

The Illusion of Control

We have seen quite clearly that people differ in self-perceptions of internal versus external control and that these self-perceptions have important consequences for various aspects of their life. If we ignore individual differences between people for a moment, we will discover that everyone has a tendency in certain chance situations to perceive an opportunity for control even when it does not exist. One study showed that dice players believe that concentration and various types of throws have an effect on the outcome.[31] But unless you believe in magic, you must agree that the outcome in a fair throw of dice is purely a matter of chance.

Effects of Personal Involvement

A number of research studies have shed light on why people sometimes act as if they have control in purely chance situations. One factor that makes people feel they have control over chance outcomes is personal involvement in the actual decision-making process. Participants in a dice game made bets in one of two conditions.[32] Half of the participants committed themselves to a bet before they tossed the dice. The remaining participants tossed the dice and then made a bet before they looked at the outcome of their toss. In reality, the probability of participants winning their bet in either game was identical. Participants, however, were willing to bet more money if they made their bets before rather than after they threw the dice. Participants somehow felt that throwing the dice after the bet would give them more control over a chance outcome than throwing the dice before the bet.

People buying lottery tickets were divided into two groups.[33] Half of the people were allowed to choose which ticket they wanted out of a box. The remaining people had their ticket chosen out of the box by an experimenter. Shortly before the lottery drawing, the people were asked how much money they would want from someone who wished to buy their ticket. In reality, all the tickets had an equal probability of winning the lottery. In spite of this fact, the people who had been allowed to choose their own ticket asked an average of four times as much for their tickets as the people whose ticket had been drawn by the experimenter.

Participants in another experiment played a game in which a stylus was moved down one of three paths.[34] If participants chose the correct path on any given trial a buzzer would sound when the stylus hit a certain point and they would win that trial. Half of the participants were allowed to manipulate the stylus themselves. The experimenter manipulated the stylus for the remaining participants but always allowed the participants to choose which path should be followed. The outcome of the game depended purely on which path was chosen and had nothing to do with manipulation of the stylus. Both groups of participants had exactly the same chance of being correct. Results showed, however, that participants who were allowed to manipulate the stylus had significantly more confidence about winning than participants who had the stylus manipulated by the experimenter. Participants in a similar experiment believed they had significantly more chance of getting a particular marble if they, rather than the experimenter, randomly drew a marble out of a container.[35]

Effects of Familiarity

People are also more likely to feel control over chance events if they are familiar with the task and feel an interest or involvement in it. Participants in the above study who were allowed to play with the stylus and the machine ahead of time were more confident that they would choose the correct path than participants who had no opportunity to play with the apparatus ahead of time. This was true even though familiarity with the apparatus had nothing to do with ability to choose the correct path. Familiarity with lottery tickets was manipulated in one experiment by giving people tickets with familiar lettering or unfamiliar and unusual symbols. In a second study, familiarity with lottery tickets was measured by the length of time people held the tickets. In both studies, people valued the familiar tickets more than the unfamiliar tickets. People also seem to value lottery tickets more if they experience the involvement of getting the ticket numbers in installments rather than all at one time.[36]

An experiment testing people's abilities at mental telepathy was set up so that a "receiving" person would try to guess which of five cards was being concentrated on by a "sending" person.[37] The receiving and sending people were in different rooms and communicated by buttons hooked up to lights. Results of this experiment showed quite clearly that the percentage of correct guesses made by the receiving people was no greater than would be expected by chance. When participants were given an opportunity to practice and talk about their images of each card before the test trials they were three times as confident about their ability at mental telepathy as when they did not have this practice. In reality, the practice sessions did not increase the participants' accuracy in "sending" the cards at all. The interesting part of this experiment is that even though the test trials were conducted in separate rooms with buttons and lights, the participants *believed* that practicing with each other would increase their success.

Effects of Past Experience

Past experiences can also influence perceptions of control over chance outcomes. College students played a game in which they guessed the outcome of a series of coin tosses.[38] The game was set up so that all students experienced an equal number of correct and incorrect guesses. However, half of the students experienced a good deal of immediate success whereas the remaining students did not experience success until later in the game. In reality, the probability of being correct in predicting a coin toss is always the same. Despite this fact, the students who experienced immediate success were significantly more likely than the students who did not experience immediate success to view themselves as having good ability in predicting the outcome of coin tosses.

In some kinds of games you have a greater chance of winning if you play against an incompetent rather than a competent opponent. This is not true, however, if the results of the game are determined purely by chance. Male college students played a game in which they made bets against an opponent who was either dapper and confident or awkward and nervous.[39] Because they were playing a chance game, the probabilities of beating both the dapper and awkward opponents were equal. The college students, however, were willing to bet significantly more money against the awkward opponent. Somehow they felt they would have a greater probability of winning a purely chance game against an awkward rather than a dapper opponent.

Some Implications

The tendency of people to perceive control over chance events has several important implications. A somewhat negative implication is the possibility of influencing people by making them feel they have control when they really do not. In gambling, business, and politics people are often falsely pacified with the notion that their will or actions may have some impact on events affecting their lives. A second implication of the illusion of control is that people appear to have a certain intrinsic motivation toward mastery and competence over their environment. We will read more about intrinsic motivation in the next section.

Intrinsic and Extrinsic Motivation

By now we have gained some knowledge about how people's behaviors reflect their perceptions of internal versus external control over the events in their lives. We have also seen that most people tend to perceive control over chance events even though such control does not actually exist. Perceived control refers to people's beliefs about internal versus external control over the outcomes of their actions. These outcomes can be positive and reinforcing or negative and punishing. Approval or disapproval of the outcomes of actions can also be understood on the basis of whether it is delivered by external sources or whether it originates within. Positive reinforcement for a person's actions can consist either in payment or approval delivered by other people or in a personal satisfaction coming from within. Similarly, punishment for an action can take the form either of aversive stimuli (such as physical pain or disapproval) delivered by other people or of negative feelings (such as guilt or self-disapproval) coming from within. Rewards and punishments that are delivered by outside agents result in what is called *extrinsic* motivation of behavior. Rewards and punishments that come from within ourselves result in what is called *intrinsic* motivation of behavior.[40] All psychologists would agree that people's behaviors are susceptible to influence from external sources. Many psychologists have argued that in addition to being influenced by external rewards and punishments, people are also motivated by intrinsic forces. Intrinsic motivation is an inner striving for competence and mastery. Psychologists who study intrinsic motivation believe that people have an innate predisposition toward self-determination. When challenges exist, they actively attempt to solve them. After mastering old challenges, they seek new challenges to satisfy their need for competence.

We will not concern ourselves with the voluminous material written by psychologists on the existence of intrinsic motivation and on arguments about how much of it is learned and how much is innate. Our discussion will focus on the conditions under which people learn to *perceive* their behaviors as being either extrinsically or intrinsically motivated. In previous chapters we examined many studies showing how people can be influenced to perceive their bodily reactions and their overt behaviors as being intrinsically motivated. Results of these studies indicated that when people perceive their bodily reactions and overt behaviors as intrinsically rather than extrinsically motivated they will interpret these reactions and behaviors as signs of their emotions or attitudes. The studies reviewed were designed to effect changes in people's bodily reactions and overt behaviors in such a way that their perception of external forces would be minimal. When people become less aware of external forces influencing their behaviors, they are more likely to interpret their actions as a product of intrinsic motivation. This rule also works in reverse. When people become more conscious of external influences on their behaviors, they are less likely to interpret their actions as a product of intrinsic motivation. We have learned a good deal about the implications of influencing people to perceive bodily reactions and overt behaviors as intrinsically motivated. We will now approach the issue from the opposite direction and read about research in which people were influenced to perceive their actions as extrinsically motivated.

Influencing the Self-Perception of Extrinsic Motivation

People who are influenced to perceive their behaviors as extrinsically motivated are less likely to view these behaviors as signs of their attitudes. They are in a position to say to themselves, "I engaged in this behavior because of certain rewards or punishments from the outside. This behavior does not necessarily reflect by true attitudes."

Monetary Payment

One method for increasing the self-perception of extrinsic motivation is to make money the apparent motivation for action. College students in two studies were individually brought into a room and given a series of challenging and interesting puzzles to solve.[41] Students in one group were told they would be paid one dollar for every puzzle they correctly solved. A second group of students was offered no payment and was not aware that other students were being paid. After they had worked on the puzzles for about an hour the students were left alone in the room for a brief rest period. At this point the students were free either to continue working on the puzzles or to look at a number of magazines that were on the table. During the rest period the students were secretly observed through a one-way mirror to see what they chose to do. The experimenters predicted that students who were not paid would perceive themselves as intrinsically motivated by the puzzle-solving task and would spend more time working on the puzzles during the rest period than students who were paid. Results of the studies supported this reasoning. Students who were not paid for solving the puzzles did spend significantly more time working on the puzzles during the rest period than students who were paid for solving the puzzles. Apparently, the paid students felt there was no reason to work on the puzzles during the rest period because they had no further external reward to gain for their efforts.

A similar study showed that college students did not perceive monetary payment as an extrinsic motivation for working on puzzles if it was given for participation in the experiment rather than for performance on the puzzles.[42] Students who received money for participating in the experiment spent the same amount of time working on the puzzles during the rest period as students who did not receive money. Students who received money only for correctly solving the puzzles spent significantly less time working on the puzzles during the rest period than students who received no money or students who received money only for their participation in the experiment.

In another series of research studies, elementary school children and college students were paid a nominal amount of money for working on either boring or interesting tasks.[43] Participants showed a significant tendency to attribute their performance on the boring tasks to the money and their performance on the interesting tasks to the enjoyment of the task. Participants were willing to spend more time on the interesting tasks for the same payment. Participants also felt that they deserved more payment for working on the boring tasks than for working on the interesting tasks.

Patients in a psychiatric rehabilitation center were divided into two groups.[44] One group of patients was paid 25¢ a week for attending vocational workshops. Patients in the second group were paid $2.00 a week for attending the workshops. Not surprisingly, patients in the second group attended the workshops more often than patients in the first group. After four weeks, payment was no longer given to the patients for attending the vocational workshops. During this period, patients in the 25¢ group attended the workshops about as often as they had before. These patients had presumably attributed their previous attendance to an intrinsic interest in the workshops rather than to the meager payment of 25¢ a week. The loss of this payment was not sufficient to influence their attendance at future workshops. Patients who had previously received $2.00 a week for attending the workshops, however, significantly decreased their attendance at the workshops. These patients had apparently attributed their previous attendance to the payment. When this payment was withdrawn, they perceived less motivation for attending the workshops.

Prizes and Privileges

Researchers have conducted a number of studies in which they manipulated children's self-perceptions of extrinsic motivation with prizes or privileges. Children who were given prizes for their behaviors appeared to have greater self-perceptions of extrinsic motivation than children who did not receive prizes for their behaviors.

Nursery school children who were playing with magic markers and construction paper were divided into three groups.[45] The first group of children was promised a Good Player Award consisting of a big gold star, a bright red ribbon, and a place to print their name for their participation. The second group of children received the Good Player Award at the end of the study in such a way that it was not contingent on playing with the magic markers. Children in the third group were not given an award. One week later the children were observed in a free play situation in which a number of toys plus magic markers were available. Children who had previously earned an award for playing with magic markers spent significantly less time with the magic markers than children who had received an award unrelated to the magic markers and children who had received no award. Apparently, the children in the first group were influenced to attribute their behavior of playing with the magic markers more to extrinsic motivation of receiving the Good Player Award than to intrinsic interest in the magic markers.

Nursery school children in a similar study were given a series of puzzles.[46] Half of the children were told that if they did a good job on the puzzles they would later be allowed to play with some attractive toys. The remaining children were given no reward for working on the puzzles. Several weeks later the children were observed in a free play situation in which the puzzles as well as other toys were available. The children who had previously been rewarded for working on the puzzles played significantly less with the puzzles during free play than the children who had not been rewarded.

Another interesting finding also emerged from this study. While originally working on the puzzles half of the children were told that they would be observed from time to time by an adult experimenter. The experimenter pointed to a nearby television camera and told the children he would be watching whenever a small light was illuminated. The remaining children were not led to believe they would be observed. During the free play session several weeks later the children who thought they had been observed played significantly less with the puzzles than the children who did not think they had been observed. Apparently, the feeling of being observed by an adult led the first group of children to perceive their work on the puzzles as motivated by the adult surveillance. They were less likely to perceive their work on the puzzles as motivated by an intrinsic interest in the puzzles.

High school students volunteered to participate in a study involving creativity and learning tasks.[47] Half of the students were told that as a reward for their participation they would be taken on an interesting tour of the psychology laboratory. The remaining students were not taken on such a tour. Results of the study showed that students who were rewarded with the tour showed significantly less interest in the study and performed worse on the creativity and learning tasks than the nonrewarded students. The nonrewarded students could perceive their motivation for being in the study as coming from intrinsic interest in the tasks. The rewarded students could explain their participation in the study as motivated by the external reward of the tour.

Ten and eleven-year-old children participating in competitive games were divided into two groups.[48] One group of children received prizes for their participation. The remaining children received no rewards for their participation. Results showed that children who received no external rewards reported significantly more enjoyment in the games than children who were given the prizes. Again, the rewarded children were more likely to attribute their participation to the prizes and the nonrewarded children were more likely to attribute their participation to enjoyment of the games.

People are most likely to perceive external rewards as extrinsic motivators for behaviors if the rewards are salient and unambiguously associated with the behaviors. We saw earlier that college students were most likely to perceive money as an extrinsic motivation for puzzle solving if the money was given specifically for working on the puzzles rather than for participating in the experiment. Similar results have also been found with children.

Nursery school children were asked to play a toy drum under one of three conditions.[49] Some children were told they would receive a prize (candy) for playing the drum. The prize was placed under a box set directly in front of the children to remind them of its presence. A second group of children was told they would be given a prize at the end of the study but were not further reminded of its existence. Children in the third group were not offered a prize for playing the drum. After about five minutes the drum-playing session was ended and the children in the first group were given their prize. The children were then given the opportunity to play with a variety of different toys and unobtrusively observed to see which toys they chose. The experimenters were interested in seeing how much attention the children would give to the drum. Results showed that children who were originally given a prize for playing the drum spent less time with the drum during the free play session than children who were promised a prize at the end of the study and children who were not promised a prize. This difference in attention toward the drum was also present when the children were tested four to five weeks later. It was concluded that children who received the prize for their drum playing were influenced to perceive their behavior as extrinsically motivated by the prize rather than by their intrinsic interest in the drum.

A somewhat different manipulation of extrinsic motivation was conducted in the following manner. Nursery school children were offered a prize (marshmallows) for playing with some drums.[50] Children in one group were encouraged to actively think about the marshmallows while playing the drums. Children in a second group were encouraged to actively think about snow while playing the drums. Children in a third group were given no special instructions. Results of this study were similar to those of the experiment reported above. Children who actively thought about the prize while playing the drums showed the least interest in the drums during a later free play period. Children who thought about snow showed the greatest interest in the drums during the later free play period. Children in the first group were apparently influenced to be very conscious that their drum playing was extrinsically motivated by the prize. Children in the second group were apparently distracted from paying attention to the prize by their active thoughts about snow. They were significantly less likely to attribute their drum playing to the external reinforcement of the prize.

External Punishment

We have seen that self-perceptions of extrinsic motivation increase when external rewards are salient and the association between rewards and behaviors is unambiguous. People can also be influenced to perceive their behaviors as extrinsically motivated if they are made aware of strong negative influences on how they act. Students working on puzzle-solving tasks were divided into two groups.[51] Students in one group were threatened with punishment from a loud buzzer if they did not complete the puzzles within a certain time. Students in a second group were encouraged to complete the puzzles during a certain time but were not threatened with punishment if they failed to do so. During a rest period the threatened students spent less time working on the puzzles than the nonthreatened students. Apparently, the threatened students had perceived part of their motivation for working on the puzzles as extrinsically motivated by the desire to avoid punishment. During the rest period they therefore had less reason to work on the puzzles than the nonthreatened students.

Verbal Praise

It was probably not surprising to learn that people are inclined to perceive behaviors for which they receive money or prizes as extrinsically motivated. How do people interpret verbal praise for their be-behaviors? Does verbal praise also decrease the perception of intrinsic motivation? One study designed to answer this question showed interesting results.[52] College students working on puzzles were divided into two groups. One group of students received verbal praise from an experimenter for successful performance on the puzzles. A second group of students did not receive verbal praise from the experimenter. Results showed that male students spent more time working on the puzzles during a rest period if they had received verbal praise. Apparently, the males did not perceive the verbal praise as a sign that their performance on the puzzles was extrinsically motivated. Rather, the verbal praise served to increase their sense of satisfaction and personal involvement. Females reacted quite differently. They spent less time working on the puzzles during the rest period if they had received verbal praise. They apparently perceived the verbal praise as a sign that their performance on the puzzles was extrinsically motivated. They therefore had less reason to work on the puzzles during the rest period. The authors of this study based their explanation of these results on the assumption that males and females are socialized differently. Males, they maintain, are given more independence and taught to interpret verbal praise as a sign of their own competence or success. In contrast, females are taught to be dependent and motivated to please others.

Verbal praise for them is likely to be a sign that they have acted in the appropriate manner required by other people. Both male and female college students were less likely to work on puzzle-solving tasks during a rest period if they had previously received verbal criticism for puzzles they could not solve. Negative criticism apparently serves to decrease feelings of intrinsic motivation for males as well as females. In the above studies, the sex of the experimenter delivering the praise or criticism did not seem to make a difference.

A study with kindergarten children showed that both boys and girls spent more time drawing pictures if they had previously received verbal praise from an adult male.[53] Conversely, kindergarten children who had previously received a prize or money for drawing pictures spent less time drawing during a subsequent test period (in which prizes or money were not given). Children also spent less time drawing pictures if they had previously been ignored. The experimenters concluded that money, prizes, and negative feelings of being ignored decrease the intrinsic motivation of kindergarten children whereas verbal praise apparently increases the intrinsic motivation of kindergarten girls and boys.

The Mechanics of External Rewards

We have now studied the self-perception of extrinsic and intrinsic motivation from both directions. Earlier in this book we learned that people can be influenced to perceive their behaviors as intrinsically motivated if they are subtly induced to engage in the behaviors with a minimum of cues for external control. In this chapter we saw that people can be influenced to perceive their behaviors as extrinsically motivated through strategies that maximize their awareness of cues for external control. Both of these approaches for studying intrinsic and extrinsic motivation require manipulations that are somewhat extreme. The research focusing on perceptions of intrinsic motivation relied on deceptions arising from false feedback, subtle inducements, and misattribution. In the research focusing on perceptions of extrinsic motivation the experimenters offered people external rewards that were often unusual or inappropriate. The use of such manipulations is valuable for gaining a theoretical understanding of the extremes of extrinsic and intrinsic motivation. However, in their everyday lives people do not normally discriminate as clearly between intrinsic and extrinsic motivation. They are more likely to view their behaviors as motivated by a combination of both. For example, people do not always interpret monetary rewards as extrinsic motivation. Before labeling and reacting to their motivation they take a variety of factors into consideration. The following review of relevant research will help clarify this issue.

Appropriateness of Reward

In two different studies high school students were divided into two groups.[54] One group of students played a coin-toss game or Stock Market game that was directly associated with winning money. Students in the second group were paid for playing a game that had no association with money. Half of the students in each of the two groups were actually given money they could keep. The remaining students were given money they had to return or were only given points. How did the students interpret their motivation in the games? Students who played a game directly associated with winning money showed significantly more interest and involvement in the game if they were allowed to keep the money. Since monetary payment was an integral part of the game it was not interpreted as an extrinsic factor influencing the students' participation. Students who played a game that was not related to monetary payment reacted in a very different manner. They showed significantly more interest and involvement in the game if they were not allowed to keep the money. Students who were paid money that was not related to the game attributed their participation in the study to the money rather than to an intrinsic interest in the game. We can conclude that the introduction of monetary rewards does not automatically generate perceptions of extrinsic motivation. People learn to make distinctions about the appropriateness or "meaning" of rewards before judging the proportion of intrinsic to extrinsic motivation.

Another study further elucidates the mechanism whereby people interpret external rewards in everyday life.[55] One group of college students was given a set of very interesting puzzles to solve. A second group of college students was given a set of very boring puzzles to solve. Half of the students in each group received monetary payment for their efforts and half of the students did not. It is not surprising that students who were not paid found the interesting puzzles significantly more enjoyable than the boring puzzles. For students who were paid, the results were very different. Students paid for doing boring puzzles were more interested in the puzzles than unpaid students working on boring puzzles. These students apparently did not consider it inappropriate to receive payment for working on a boring task and they reacted to the payment in a favorable manner. Students paid to solve interesting puzzles had less interest in the puzzles than unpaid students working on similar puzzles. Because the interesting puzzles were enjoyable to work on in themselves, the monetary payment apparently seemed unnecessary and inappropriate. This experiment helps to clarify the research we reviewed in the previous section. External rewards can increase the perception of extrinsic motivation if they are given for a task that is interesting enough to be done for its own sake. External rewards can increase the perception of intrinsic motivation if they are given for behaviors that might otherwise not be performed.

Rewards as Bribes

Up to this point, we have examined the influence of external rewards on perceived extrinsic motivation from the perspective of the self-perception of causes of behaviors. External rewards can also enhance perceptions of extrinsic motivation by making people think they are being paid off or bribed. People are likely to interpret the overt attempts of others to control their behaviors with external rewards as a threat to their freedom and to react negatively when this interpretation is made.[56]

Rewards as Distractions

External rewards can have other negative effects. They can decrease future interest in an activity by giving the activity a negative valence. They can be distracting by causing a person to pay more attention to the rewards than to the activity. They can also cause anxiety over the anticipation of receiving the reward, and frustration if the reward is reduced or delayed.[57]

The following study examines the distracting effect of external rewards. Children ranging in age from four years to eleven years were given a series of problems requiring discrimination learning.[58] Children in one group were given an M&M each time they made a correct response. Children in a second group were told whether or not their responses were correct, but they were not given a reward. For children in a third group, an M&M was placed in a bowl for every correct response they made. These children knew that the function of the M&Ms was to tell them which responses were correct and that the candies would not serve as a reward they could keep. Results of this study showed that children who were not exposed to the M&Ms performed best on the discrimination learning tasks. The fact that the learning performances of children who received M&Ms as rewards and of children who received M&Ms as feedback were similar suggests that in this study the M&Ms served mainly as a distraction. Children in the M&M groups apparently did not do as well on the discrimination learning tasks because the M&Ms distracted them.

Another study showing a negative influence of external rewards was conducted in the following manner. Children in the sixth grade were asked to teach first-grade children how to play a simple but interesting game.[59] The sixth-grade children were very enthusiastic about this assignment and quite willing to participate with no further inducement. Half of the sixth-grade children were encouraged to teach the game solely because of their own interest. The remaining sixth-grade children were encouraged to teach the game and also promised a free movie ticket if they did a good job. Results showed that children who were not paid were significantly more successful in teaching the game than children who were rewarded with the movie ticket. The rewarded children were more demanding and critical toward the first-graders than the nonrewarded children. The nonrewarded children were significantly warmer in their instructional tone and were able to teach the game to the first-graders in significantly less time and with significantly less effort. It appears that the external reward in this study served to distract the sixth-grade children and interfere with a task they otherwise could have done in a relaxing and non-goal-directed manner.

Some Conclusions and Implications

Summarizing the Effects of External Rewards

We have considered many situations in which external rewards led to the self-perception of extrinsic motivation and a consequent decrease in normally intrinsically motivated behaviors. It should be noted that there are many contexts in which external rewards will not result in decrements of behavior. If people are made to feel guilty or indebted by large external rewards, they may attempt to work harder to justify or compensate for the rewards. Participants in the research we have examined most likely reacted to salient external rewards by decreasing their behaviors because opportunities for compensation were irrelevant or unavailable.[60]

In short, external rewards can influence the self-perception of extrinsic motivation in several different ways. In some situations external rewards influence people to attribute their actions to extrinsic causes ("I behaved in this way to receive the reward"). In other situations people may perceive a reward as a bribe or threat to their freedom. It is also possible for external rewards to be distracting or cause unpleasant feelings of anxiety or frustration. Psychologists do not always agree on how best to apply these explanations to specific situations.[61] Because there are so many individual differences between people, it may not be possible to make accurate predictions about when and how each of us will be influenced by external rewards. We do know, however, that inappropriately large, obvious external rewards tend to decrease intrinsic motivation. With our current knowledge it is possible to make some valuable conclusions and recommendations about the self-perception of extrinsic and intrinsic motivation.

Implications for Education

To attempt new challenges "for their own sake," a person must have had a reasonable amount of success with new challenges in the past. As we have seen, external rewards are not necessarily incompatible with self-perceptions of intrinsic motivation. A person's intrinsic motivation for working on a job would not be increased if he or she experienced a cut in pay. It is entirely possible for people to work at a task because they enjoy *both* the task and the money they earn for their efforts.[62]

Even though children have a great curiosity and interest in mastery, we would not think it feasible to leave them alone in a well-furnished classroom to develop their own curriculum for learning. They need guidance from external sources. External reinforcement in education is useful for clarifying learning objectives and giving feedback to students about how well they are doing. Many times children will not attempt certain tasks unless they initially receive external reinforcement for doing them. After experiencing success with the tasks the children will often continue to do them because they have developed an intrinsic interest in them.[63]

In view of the fact that external rewards can cause decrements in performance if they are misused, the following suggestions may be of value. External rewards should be used in programs designed to provide students with the experience of success. Learning behaviors that students do not originally know how to perform are at first motivated with external rewards and ultimately motivated by the experience of mastery and competence. We have seen that it is disadvantageous to put too much emphasis on external rewards and too little emphasis on feelings of satisfaction. It is therefore more desirable to use subtle forms of social approval or enjoyable activities as rewards than to incorporate highly distracting rewards that seem inappropriate for the amount of effort being expended.

Implications for Work Organizations

We have learned that external rewards are most likely to reduce self-perceptions of intrinsic motivation if they are given for behaviors that are intrinsically interesting and if the rewards are interpreted as inappropriate. Most jobs in industrial organizations are not interesting enough to be done for their own sake. In addition, payment for working in an industrial organization is certainly not considered inappropriate. For these reasons, a strategy for increasing self-perceptions of intrinsic motivation in work organizations would focus more on methods of increasing intrinsic interest in the jobs than on changes in the external reward structure.[65]

There are several possible approaches to increasing the intrinsic interest of jobs. Jobs that include a variety of tasks are more interesting than jobs focusing on one activity. Periodically rotating workers from one job to another can enhance the interest of the work. Jobs including decision-making or exploration are generally more interesting than jobs restricted to repetitive activities. Jobs are often more interesting if they foster social interaction. Jobs workers can identify with "wholeness" are likely to be more interesting than jobs that are part of an ambiguous chain. Workers are more satisfied if they can complete an identifiable module of work or at least appreciate the relationship between their task and the final product. Jobs are more interesting if they seem relevant and important and if workers have personal responsibility for their accomplishments. Workers who are aware of the quality of their performance can take personal satisfaction in work well done.[66]

SEVEN

Self-Perception of
Success and Failure

We have examined various ways in which the self-perception of internal versus external control helps to determine people's reactions to experiences of success and failure. The degree to which people attribute success and failure to either internal or external factors also affects their future aspirations, self-satisfaction, persistence on tasks, and ultimate achievement. In this chapter we will consider a number of other factors influencing people's perceptions and reactions to success and failure. After scrutinizing the explanations people give to themselves for experiences of success and failure, we will see how these explanations for success and failure relate to motivation for achievement. Finally, after reviewing research comparing male and female experiences of success and failure, we will learn how boys and girls are socialized to react to success and failure in different manners.

Components of Success and Failure

Bernard Weiner and his colleagues have suggested that the self-perception of success and failure can be understood in terms of the relative weight a person accords the following factors: ability, difficulty of task, luck, and effort.[1] People generally define their ability on the basis of past experiences with the same or similar tasks. If they have

151

been successful in the past they are more likely to see themselves as having ability than if they have failed in the past. There is also some evidence that successful performance during early trials of a task results in the perception of greater ability than successful performance during later trials of a task.[2] People usually judge the difficulty of a task by observing how well other people do on it. Social norms also define which tasks are supposed to be very difficult and which are easy. Luck is judged on the basis of past experience and from what people tell us. Random success on a task appears to be based more on luck than consistent success or failure. Finally, evaluations of effort take into account the effects of our efforts on the outcome of the task. Success and failure are perceived as a function of effort when there is a fairly clear relationship between how hard we try and how well we do. One study showed that an increase in the proportion of successful performances over time indicates to most people more effort than a decrease in the proportion of successful performances over time. This is true even if the total accomplishment is the same.[3]

Attributions and Satisfaction

An analysis of luck and effort shows that these explanations for success and failure are changeable and unstable. People are most likely to use luck or effort to explain success and failure that is inconsistent with past experience or unexpected. By contrast, difficulty of task and ability are generally stable explanations for success and failure that is consistent with past experience and expected.[4]

Most people attribute consistent failure to "low" ability and "high" difficulty of task. Failure following consistent success is most often attributed to bad luck. Failure following alternating success and failure is most often attributed to lack of effort and bad luck.[5]

When people are sure they will succeed, the experience of this anticipated success leads to great satisfaction. In conditions of less certainty, more satisfaction appears to come from unexpected success. More dissatisfaction generally comes from unexpected failure than from expected failure.[6] The positive effects of unexpected success and the negative effects of unexpected failure are greatest when the required levels of performance are determined by an external agent. If people are able to set their own standards of performance, the impact of unexpected success and failure is not so great.[7] People who were given a choice of which problems to solve did not experience as much satisfaction with success as people who were not given a choice.[8] Having a choice apparently made the people feel they had "unfairly" influenced the situation.

Performance on tasks is generally enhanced by experiences of success and retarded by experiences of failure.[9] However, failure can enhance performance on tasks if it is attributable to not trying hard enough rather than to self-doubts about ability. People who ultimately expect to succeed can be motivated by failure to increase their efforts.[10]

The relative effects of success and failure on performance are also influenced by the amount of relevance these experiences have for predicting future success or failure. For people expecting to do well on a task, an experience of success will be most effective in enhancing performance and satisfaction with the task if the experience is relevant for predicting future success. Success that is irrelevant to future performance is not as meaningful or satisfying. People who expect to do poorly on a task appear to be uncomfortable with experiences of success that are relevant to their future performance because this success is unexpected.[11]

Performance of Other People

Other people's performance on a task serves as a guideline for evaluating the difficulty of the task as well as for evolving self-perceptions of effort, ability, and luck. People are likely to attribute success and failure to the difficulty of the task if other people who are similar to them succeed and fail in the same manner. They are also likely to consider the outcome a result of the difficulty of the task if they succeed where dissimilar people fail or if they fail where dissimilar people succeed.[12]

By contrast, people are most likely to attribute outcomes to their own efforts if they succeed where similar people fail or if they fail where similar people succeed. With two dissimilar people, the reverse is true. They are more likely to attribute outcomes to their own efforts if both of them succeed or if both of them fail.[13]

Most people consider ability an important factor affecting the outcome of either a task on which they do well and other people do poorly or a task on which they do poorly and other people do well. If a person fails on a task altogether, his or her self-perceptions of luck are not influenced by the performance of other people. When a person succeeds, he or she is likely to feel lucky if other people fail but not if other people also succeed.[14]

Performance of other people also influences efforts and expectations of success. People are most likely to expend effort on tasks of intermediate difficulty. If a task is so easy that everyone does well or so difficult that everyone else fails, a person is likely to view strong effort as a waste of energy.[15]

People are more likely to predict success for themselves if other people do well on a task than if other people fail. Moreover, people are most likely to predict success for themselves if they attribute previous success by others on a task to the relative ease of the task. They are least likely to predict success for themselves if they attribute the previous success by others to luck.

When other people fail on a task, people are most likely to predict success for themselves if they think that lack of effort caused the others to fail. They are least likely to predict success for themselves if they think the other people failed because the task was too difficult.[16]

Participants in a study performed a task of skill on which everyone got the same score.[17] When the results were changed so that one person in the group did more poorly than the others, the value of the task increased in the eyes of the participants. When the results showed one person doing better than the others, the value of the task declined in the opinion of the participants. If the task involved luck rather than skill, the performance of another person did not matter.

Taking Credit for Success

Several research studies have shown that people are more likely to explain success on a task as a result of their ability and failure on a task as a result of bad luck.[18] This type of reaction, if not too extreme, is probably adaptive because it encourages a positive outlook on one's ability.

The tendency to attribute success to oneself was illustrated in a study in which college students attempted to teach mathematical concepts to elementary school children.[19] When the children showed great improvement, the college students had a strong tendency to attribute that improvement to their teaching ability. When the children did not improve their skill at solving the mathematics problems, most of the college students attributed the children's performance to the ability of the children or to limitations in the teaching situation, such as lack of time or facilities.

Other studies have found that people are less inclined to take credit for success if their positive self-evaluation might be questioned at a later time. Male high school students attributed less ability to themselves when they knew that they would be performing a task in the future than when they had already performed the task.[20] The students apparently felt safer not giving themselves too much credit for an accomplishment they had not yet demonstrated. A similar study showed that college students evaluated themselves as significantly more competent when their success or failure on problem-solving tasks would be anonymous rather than open to public knowledge.[21]

Female college students were interviewed and then asked how well they felt they had done in the interview.[22] If the students knew they were going to be evaluated by the interviewer they did not give themselves a particularly high rating. The students apparently wanted to prevent loss of esteem in the event that the interviewer's evaluation might be unfavorable. When the students were told that there would be no evaluation by the interviewer, they were more positive (but not unreasonably positive) in their self-evaluations.

Female high school students were exposed to an experience of success on a test for personal sensitivity.[23] The students were then given a task on which they had to make judgements of people in photographs. Students did not experience discomfort if they experienced success on both of the above tasks. If students experienced success on the first test and were then led to experience failure on the second task, the inconsistency made them feel uneasy. One group of students experiencing success on the personality test and failure on the photograph rating task was led to believe that they would be retested on the personality test in the future. These students experienced discomfort because their previous success on the personality test was going to be reevaluated. To spare themselves a loss of self-esteem, they actually faked their answers on the photograph rating task to make themselves look bad. The students presumably felt that if they did poorly on the photograph rating task they would have less to lose if they did not succeed on the second test for personal sensitivity.

Success can also hinder performance if it is experienced by people with very low self-esteem. Female college students were tested on a task involving motor coordination.[24] It was arranged that all students would succeed. For most of the students this experience of success led to better performance on later trials of the task. This was not true for students who had weak feelings of self-acceptance and low self-esteem. Students with low self-esteem who experienced success and were led to attribute the success to their personal skill did not improve their performance in later trials. These students were apparently made uncomfortable by the unexpected experience of success and they regulated their future performance so that this success would not continue.

When students with low self-esteem were led to attribute their success on the tasks to luck the results were very different. The students did not appear to experience the same discomfort of unexpected success. They derived some personal satisfaction from the success because they did not have to take full responsibility for that success as a result of their personal skill. These students did not hold back their performance on the tasks during future trials.

Whether or not people attribute success to ability and failure to luck also depends on the nature of the task. College students who were tested on a radar detection task were found to attribute success on the task to effort and failure on the task to difficulty of the task.[25] What happened here, most likely, was that the radar dectection task turned out to be quite difficult. When students succeeded on this difficult task it did not seem justified to believe that it was a function of their ability. When students failed, it seemed to be unrealistic to blame this failure on bad luck.

Patterns of Success and Failure

People's reactions to success and failure seem to be very much influenced by the patterns in which these experiences occur. Participants in one study were more willing to continue working on a cognitive task when they had experienced gradually increasing success rather than constant total success.[26] Constant success was boring and eliminated any challenge the task might have. Whether or not experiences of failure were consistent or gradual did not seem to make a difference to participants. They reacted to any kind of failure with generally low levels of persistence.

Research has shown that people who experience gradual improvement on a test of reaction time perform better and are more confident and satisfied about their performance than people who experience sudden improvement on the task.[27] It is possible that gradual improvement, more than sudden improvement, imparts a sense of active mastery and competence. Sudden improvement has the appearance of chance or luck and may create a feeling of unpredictability about one's ability.

Self-Perception and Motivation
for Achievement

In Chapter Six we learned that people with high achievement are more likely than people with low achievement to perceive the outcomes of their actions as internally controlled. People who are oriented toward achievement also differ from people who aren't in their self-perceptions of success and failure. Research with elementary, high school, and college students has shown that students who are highly motivated to achieve attribute successful accomplishments to their own personal ability significantly more often than students with low motivation for achievement.[28] Students with low motivation for achievement are more likely to attribute success to factors in the external environment. It is interesting that students with high motivation for achievement do not lose confidence in their ability after experiences of failure.

They tend more than students with low motivation for achievement to attribute experiences of failure to lack of effort. Students with low motivation for achievement are more likely to perceive failure as an indication of insufficient ability.

A study with college students found that most students with high motivation for achievement attributed experiences of success to their ability and effort.[29] Students with low motivation for achievement were more likely to attribute experiences of success to luck. The college students in this study also became more involved and experienced more success on a task when they were told that the amount of effort they expended would make a difference. When students believed their efforts would have no effect on success they did not try as hard.

Graduate students and college professors who were ambitious and had great expectations for success were compared with graduate students and college professors who had little faith in their own competence and only slight expectations for success.[30] Although both groups of students and professors experienced anxiety, the competent and ambitious students and professors were much less likely to blame themselves when they experienced failure.

People with high motivation for achievement are more willing to reward themselves for a successful performance than people with low motivation for achievement.[31] This is probably because people with high motivation for achievement attribute success to themselves and are able to take satisfaction in their accomplishments. People with low motivation for achievement are more likely to attribute success to external factors and therefore do not experience as much personal satisfaction from a successful performance.

We are most likely to reward people for a successful performance when they have worked hard. Whether or not they have high general ability is not so important. We are most likely to punish people for a poor performance when they have not worked hard. This is especially true for people with great ability. When people with little ability perform poorly we are more likely to give them the benefit of the doubt for "trying." People with ability who fail must prove that they did not fail because of lack of effort.[32]

We have seen that people who attribute success to their ability and effort are more likely to expend effort for a successful performance than people who attribute success to luck or to the ease of the task. In confronting failure, the people who are least likely to give up are those who attribute failure to lack of effort or bad luck. People who think that failure is a sign of lack of ability or difficulty of task are not as likely to keep trying.[33]

College students were exposed to an experience of failure on a cognitive task.[34] Half of the students had been given a placebo pill that would supposedly interfere with their performance on the task. The remaining students did not receive a pill they could blame for their failure on the task. The experimenters were interested in seeing what effects the placebo pill would have on students with high and low motivation for achievement. Persistence in the face of failure was very different for the two different groups of students.

Students with low motivation for achievement tend to attribute failure to lack of ability. However, students with low motivation who had taken the placebo pill could attribute some of their failure to the pill rather than to their lack of ability. They were less discouraged and worked harder in the face of failure than students with low motivation for achievement who had not taken the placebo pill.

Students with high motivation for achievement tend to attribute failure to lack of effort. Highly motivated students who had taken the placebo pill were discouraged because the pill would supposedly decrease the power of their efforts. They did not perform as hard in the face of failure as students with high motivation for achievement who did not have the placebo pill to reduce the effectiveness of their efforts.

Fear of Success

Sex-role stereotypes in American society suggest that it is most appropriate for males to be aggressive, independent, dominant, and unemotional and for females to be tactful, gentle, neat, and aware of other people's feelings.[35]

An interesting example of the proliferation of sex-role stereotypes was recorded by researchers who asked parents to describe their newborn boys and girls on a rating form.[36] The experimenters had independently determined that the actual birth weights and lengths of the boys and girls were equivalent. Physicians' ratings of color, muscle tonicity, reflexes, and heart-rates were also equivalent for the babies of both sexes. In spite of this fact, both male and female parents described baby girls as being significantly softer, finer featured, littler, and more inattentive than baby boys.

The prevalence of sex-role stereotypes in American society prompted Matina Horner to hypothesize that American women are in a position to experience anxiety and discomfort about being too successful. Women who contradict feminine stereotypes by achieving success are vulnerable to social rejection and feelings of being unfeminine. To examine this idea, Horner devised a test of reactions to male and female success.[37] She asked female college students to write a brief story in response to the following statement about a female:

After first term finals, Anne finds herself at the top of her medical school class.[38]

Male college students were asked to write a brief story about a male in the same situation:

After first term finals, John finds himself at the top of his medical school class.[39]

Horner's results showed that 66 percent of the female students and only 9 percent of the male students wrote stories expressing negative feelings about success by a person of their own sex. Many of the females rationalized Anne's success by describing her as unfeminine and personally undesirable. Another reaction by females was to end the story with Anne dropping out of medical school to get married and raise a family. Some females denied Anne's success by suggesting that Anne was a nonexistent person created by a group of medical students who took turns taking exams and writing papers under a false identity.

A review of the research undertaken since Horner's original study suggests that the rejection of success demonstrated by female students is linked to sex-role stereotypes.[40] Male students as well as female students are inclined to reject success in medical school for Anne but not for John. In our society, success in medical school is apparently an accomplishment that is still reserved for males. A study with Australian college students also found happiness with success closely related to sex-role stereotypes.[41] The Australian students gave ratings for male-dominated jobs showing that men would be expected to be happier about success and unhappier about failure than women. In female-dominated jobs women were expected to be happier about success and unhappier about failure than men. There was also evidence that failure is especially aversive to men in male-dominated occupations and that women who succeed in male-dominated occupations will experience feelings of happiness.

In a second measure of fear of success psychologists asked people to respond to statements such as the following:

Often the cost of success is greater than the reward.

I believe that successful people are often sad and lonely.

I am happy only when I am doing better than others.

Achievement commands respect.

It is extremely important for me to do well in all things that I undertake.[42]

People who agree with the first two statements tend to fear success. People who agree with the last three statements demonstrate a positive attitude toward success. Research has shown that female college students generally show greater fear of success on these kinds of questions than male college students. College students whose answers to these questions indicate a fear of success also perform more poorly on cognitive tests.[43]

Because people's attitudes toward sex-role stereotypes are constantly changing it is not appropriate to assign percentages to males and females who fear and do not fear success.[44] We can gain a further understanding of fear of success by studying how people in our society treat successful males and females and by learning about how males and females perceive their success.

Reactions to Male and Female Success

More often than not, successful males are valued more highly in American society than unsuccessful males. What about successful females? Are females valued for their achievements or do they suffer negative reactions for violation of sex-role stereotypes?

College students listened to a tape-recorded interview in which either a male or a female was being interviewed for a scholarship program.[45] For half of the students the person being interviewed appeared to be highly competent with strong qualifications for the program. The remaining students heard a person being interviewed who was incompetent and not qualified for the program. When asked to evaluate the person being interviewed both male and female students gave the most favorable ratings to the competent male and the least favorable ratings to the incompetent male. The competent female was evaluated more favorably than the incompetent female, but the difference was not as important. This study suggests that competent females do not suffer negative evaluations for being competent but that people do not value competence in females as much as competence in males.

College students in a similar study observed a videotaped interview in which a female was being interviewed for an academic position of student advisor.[46] Half of the students saw a female who was competent and highly qualified. The remaining students saw a female who was incompetent and not well qualified. Again, the competent female was preferred by both male and female students over the incompetent female.

Evaluations were made of hypothetical females who had one of four possible combinations of "high" or "low" motivation to succeed and feminine or masculine sex-role orientation.[47] The female who was highly motivated to succeed was described as actively committed to a competitive career in graduate school. The female with low motivation to succeed was described as disinterested in a career that would involve active competition. The female with a feminine sex-role orientation was described as willing to prepare meals for a family, inclined to act helpless at certain times, and willing to take care of a baby. The female with a masculine sex-role orientation would supposedly be willing to engage in fist fights if necessary, and would not see it her duty to prepare meals or take care of a baby. College females who evaluated the four different types of females expressed greatest liking for a non-success-oriented female with feminine sex-role preference. College males were most attracted to a success-oriented female with a feminine sex-role preference.

Women can receive positive evaluations if they successfully perform a male-stereotyped behavior in an emergency.[48] People gave more credit to a woman than to a man for quick and efficient action in alerting the police after a robbery. This reaction was possibly due to the fact that women are not expected to perform well in such situations and are therefore given special praise when they do. It is interesting that women were given more credit for their actions if they were alone than if they were with a man. Women who took efficient action in the presence of a man were apparently seen as inappropriately usurping the masculine role. In sum, it appears acceptable for women to adopt masculine roles in emergencies if they are alone. Women in the company of a man are most accepted if they leave the masculine role to the man.

The above studies suggest that competent females do not suffer negative evaluations when they are being evaluated from a theoretical perspective. It is still possible that people might be threatened by competent females with whom they have personal interaction. An interesting study relevant to this notion found that female high school students in noncoed high schools had significantly less fear of success than female high school students in coed high schools.[49] Females who had also attended noncoed elementary schools manifested the least fear of success. It has been argued that females in noncoed schools do not have to suffer the negative reactions resulting from competition with males. Fear of success is present in women when they are uncertain of the reactions they might receive for being successful. Because of the fear of rejection, women are often reluctant to enter competitive situations. One study found that women working on a task had lower expectancies for how well they would do and less confidence about their performance when they competed in a group than when they worked alone.[50] Men did not reduce their expectancies and confidence when they were working on the task in a competitive situation. Another study showed that women suffer greater loss in self-esteem in competition when they are rejected by males rather than by females.[51] Men (or women) who feel that successful women threaten their position or beliefs are most likely to derogate thóse women. There is a good deal of ambivalence about successful women that our society still needs to resolve.

Self-Perceptions of Success

People who have a great fear of success are more likely than people with a slight fear of success to explain their success on a task by saying that the task was easy or that they were lucky. People with little fear of success are most likely to attribute success on a task to their ability and their effort.[52] Because women are more likely to fear success than men, they are also more likely to view their experiences of success as a function of external rather than internal factors.

College students were asked to evaluate the performance of people on "masculine" and "feminine" tasks.[53] Success of women on feminine tasks was generally attributed to their ability whereas success of women on masculine tasks was generally attributed to luck. Success of men on both masculine and feminine tasks was attributed to ability. Students in the study also gave higher prestige to success on the masculine task and evaluated successful men as more intelligent than successful women. When asked to predict their own performance, male students felt they could do well on both masculine and feminine tasks. Female students did not feel they could do particularly well on masculine tasks.

When college students were led to succeed or fail on a cognitive task, females were significantly more likely than males to attribute success to good luck and failure to bad luck.[54] Males and females were equally likely to perceive themselves as having ability after experiences of success. After experiences of failure, however, males continued to attribute more ability to themselves and to have higher expectancies for future performance than females.

Researchers have found similar results with elementary school children.[55] Elementary school boys are more likely than girls to attribute experiences of success to their ability and to attribute experiences of failure to bad luck. Girls are less likely to take credit for success and more likely to blame themselves for failure by lowering estimates of their ability. Boys remain more optimistic than girls after experiences of failure and continue to have high expectancies for future performance. Boys also feel more satisfied than girls for the opportunity to work on a challenging task.

If men attribute success to skill whereas women attribute success to luck it is likely that men and women will differ in their preferences for tasks based on skill or luck. Data compiled at county and state fairs to determine which sorts of games would be preferred by males and females showed that males were significantly more likely than females to play games of skill, such as coin-in-dish, ring toss, and uprighting a bottle with a ring attached to a fishing pole.[56] There was no difference between males and females in the choice of games of luck, such as roulette. Females preferred bingo significantly more than males. A laboratory study asking college students to choose between games of skill and luck found a significant preference given by males to games of skill and by females to games of luck.[57] Males in this study were also significantly more likely than females to predict that they would succeed. In both studies males were more persistent in skill games and did not give up as easily as females.

Socialization of Differences According to Sex

Now that we are aware of the differences between the ways in which males and females perceive success and failure, we might well ask how these self-perceptions develop. It is not possible in this chapter to review the vast literature on the socialization of sex differences.[58] However, we can consider the research specifically related to children's experiences of success and failure.

Studies have shown fairly clearly that successful women are women who are able to define achievement as an acceptable feminine behavior. Because our society has not traditionally associated achievement with femininity women find their motives for achievement and femininity in conflict. Some undesirable outcomes of this conflict are women's fear of success and other compensatory reactions by women such as concealing accomplishments and playing dumb or overemphasizing their commitment to valued feminine qualities related to physical appearance, pleasant personality, and domestic activities.[59]

By the time they are in elementary school children have learned to view social, verbal, and artistic skills as feminine, and mechanical, spatial, and athletic skills as masculine. Girls in elementary and junior high school are taught not to value or expect success in masculine skills. Boys are less likely to avoid success in feminine skills. This is especially true for boys from more privileged socioeconomic backgrounds.[60]

Lessons from Parents

Boys and girls develop motivation for achievement when they receive reinforcement from their parents for setting high standards for themselves, when they are encouraged to achieve and when they have parents who serve as models for achievement. These aspects of child rearing are experienced less frequently by girls than by boys because they conflict with traditional views of femininity. Fewer girls than boys are encouraged to have high expectancies for success, establish high aspirations, or develop the ability to accept failure.[61]

Lessons from Teachers

Your own experiences and observations have probably made you realize that most parents expect and teach boys to achieve more than girls. It may surprise you to learn, however, that boys and girls develop important differences in self-perceptions of success and failure in school. A study of interactions between elementary school children and their teachers showed that boys and girls receive the same amounts of positive and negative evaluations by teachers, but the nature and goal of these positive and negative evaluations are strikingly different. A large proportion of the negative evaluations received by boys are based on their conduct in class and have nothing to do with the intellectual quality of their work. Negative evaluations received by girls, in contrast, are based largely on the intellectual quality of their work. This discrepancy in negative evaluations leads to some important differences in socialization. Boys learn to expect negative reactions by teachers to their behaviors in the classroom, but they do not interpret the teachers' negativity as a reflection of their lack of ability. Girls, on the other hand, become quite sensitive to negative feedback as an indication of lack of ability.

Positive evaluations by teachers are also used differently for boys and girls. Boys are given positive evaluations almost exclusively for the intellectual quality of their work. Girls more often receive positive evaluations for good behavior and other nonintellectual aspects of performance.

Because boys learn to perceive positive evaluations from teachers as a sign of their ability and negative evaluations from teachers as irrelevant to their ability, they learn to discount past failure and emphasize past success in determining their future aspirations. They learn not only to attribute success to ability and failure to lack of motivation, but also to have high estimates of their potential for future achievement. Girls learn to attribute success to luck and failure to lack of ability, and to develop conservative estimates of their potential for future achievement.[62]

When elementary school children are given negative evaluations by their peers rather than by their teachers, boys suffer more than girls. This is most likely because boys are more peer oriented than girls.

There is often conflict between those behaviors of boys that elicit the approval of their peers and those behaviors that elicit adult approval. In elementary school, boys have a greater tendency than girls to opt for approval from their peers.[63]

Lessons from Children's Books

Children also learn sex-role differences in storybooks. A 1972 study of children's books that had won awards from the American Library Association found the following.[64] More than twice as many children's books had males rather than females in the titles. Close to one-third of the children's books had no female characters at all. The children's books had eleven times as many pictures of males than of females.

Plots of children's books typically involve some form of adventure by a male protagonist. Males in children's books are portrayed as active, physical, and independent. Females are most often inconspicuous, passive, and immobile. Females are most often shown indoors while males are most often shown outdoors. Males in children's books often work together with a strong sense of camaraderie. Females in children's books rarely work or play together.

Sex-role stereotypes in children's books are very strong. Women are identified almost exclusively as mothers and wives. Females in children's books are motivated toward pleasing and serving men. They cook, clean house, bring food to men, and are sweet, pretty, and dependent. Women who are not mothers and wives are fairies or fairy godmothers. Fairy godmothers are usually the only female characters with an active leadership role.

Men in children's books play active roles. They are storekeepers, housebuilders, fishermen, farmers, policemen, judges, doctors, and heroes of all different kinds. Males in children's books rescue others. Females in children's books are rescued.

Mothers in children's books hug and take care of children when they are sick, but they are also restrictive and shout at children for making noise and getting dirty. Fathers in children's books take children out to have a good time and teach children how to do things that are fun. Fathers do not engage in household work or mundane aspects of child care.

An experiment in which nursery school children listened to a story that was read to them by an adult experimenter demonstrated the influence of children's books on children.[65] Some of the children in the study heard a story depicting achievement by a boy. Other children heard a story depicting achievement by a girl. A third group of children heard a neutral story about animals. After hearing the story, the children were given a challenging task. Both boys and girls were most likely to show persistence with the task if they had recently heard a story depicting achievement by a child of their own sex. Children who persisted most on the task tended to be children who had good recall of the story in which a child of their own sex had succeeded. Hearing a story showing achievement by a child of the opposite sex did not increase the children's persistence on the task. The above results were stronger for boys than they were for girls. However, the persistence of both boys and girls was influenced by a children's story to which they had recently been exposed.

Learning to Succeed

We can summarize the results of research in the self-perception of success and failure by outlining the characteristics of people who are most inclined to experience success. Successful people were generally raised on experiences of success. They were encouraged at home and in school to set high standards for themselves. Successful people have learned to interpret success as a sign of their ability. When successful people fail, they are more likely than unsuccessful people to blame the failure on their lack of effort rather than on their lack of ability, and to seek out alternative responses that will help them overcome the failure.

We now have a good background for understanding the factors influencing people's self-perceptions of success and failure. In Chapter Eight we will look at some extreme forms of success and failure. One extreme of failure is what psychologists refer to as "learned helplessness." At the other end of the spectrum are the techniques developed by psychologists for teaching people to gain greater self-mastery and self-control.

EIGHT

Learned Helplessness
and Self-Control

We have seen that the self-perception of internal versus external control has an effect on conformity, personal effectiveness, achievement, social activism, personal adjustment, and reactions to success and failure. In this chapter we will consider some extreme instances of the perception of external control that causes people to feel helpless about what happens in their lives and to develop symptoms of depression. We will also review research indicating that women (and presumably other minority groups) are more vulnerable to feelings of external control because of prejudices limiting their chances for success in our society. Later in this chapter we will learn how people can develop increased internal control with behavior rehearsal, self-observation, stimulus control, self-reinforcement, and self-punishment. It will be argued that people's success in mastering new behaviors, coping with aversive experiences, and remaining persistent in the face of obstacles is strongly influenced by their feelings of self-efficacy.

External Control in Extreme Situations

The following descriptions of extreme external control were compiled by W. B. Cannon:

> A Brazilian Indian condemned and sentenced by a so-called medicine man, is helpless against his own emotional response to this pro-

nouncement—and dies within hours. In Africa a young Negro un-knowingly eats the inviolably banned wild hen. On discovery of his "crime" he trembles, is overcome by fear, and dies in 24 hours. In New Zealand a Maori woman eats fruit that she only later learns has come from a tabooed place. Her chief has been profaned. By noon of the next day she is dead. In Australia a witch doctor points a bone at a man. Be-lieving that nothing can save him, the man rapidly sinks in spirits and prepares to die. He is saved only at the last moment when the witch doc-tor is forced to remove the charm.[1]

R. Herbert Basedow has provided a similar account:

The man who discovers that he is being boned by an enemy is indeed, a pitiable sight. He stands aghast with his eyes staring at the treacherous pointer, and with his hands lifted to ward off the lethal medium, which he imagines is pouring into his body. His cheeks blanch, and his eyes become glassy, and the expression of his face becomes horribly distorted. He attempts to shriek but usually the sound chokes in his throat, and all that one might see is froth at his mouth. His body begins to tremble and his muscles twitch involuntarily. He sways backward and falls to the ground, and after a short time appears to be in a swoon. He finally com-poses himself, goes to his hut and there frets to death.[2]

Bruno Bettelheim described prisoners in Nazi concentration camps who had resigned themselves to external control in the following manner:

Prisoners who came to believe the repeated statements of the guards—that there was no hope for them, that they would never leave the camp except as a corpse—who came to feel that their environment was one over which they could exercise no influence whatsoever, these prisoners were in a literal sense, walking corpses. In the camps they were called "moslems" (Muselmänner) because of what was erroneously viewed as a fatalistic surrender to the environment, as Mohammedans are sup-posed to blandly accept their fate. But these people had not, like real Mohammedans, made an act of decision and submitted to fate out of free will. On the contrary, they were people that were so deprived of affect, self-esteem, and every form of stimulation, so totally exhausted, both physically and emotionally, that they had given the environment total power over them.[3]

Fifty-five women were asked upon admission to an old-age home how much freedom of choice they felt they had in moving to the home.[4] Of the 17 women who said they had no alternative except to move into the home, 8 died after four weeks in residence and 16 were dead within ten weeks. In contrast, only 1 of the 38 women who felt they had other choices open to them died within the same period of time. A second study compared 22 elderly people who were placed in an old-age home by their families with 18 elderly people who applied to the homes on their own. After one month, 19 of the people in the first group were dead. Only 4 people in the second group had died within the same period. Research has shown that the mortality rate can increase as much as 100 percent among elderly people forced to change institutional settings without sufficient time to become familiar with their new environment.[5]

The above examples point out the powerful effects of loss of personal, or internal, control. You are probably aware of some of the countless other cases of extreme external control that have been recorded throughout history. Observational studies such as the ones above provide an overview of the loss-of-control phenomenon. A review of experimental studies will enable us to place extreme external control into a theoretical context and learn how it relates to our study of self-perception.

Learned Helplessness in Animals

Martin Seligman and his colleagues have defined situations in which people and animals experience extreme loss of control over their lives as a case of "helplessness." This type of helplessness is the result of organisms learning that they have no chance of modifying their present situation. Any responses they might attempt in controlling the outcome of their lives are futile and doomed to failure.[6]

Teaching Helplessness

Let's say that you put a dog into a box that is divided into two compartments by a barrier. The floor of one compartment is made of a metal grid through which you can deliver electric shocks. If you deliver shocks, the dog will yelp and squeal and sooner or later jump over the barrier to the other compartment in order to escape the shock. If you precede each shock with a tone or a light signal, the dog will learn to jump over the barrier before the shock is delivered.

Now let's assume that you deliver electric shocks to a dog in such a way that the dog has no way of escaping. No matter what the dog does, it receives the shocks. After exposing the dog to a number of these experiences of helplessness, you place it in the above apparatus. You turn on the electric shock and watch to see the dog's reaction. More than likely, the dog will sit in the shock compartment and take the shock without even trying to escape. The dog has learned that it is helpless and unable to do anything about electric shock.

To show that this helplessness is learned rather than caused by stress from exposure to electric shocks, you can do the following experiment. Give one group of dogs a series of electric shocks which they can escape by making some sort of response. Give a second group of dogs an identical amount of shocks. The shocks for the second group of dogs are exactly the same in duration and intensity as the ones for the first group of dogs. The only difference is that they are controlled by you and are independent of any action on the part of the dogs. After this training, put the dogs in the box with the barrier. The dogs in the first group will readily learn to escape the shock in one compartment by jumping over the barrier. The dogs in the second group will sit in the shock compartment, take the shock, and never learn to jump over the barrier. Similar demonstrations of learned helplessness have been conducted with cockroaches, fish, birds, rats, mice, cats, and monkeys.[7]

Curing Helplessness

If you feel guilty about teaching the dogs to be helpless in the face of electric shock, how can you "cure" them? Since the helpless dogs won't even try to escape the shock, you will at first need to be very directive. You can lower the barrier and literally drag the dogs into the "safe" compartment. At first, the dogs will not cooperate and might even resist you. During the course of some 25 to 200 draggings, the dogs will slowly begin to cooperate and will begin to respond to a slight nudge or pull by getting themselves over to the safe compartment. With patience, you can finally teach the dogs to escape the shocks of their own accord.[8]

Preventing Helplessness

If you knew someone else was going to try to teach a certain dog to be helpless, you could "immunize" the dog in the following manner. Place the dog in a situation where it is possible by some sort of action to escape electric shocks. With this previous experience of self-control, the dog will later be much less likely to develop helplessness when confronted with an experience of unescapable shock.[9]

Learned Helplessness in Humans

Although research on learned helplessness in animals does not generally rely on conditions as extreme as those described earlier in the comparative observational studies with humans, it still might cause some ethical concern. Psychologists conducting experimental studies of learned helplessness in humans have attempted to design experiments that shed light on the development and treatment of learned helplessness without causing harm to the participants. Before reading about these experiments, it will be worthwhile to remember that helplessness is defined as a condition in which people (or animals) have learned that certain consequences in their lives are beyond their control. Learned helplessness is not caused by the mere experience of aversive or unpleasant events. Learned helplessness is caused by experiencing unpleasant events in a situation where there is no action one can take to alter them. In a later situation, it may be realistically possible for a person to control aversive outcomes by behaving in a certain way. Because of the early experience of external control, however, the person still believes or perceives that the possibility for internal control does not exist. It is this perception that one's actions cannot affect the environment (when they really can) that is of greatest interest to us. In some circumstances, learned helplessness relates to people's perceptions that they cannot control the aversive outcomes in their lives. Learned helplessness can also relate to a lack of perceived control over positive outcomes. We will explore research analyzing both kinds of learned helplessness.

Perceptions of Skill Versus Luck

One method for studying learned helplessness in humans is to manipulate perceptions of whether or not outcomes of performance are due to skill or luck. People who believe that the outcomes of their actions are controlled by luck will experience more learned helplessness than people who believe that the outcomes of their actions are controlled by skill.

Participants in a study were seated in front of a panel with twelve buttons and given a series of electric shocks.[10] During each exposure to shock a different nonsense syllable (three letters with no meaning) was projected on the wall. One group of participants was told that they could turn off the shock by learning to press the correct button associated with each of the nonsense syllables. They were led to believe that escaping the shocks was a matter of skill. A second group of participants was told that there was no way to learn which was the correct button. They could supposedly only escape the shock by correctly guessing which button to press. These participants were led to believe that escaping the shocks was a matter of luck. In reality, the experiment was set up so that both groups of participants escaped an equivalent number of shocks. The only difference between the "skill" participants and the "luck" participants was their belief about *why* they had escaped the shocks.

After this experience, all of the participants were tested on how well they could recognize the nonsense syllables as they were flashed on the wall for very short periods of time. Results showed that the skill participants had learned to recognize the nonsense syllables with significantly greater accuracy than the luck participants. The authors concluded that people will attempt to cope with threatening situations much more if they believe they can do something about what is happening than if they do not.

Participants in another study were given a perceptual problem to solve.[11] Half of the participants were told that the task was set up so whatever success they had would be a matter of luck. The remaining participants were told that whatever success they had on the task would be a matter of their personal skill. In reality, it was arranged that luck and skill participants would succeed and fail an equal number of times. Because their perceptions of this success and failure were not the same, the luck and skill participants reacted in different manners. Skill participants were much more likely than luck participants to use their past success and failure as an indication of how they would perform on future problems.

The above studies show that people will learn better and use their past performances to greater advantage if they believe their success or failure is determined by skill rather than luck. There is also evidence that people will experience less stress in aversive situations if they believe they have some personal control over the outcomes of the situation.[12] When a feeling of personal control over aversive outcomes does not automatically lead to a reduction in stress, it is still useful for coping behaviors in the future.[13] If people feel no personal control over aversive events they become increasingly anxious. People who learn to associate anxiety with luck or chance may not engage in adaptive behaviors in future stressful situations even if it is possible to do so. People who maintain a belief in personal control during stressful situations will not give up and will still be able to exercise adaptive behaviors in the future.[14]

Teaching Helplessness

College students were divided into three groups.[15] Students in the first group were exposed to an unpleasant tone which they could turn off by learning to give four presses to a button on a panel in front of them. Students in the second group were exposed to the unpleasant tone and the button but there was no way for them to learn how to make the tone go off. Students in the third group were not given prior experience with the unpleasant tone. Later, all students were exposed to a second unpleasant tone. This tone could be turned off by learning how to move a knob in a certain direction. Results showed that students in the second group did significantly more poorly than other students in learning how to turn off the second unpleasant tone. These students had previously been taught to be helpless and to perceive that they had no control over unpleasant tones. Students in the first group were significantly better than students in the second group and somewhat better than students in the third group in learning how to turn off the second unpleasant tone. These students had previously learned that they could exercise control over unpleasant tones.

College students in a second experiment were first taught that they either could or could not turn off an unpleasant tone.[16] Later, the students were given an anagram test. Results showed that students who had previously learned to be helpless in turning off an unpleasant tone did more poorly on the anagram test than students who had learned to turn off the tone or students who had not been exposed to the tone. This experiment is interesting because it shows that learned helplessness in turning off an unpleasant tone can generalize to unsuccessful performance on an unrelated task.

In a third experiment, college students were exposed to a discrimination learning task.[17] The experimenters arranged for students in one group to experience success in learning the task. Students in a second group experienced failure with the discrimination task. Students in a third group were not exposed to the discrimination learning task. Later, all the students were placed in a situation where it was possible to learn how to turn off an unpleasant tone. Students who had previously experienced helplessness with the discrimination task were significantly slower in learning how to turn off the unpleasant tone than other students. Students who had previously experienced success with the discrimination learning task did slightly better in escaping the unpleasant tone than students who were not exposed to the discrimination learning task. This experiment also shows that helplessness learned in one situation can influence performance in other situations. Other research has concluded that learned helplessness is more likely to occur if people experience failure on tasks they consider to be important rather than unimportant and if people attribute lack of success in escaping an aversive outcome to their own inadequacy rather than to external factors in the environment.[18]

Experiments showing how helplessness can be learned have also been conducted with children.[19] Two adult experimenters tested fifth-grade children on the construction of block designs. One experimenter administered problems that the children could solve. The second experimenter always gave the children problems that could not be solved.

After this experience with success and failure, both experimenters gave the children additional problems that could be solved. Results showed that the children performed significantly better when the second set of problems was given by the adult with whom they had previously experienced success. Even though all of the problems in the second set were soluble, children who had previously experienced failure with one of the experimenters continued to *expect* failure and therefore did not perform as well. Children whose future performance was most likely to suffer from the experience of failure were children who tended not to take personal responsibility for the outcomes of their performance. They were more likely than children who did not suffer so much from failure to attribute their success and failure to external factors.

Learned Helplessness and Depression

The behavioral deficits associated with learned helplessness are related to clinical depression because they show how people can be influenced to lose their initiative and give up all hope of dealing with their environment. Several research studies have associated learned helplessness with depression.

Psychologists conducted a replication of the experiment in which people were first exposed to experiences of helplessness or success in escaping an unpleasant tone and then given an anagram test to solve.[20] As in the original experiment, people who had learned to be helpless in escaping the unpleasant tone did significantly more poorly on the anagram test than people who had experienced success in escaping the unpleasant tone. In addition, people experiencing helplessness in escaping the unpleasant tone reported significantly greater feelings of depression, anxiety, and hostility on a personality test than people who previously experienced success.

In another variation of this experiment, people experiencing helplessness in escaping unpleasant tones had significantly lower autonomic arousal (by measures of skin conductance) than people experiencing success in escaping unpleasant tones.[21] The experimenters interpreted the low autonomic arousal shown by people experiencing helplessness as a sign of the decreased involvement and motivation characteristic of people suffering from clinical depression.

People who experienced helplessness over unsolvable problems or an inescapable noise were compared with people who were shown to be highly depressed on a personality test.[22] In contrast with generally normal people, the people who experienced helplessness and the clinically depressed people gave similarly poor performances on an anagram test. The researchers concluded that helpless and clinically depressed people have the same tendency to perceive that the outcomes of their actions are beyond their personal control. Depressed people had significantly greater success on the anagram tests if they were convinced not to blame themselves for their failures.

Several studies have found correlations between attitudes of helplessness in one's life and predisposition toward suicide. People who had made serious attempts at suicide were more likely than people who had made less serious suicide attempts to agree with the following kinds of statements:

I might as well give up because I can't make things better for myself.

My future seems dark to me.

I never get what I want so it's foolish to want anything.

All I can see ahead of me is unpleasantness rather than pleasantness.[23]

In addition to depression, learned helplessness can cause other maladaptive symptoms. Participants in an experiment were exposed to bursts of loud aversive noise while working on a numerical task.[24] Half of the participants were told that they could press a button to turn off the noise bursts if they wanted to, but that it would be preferable if they worked on the problems with the noise present. As it turned out, these participants were willing to withstand the noise "of their own free choice." The remaining participants were not provided with a button and suffered the noise in a way that was "beyond their control." Results of the experiment showed that participants who did not have feelings of control over the aversive noise were significantly more likely to report symptoms such as headaches, upset stomachs, chest pains, flushed face, and dizziness while they were working on the numerical task. Lack of perceived control over the aversive noise apparently led those participants who experienced the "uncontrollable" noise to perceive their discomfort in terms of bodily symptoms.

External Control of Positive Outcomes

If we had the choice between experiencing either negative or positive outcomes in our lives, we would surely choose positive outcomes. However, even positive outcomes can cause feelings of helplessness if they occur in a manner that is independent of our actions. Very attractive people sometimes suffer because they are rewarded for their beauty rather than for their accomplishments. Famous people often complain because they receive attention for what they did in the past. Rewards for past behaviors do not help to stimulate accomplishments that will be satisfying in the present or future. People thrive on positive outcomes, but these outcomes are most meaningful when they are a result of something they have done. Positive outcomes that are independent of a person's actions do not contribute much to his or her sense of worth or competence.

Consider a simple study with hungry rats.[25] Half of the rats had food delivered to them "out of the sky" through a hole in the roof of their cage. The remaining rats received food only for coming close to pressing a bar. When all of the rats ultimately had to learn to press a bar for food, rats in the first group were severely retarded. Their previous experience of receiving food independently of their behaviors interfered with their later learning that food would be contingent upon their behaviors.

A group of elementary school children received random approval from an adult.[26] The approval was not related to anything the children did. Later the children had to learn how to perform a task and they were given social approval whenever they made a correct response. These children were retarded in their learning because they had previously learned that social approval was independent of anything they did. Social approval is only useful in teaching people to make correct responses if they learn that their responses control that approval.

Overcoming Learned Helplessness and Depression

Depression is defined by the American Psychiatric Association as an "emotional state with retardation of psychomotor and thought processes, a depressive emotional reaction, feelings of guilt or criticism and delusions of unworthiness."[27] People who are depressed and have the "blahs" often recognize that the best thing to do is get involved in a project and accomplish something. It doesn't matter so much what they do as long as they are able to experience success and competence. People with high self-esteem are people who *do* things and then feel good about having done them. Criticisms of educators for emphasizing individual performance rather than individual feelings are somewhat misguided. Experiences with success and internal control are the cause rather than the result of good feelings and self-esteem.[28]

Most people have strategies for overcoming depression through activities in which they can exercise internal control. Later in this chapter we will learn about methods psychologists have developed for helping people to increase their experiences of power and control over their lives. First we will look at specific programs for treating learned helplessness in experimental settings. The psychologists who conducted the experiments for teaching helplessness to college students and children also formulated programs for alleviating learned helplessness.

College students were exposed to an unpleasant tone.[29] The students had a button in front of them but did not realize that the button was disconnected and had nothing to do with the unpleasant tone. As a result, the students came to feel there was no way they could learn to turn off the tone. After this experience with helplessness, the students were divided into three groups. Students in one group were given the opportunity to correctly solve 12 cognitive discrimination problems. Students in a second group had the experience of correctly solving 4 problems. Students in the third group did not have the successful problem-solving experience.

Later, all of the students were put in a situation where it was possible to learn how to move a lever to turn off an unpleasant tone. Students who had been given the chance to experience success in problem solving did significantly better in learning how to turn off the tone than students who had not had this experience. The students who had successfully solved 12 problems did somewhat better than the students who had correctly solved only 4 problems.

A parallel study was conducted with students who were rated as highly depressed on a personality test. (Remember that clinically depressed people are similar in their performance to people who have been taught helplessness.) Like the nondepressed students, the clinically depressed students did significantly better in learning to turn off an unpleasant tone if they had successfully solved a number of cognitive discrimination problems.

The above experiments show that experience with success can alleviate decrements in performance that are caused by learned helplessness. Experiences with success can also increase people's expectancies of success. People who experience helplessness will perform less successfully in the future because they believe that their actions are ineffective. People who experience success can overcome learned helplessness by again perceiving their behaviors as potentially effective in causing desired outcomes.

Children who were identified in school as being extremely helpless were exposed to a program designed to reduce this helplessness.[30] Psychologists had originally characterized the children as having high expectations of both failure and the types of performance decrements demonstrated in experiments where helplessness was artificially taught. The helpless children were divided into two groups. Children in one group were exposed to a series of problem-solving tasks in which they experienced nothing but success. Helpless children in the second group experienced a good deal of success with problem-solving tasks but they also experienced some failure. When they failed, they were told that the failure was under their control and that they could avoid failing if they tried harder.

Results of this experiment showed that all of the helpless children improved their performance on tasks on which they could succeed. Only the helpless children in the second group, however, had learned to continue trying and not give up after experiencing failure. The researchers concluded that learned helplessness in children can be alleviated by allowing them to experience success and by teaching them to take personal responsibility for failure. Failure, in itself, will not cause helplessness if people learn that it is possible to avoid failure by trying harder and by learning new behaviors. Success can make people most persistent in their future performance if they attribute it to their own efforts. Experiences of success with a small taste of failure lead to more persistence in future problem-solving tasks than experiences of success with no failure.

We have seen that the loss of personal control has a powerful negative effect on institutionalized elderly people. Retirement, physical decline, and institutionalization all result in a loss of personal control. Many recent books and articles discuss the importance of allowing elderly people to retain internal control over their lives, emphasizing that it is essential for older people to experience activities and opportunities for decision making through which they can continue to exercise feelings of competency.

Elderly people living in a retirement home were put in contact with a college student who would visit them individually to chat and become acquainted.[31] The students made appointments with the elderly people and visited with them during these times. Elderly people receiving the student visitors did better than elderly people who had no student visitor on a number of measures. The elderly people with visitors reduced their daily requirement of medication, rated themselves as being significantly happier, and involved themselves in significantly more enjoyable activities. Elderly people who were visited by a student on a random schedule did not improve as much as elderly people who actively participated in arranging a schedule and were able to look forward to the visits. Apparently, part of the value of the visitors consisted in giving the elderly people a feeling of control over their own lives.

Elderly people in another nursing home were divided into two groups.[32] One group of elderly people was provided with the opportunity to make suggestions for changes in the home and allowed to choose how their rooms would be decorated and how they would spend their leisure time. Elderly people in a second group were told that the staff of the nursing home was working to make life as pleasant as possible for them, but they were not given any responsibility for structuring their own lives. After about one month, elderly people in the first group were much more socially active and rated themselves as being significantly happier than elderly people in the second group. It appears that being well cared for by others is not nearly as important as being able to care for oneself.

Prejudice Against Females

In Chapter Seven we learned how males and females are socialized to have different perceptions of success and failure. We also saw that competent women are preferred over incompetent women, especially if they maintain a feminine sex-role orientation. Even though most people favor competent women over incompetent women, they still do not view them as positively as competent men. Women compared directly with men often suffer negative evaluations and self-perceptions. People who experience negative self-perceptions are vulnerable to helplessness because they are less likely to feel active control over their lives.

Stereotyping

College students at the University of California were asked in 1957 to rate the overall worth and value of men and women.[33] About 70 percent of the college women and 50 percent of the college men said that men and women were equal. However, 24 percent of the women and 40 percent of the men said that men were somewhat superior. Only 6 percent of the women and 10 percent of the men said that women were somewhat superior. When the students were required to choose between either men or women as being superior, over 80 percent of the women and 90 percent of the men judged men as superior. Results of this study also showed that college students would choose more favorable adjectives and list more favorable characteristics for males than for females.

A study of college students in 1968 found that behaviors stereotypically associated with males were seen as more socially desirable than behaviors stereotypically associated with females.[34] Behaviors associated with males included being aggressive, independent, objective, competitive, and active. Behaviors associated with females included being talkative, gentle, tactful, neat, and tender.

Female college students were asked in 1967 to evaluate six 1500-word articles in the fields of linguistics, law, art, dietetics, education, and city planning.[35] Half of the students believed the articles had been written by men and half of the students believed the articles had been written by women. Significantly more favorable evaluations were given to the linguistics, law, and city planning articles when they were purportedly written by a man rather than by a woman. The students gave equal ratings to male and female authors in fields of art, dietetics, and education.

Female college students in 1971 were asked to judge a series of paintings.[36] Students were randomly told that half of the paintings were by a male artist and half of the paintings were by a female artist. Students were significantly more favorable toward paintings that were identified with a male artist. Only if students were told that a painting had won a prize were they willing to give female and male artists equal ratings.

College students in 1974 were asked to list all of the words they could think of to denote males and females.[37] The experimenters thought that prejudice against males or females would be indicated by the proportion of favorable versus unfavorable words the participants listed. Both male and female college students listed significantly more words for females than for males. In addition, the words listed for females were rated as a whole to be significantly more negative and unfavorable than the words listed for males. The most commonly listed positive words for males and females were man, husband, father, and woman, lady, mother. The most commonly listed negative words for males and females were bastard, stud, and bitch, whore, slut. Similar results were found with elementary and high school students.

Photographs of women who were active and not active in the feminist movement were rated for attractiveness by college students.[38] Students found no differences in attractiveness between feminist and nonfeminist women when the identity of the photographs was withheld. College students who were asked to choose pictures of women they *thought* were involved with the feminist movement had a significant tendency to choose the unattractive pictures. Apparently feminist women are falsely stereotyped as being less attractive than nonfeminist women.

Judgments of Mental Health

A group of psychiatrists and clinical psychologists was asked to specify traits characteristic of healthy and well-adjusted men, women, and adults.[39] The clinicians' opinions about what makes a healthy man and what makes a healthy adult were similar. The clinicians' descriptions of a healthy woman and a healthy adult, however, were very different. Healthy women were judged as possessing feminine traits that, in our society, are not valued as much as masculine traits. Healthy men and healthy adults were perceived as being independent, aggressive, competitive, skilled, and ambitious. Women who were supposedly healthy were described more often as submissive, dependent, easily influenced, and nonobjective. The authors of this study concluded that women in our society are put into a bind. To be considered "healthy," they are expected to manifest the traditionally acceptable feminine behaviors, which, however, are not valued. A woman who adopts male behaviors that are valued is in danger of being judged unfeminine or "unhealthy." A woman who adopts feminine behaviors in order to be seen as feminine and "healthy" is engaging in behaviors that are not valued.

College students were asked to give their evaluations of different instances of stress.[40] When considering the case of a male or female under pressure of an important examination, the students were more likely to accept negative reactions from males. Females who reacted to examination pressure with aggression, social withdrawal, headaches, or blank spells were more often judged to need the help of a psychiatrist than males who reacted to examination pressures in a similar manner. In cases of rejection by a fiancé, females were given more leeway than males to react in a stressful fashion. On the whole, greater pathology was attributed to females for aggressive behavior than to males. Males were judged as somewhat more pathological than females when they reacted to stress with headaches and nausea.

Hiring Practices

It is common knowledge that women have less representation than men in upper-echelon jobs. In 1974, 61 percent of male white-collar workers and only 32 percent of female white-collar workers were employed in professional and managerial occupations.[41] In many instances, it is possible that men rather than women are hired for jobs because men have more experience and training. Women also suffer, however, purely on the basis of stereotyping by sex. Women are vulnerable to helplessness when job hiring is based on sex-role stereotypes rather than objective qualifications. It is possible to increase one's personal qualifications with personal action and effort, but the negative influence of sex stereotypes is often beyond a person's internal control. A number of studies have shown how sex stereotypes can influence hiring practices and evaluations of performance on the job.

Students in management and business courses were asked to rate the most important qualifications of a white-collar worker.[42] When the white-collar worker was supposedly a man, the most important qualities related to motivation, ability, and interpersonal relations. A male white-collar worker was thought to be most qualified if he had a desire to get ahead, was self-confident, could withstand pressure, and could deal effectively with other people. When the white-collar worker was supposedly a woman, the most important qualities related to personality, appearance, and a minimum of skills and education. A female white-collar worker was thought to be most qualified if she was married, had a pleasant personality and pleasant voice, was well-dressed and attractive, and she had four years of college and excellent clerical skills.

Another example of sex stereotyping in employment was shown in the following study. Men who served in management positions in companies throughout the United States were asked to list the characteristics most typical of women in general, men in general, and people who are successful in company management.[43] The qualities listed for men in general and successful managers were very similar. The most common traits chosen for men and successful managers were aggression, leadership ability, emotional stability, and self-reliance. There was very little relationship between the characteristics used to describe women and the traits seen as necessary for successful managers. Women were judged as more qualified than men only in terms of their supposedly greater understanding, helpfulness, and neatness.

The above studies illustrate the sex-role stereotyping that exists in various areas of white-collar employment. Researchers have also found evidence that such discrepancies between the occupational stereotypes of men and women influence hiring practices. Job recruiters were asked to evaluate male and female applicants for the positions of editorial assistant and personnel technician.[44] The male and female applicants had identical qualifications. In spite of this fact, the job recruiters most often rated the males as appropriate for the job of personnel technician and judged the females as appropriate for the job of editorial assistant. This study shows that hiring decisions about equally qualified men and women can be biased by sex stereotypes.

A number of other studies have uncovered clear prejudice against hiring women whose qualifications are equal to those of men. Letters describing job applicants were sent to the hiring committees of 228 colleges and universities in the United States.[45] Half of the letters referred to an applicant who was male and half of the letters referred to an applicant who was female. In all other respects the letters were identical. The members of the hiring committees were asked to judge the academic rank that was appropriate for each job applicant. Female applicants were most often recommended for the position of assistant professor. Male applicants were most often recommended for the higher position of associate professor. Several male applicants but no female applicants were judged qualified to serve as full professors. Two similar studies found that college recruiters and business students were more favorable toward hiring a man rather than a woman for management positions even when the job qualifications of the applicants were identical.[46]

Male business students were asked to make a number of administrative decisions while playing the role of personnel director for a large bank.[47] The male students were significantly more likely to recommend promotion for male employees than for female employees even though it was assumed the qualifications of the men and women were equal. The students also gave significantly higher ratings to male employees on potential for customer and employee relations. When asked who should attend a personnel conference, the male students were significantly more likely to recommend a male. The students were also more likely to accept the judgment of a male supervisor than a female supervisor that a particular employee should be fired.

Some Conclusions

The research studies we have considered in this section illustrate the negative stereotyping of women occurring in the past twenty years. These studies do not imply that everyone in all situations acts on the basis of negative stereotypes of females. Other research studies have failed to uncover prejudice against women. The importance of the research reviewed above is to show that where negative stereotyping does exist, it can place females at a disadvantage and give them less sense of worth and personal control in their lives.

Strategies for Self-Control[48]

Numerous experiences of survival have been recorded by people who floated on a raft for months at sea, waited for rescuers in a blizzard high in the mountains, or suffered imprisonment and torture at the hands of fellow human beings. One theme common to all of these accounts of survival is the importance of the will to live and the strength never to give up. The phenomenon of the will to live is related to our study of learned helplessness because it is based on the feeling that if we talk to ourselves and convince ourselves that we can survive, our efforts will ultimately pay off. The ability to survive in extreme situations depends on never giving up the sense of internal control. If you have an opportunity to read reports about survival experiences, you will be struck by the parallels between the accounts of the survivors and the knowledge you have gained about the scientific study of learned helplessness. Because our focus in this book has been on scientific research, we will leave the description of survival to the many books that have been written on this topic. We will continue to focus on scientific research by considering a brief summary of techniques psychologists have developed for teaching people to increase the amount of personal control they have over their lives. By learning and practicing these techniques people can learn to reduce their feelings of helplessness and maintain a life with greater self-perception of internal control.

In Chapter Three we studied methods of learning to live successfully with bodily reactions and perceived emotions. The strategies for positive control over bodily reactions included self-relaxation, adaptive relabeling, and the use of cognitive strategies. In this section we will read about methods for learning to deal more effectively with overt behaviors. Overt behaviors can be brought under greater personal control with techniques of behavior rehearsal, self-observation, stimulus control, self-reinforcement, and self-punishment.

Behavior Rehearsal

We saw many interesting examples in Chapter 5 showing how it is possible to influence people's attitudes by inducing them through subtle measures to change their behaviors. People can use the same techniques on themselves. If they try out or rehearse new behaviors, they can learn to use these new behaviors to alter their self-perceptions. If a person has specific new behaviors or actions he or she wishes to try, it is often useful to practice first with another person. The other person can be a professional therapist or a friend. To rehearse a behavior, you must first decide upon the desired new behavior or reaction and then set up a role-playing situation in which you can practice it. If you are interested in trying out different ways of interacting with a date, you would play your role and the other person would play the role of the date. If there are new behaviors you want to try at work, the other person could play the role of your co-workers or boss.

An application of behavior rehearsal that has received a good deal of attention recently is "assertiveness training." Many of the popular books written on assertiveness training suggest exercises that enable people to practice interacting with each other in the assertive ways they would like to behave in various situations. The participants may set up a dialogue in which one person takes the role of a car mechanic who is charging an unreasonable fee, and the other person practices methods for being more assertive in getting a fair deal. Other instances where more assertiveness may be desired include interacting with a person of the opposite sex, dealing with one's boss, or dealing with one's parents or children. Research has shown that active rehearsal of assertive behaviors is significantly more effective in changing future actions than just thinking or talking about assertiveness.[49] It has also been found that people gain the most from behavior rehearsal when they receive encouragement and coaching about which behaviors might be best for them to attempt. For people who are very nonassertive it is helpful to practice expressing anger by shouting and hitting a cushion with one's hand or a polyethelene club.[50]

Self-Observation

To gain control over our behaviors, it is necessary to have an objective method of recording the progress we are making. If we do not keep a record of our behaviors it is too easy to think we are making certain changes when we really are not. A daily weight chart is much more accurate for measuring the effects of a diet than subjective impressions of changes in weight. A daily or hourly record of cigarettes smoked, outbursts of anger, or pages studied for a class is considerably more accurate than one's memory about these behaviors. Developing a method for recording behaviors is not only essential for an objective measure of progress, but also useful for providing an awareness and confidence in the power to bring these behaviors under internal control.

College students who were smokers were divided into two groups.[51] One group of students kept a record of how many cigarettes they smoked in class. The remaining students kept a record of how many times they had an urge to smoke but did not choose to light up at that particular time. After two weeks of this treatment, the first group of students smoked more than before and the second group of students smoked less. By observing themselves smoking, the first group of students apparently became more aware of the desire to smoke. By observing themselves not smoking, the second group of students apparently became more aware of their ability to choose not to smoke.

An elementary school student who whined a lot in class was given a chart with cartoons of a smiling face and a crying face.[52] The child learned to record his whining and smiling on these cartoons during the course of each day. At the beginning of the self-observation treatment, the child whined an average of two and a half times an hour. After about ten days of self-observation, the whining was virtually eliminated.

A psychologist wishing to lose weight recorded the number of bites of food he took each day.[53] Initially, 184 bites were maintaining a body weight of 250 pounds. By reducing the number of bites of food per day over a period of several weeks, the psychologist was able to lose 31 pounds.

An 18-year-old male with nervous tics was instructed to keep track of each tic with a hand counter.[54] The recording treatment and subsequent self-awareness of the behavior reduced the number of tics to zero.

A number of studies have shown that self-observation has a positive effect on study habits. In one experiment, participants ranging from elementary school to college students were instructed to keep a record of the number of minutes they studied each day.[55] This self-observation caused them to increase the amount of time they spent studying as well as their exam scores.

Self-observation is valuable for providing a record of the behaviors we wish to control. Self-observation is most useful for controlling behaviors that provide immediate reinforcement. The observation of a noticeable change in weight, cigarette smoking, or studying can be gratifying enough to make us continue self-observation in the future. In many instances, however, self-observation does not offer enough reinforcement in itself to sustain a change in behavior and some sort of other encouragement is necessary. For this reason, it is usually advisable to combine self-observation with a program in which we give ourselves rewards for doing a good job and possibly punish ourselves when we are doing a bad job.[56]

Stimulus Control

Think about the last time you visited a friend's house and a bowl of nuts or potato chips was placed in front of you. You probably ate some. If you are a smoker and someone offers you a cigarette it is likely that you will smoke it. If you are looking at a pocket calculator you will most probably try out a single problem. People's behaviors are very much controlled by external situations. This does not imply that they cannot exert internal control, because they can often do things to change the external situations. They place letters to be mailed in a spot where they will see them and write notes to themselves or tie strings around their fingers to remind themselves of various things they want to accomplish.

People who wish to control their eating behavior can control the external cues for eating in the following ways. They can limit their eating to certain hours at one table in the same room. In this way they bring their eating under the control of their own time schedule and their presence at the table. As a result, they make eating independent of previously uncontrollable cues such as television watching, reading, or talking on the phone. In addition, they should limit ahead of time the amount of food to be eaten by placing a finite portion of food on the plate and eating *only* that measured portion. Fattening foods are less likely to be eaten if they are not available. It is probably best to shop for food on a full stomach. Chewing slowly and swallowing one bite of food before putting the next bite on the fork make it easier to eat less. While learning to make eating contingent on only a time schedule and a certain table it is necessary to develop alternative responses to the cues that previously encouraged eating. Emotional upsets might be "pacified" with exercise, self-relaxation, or self-rewards that don't involve eating. Television watching and card playing should be enjoyed without food or at most with small amounts of nonfattening foods.[57]

The stimuli for smoking can be brought under control by restricting smoking to a special chair. Another technique for controlling smoking is to use a small portable timer and light up a cigarette only at the tone of the timer. The smoker can gradually extend the time between tones. The point of these techniques is to exert personal control over the external cues for smoking. Smoking is usually under the control of independent external cues, such as studying, finishing a meal, social drinking, and tension.[58]

To control the stimuli for studying, you can set aside a certain desk for nothing but studying. The strategy is to find a quiet, nondistracting spot in which to study and go there at specified times during the day.

At that desk, you *only* study. You eat, daydream, and visit with other people all in a different place.[59]

Sulking or pouting can be restricted to a "sulking stool." Such a technique makes the sulking behaviors objective and limits sulking to a situation that is less detrimental to interpersonal relationships. A person wishing to sulk may do so on the sulking stool, but it is understood that sulking will not be allowed in any other situations.[60]

It is also possible to control the stimuli for positive feelings. Elementary school teachers found that they would often look at the clock in the classroom when they were tired or agitated to see when the next break would come.[61] A smiling face was placed near the clock to serve as a cue for smiling and thinking positive thoughts. Whenever the teachers looked at the clock they were reminded to engage in these positive behaviors.

Self-Reward

One method for encouraging the use of behavior rehearsal, self-observation, and stimulus control is to provide reinforcement in the form of a reward for doing a good job. The best system for doing this is to keep an accurate record of the behavior you wish to change. You can then reward yourself each time you make a specific amount of progress in changing that behavior. You might reward yourself for specific reductions in weight, specific decreases in the number of cigarettes smoked, or specific decrements in sulking or increments in smiling. Or it might be more efficient to offer yourself rewards for a specific amount of time or energy devoted to your self-control program. You would then reinforce yourself for a certain numbers of hours spent in study, distance or time of jogging, or hours spent practicing a musical instrument. The rewards could include treating yourself to various goods or allowing yourself to engage in enjoyable activities. Or you could give yourself points to accumulate for a future reward.

The behavioral changes required for reinforcement must be ambitious enough to guarantee progress but not so strict as to make it impossible to receive the reward. If it is difficult to maintain self-discipline, a contract can be drawn up with a second person who administers the rewards. While attempting a new behavior, it is possible to reinforce the desired change in a covert manner by thinking positive and pleasant thoughts. You can anticipate how good it will feel to get the reward. You can also imagine the positive outcomes of your efforts, such as how good you will look after losing weight or how healthy you will be after jogging or quitting smoking.[62]

Self-Punishment

To decrease certain behaviors it is often useful to employ some form of self-punishment. Attempts have been made to provide people with a portable electric shocker for shocking themselves whenever they have an urge or desire to engage in behaviors they wish to decrease. Another form of punishment is to deprive oneself of a privilege for thinking about or engaging in an undesired behavior. Psychologists have devised programs in which people are instructed to tear up a one-dollar bill when they have undesirable thoughts or engage in unwanted behaviors. Another technique is to draw up a contract with a second person giving him or her a certain amount of money to withhold until an agreed upon behavioral change has been accomplished.[63]

Covert self-punishment is also useful for decreasing an unwanted behavior. The idea of covert punishment is to think about the negative implications of an undesired behavior and to associate the urges for this behavior with unpleasant emotional reactions. This technique is similar to the use of cognitive strategies for effecting positive outcomes (see Chapter Three). A graphic description of covert punishment is provided in the example below. People wishing to stop smoking are trained to imagine the following scene as vividly as possible whenever they experience the desire for a cigarette.

> You are sitting at your desk in the office preparing your lectures for class. There is a pack of cigarettes to your right. While you are writing, you put down your pencil and start to reach for the cigarettes. You get a nauseous feeling in your stomach. You begin to feel sick to your stomach, as if you are about to vomit. You touch the pack of cigarettes and bitter spit comes into your mouth. When you take the cigarette out of the pack some pieces of food come into your throat. Now you feel sick and have stomach cramps. As you are about to put the cigarette into your mouth, you puke all over the pack of cigarettes. The cigarette in your hand is very soggy and full of green vomit. There is a stink coming from the vomit. Snots are coming from your nose. Your hands feel all slimy and full of vomit. The whole desk is a mess. Your clothes are all full of puke. You get up from your desk and turn away from the vomit and cigarettes. You immediately begin to feel better being away from the vomit and the cigarettes. You go to the bathroom and wash up and feel great being away from the vomit and the cigarettes.[64]

Covert punishment for overeating can be implemented by imagining oneself being blown up like a balloon or picturing scenes of ugly yellow fat. A combination of self-reward and self-punishment was employed in a procedure where overweight people stored unsavory bags of pork fat in their refrigerators which they could remove piece by piece whenever they lost a certain amount of weight.[65]

Self-Perception of Efficacy

The techniques for developing self-control over overt behaviors described in this chapter and the strategies for adapting to bodily reactions that were outlined in Chapter 3 can both provide people with a greater sense of control over their lives. Albert Bandura has developed a theory in which he proposes that people's perceptions of self-efficacy have strong influence on their success in mastering new behaviors, coping with aversive experiences, and remaining persistent in the face of obstacles.[66] We have seen that learned helplessness greatly reduces or entirely destroys perceptions of self-efficacy. Techniques for effective control of bodily reactions and overt behaviors enable people to strengthen their perceptions of self-efficacy. Many psychologists believe that psychotherapy is most effective when it focuses less on teaching specific responses to specific problems and more on developing problem-solving strategies that can be used as coping mechanisms in a variety of situations.[67] A number of recent studies have demonstrated the value of helping people to increase their feelings of self-efficacy.

Bandura and his colleagues compared different methods of treating male and female adults who suffer from fear of snakes.[68] Participants in one group first watched the therapist look at a nonpoisonous snake, approach the snake, touch the snake, hold the snake, and let the snake crawl freely in the room. These participants were then encouraged to follow the same procedure in adapting to the snake, and to progress at whatever pace was most comfortable for them. The treatment session was designed to be challenging and to provide participants with an experience of self-directed mastery and enhanced personal efficacy. Participants in a second group observed the therapist approach and touch the snake but were not given the experience of going through the process themselves. A third group of participants did not receive treatment and served as a control group.

Results of the study showed that participants in the first group (observation and practice) improved the most in their ability to approach and touch nonpoisonous snakes. Participants in the second group (observation only) did not improve as much as participants in the first group but showed significantly more improvement than participants in the control group. A second important finding of this study was that participants in the first group also experienced the greatest increase in feelings of self-efficacy. Participants who observed the therapist and then touched the snake themselves had the highest expectations for success in approaching and touching nonpoisonous snakes in the future. Participants in the second group had feelings of self-efficacy that were higher than participants in the control group and lower than participants in the first group. An additional finding was that feelings of self-efficacy correlated highly with success in approaching and touching the snakes in future tests. In general, participants who *believed* they would be successful in approaching and touching the snakes *were* successful.

A program for increasing self-efficacy has also been developed to help people gain self-control over exaggerated feelings of anger.[69] The program consists in teaching people to identify situations that cause them to feel angry and to become aware of their bodily responses during these situations. The awareness of anger-provoking situations and related bodily feelings can then serve as a cue for implementing coping strategies such as adaptive relabeling and self-relaxation as well as adaptive behaviors previously rehearsed with a friend or therapist. The coping strategies and adaptive behaviors can be maintained in one's daily life with self-observation and self-reward.

Another example of the effect of feelings of self-efficacy was shown in a study designed to enhance people's ability to cope in crowded situations.[70] Adult women who were entering a crowded grocery store were approached by an experimenter who offered to pay them three dollars for participating in a study in which they would be given thirty minutes to select (but not buy) fifty household items on a list while attempting to make the total price as low as possible. At the end of thirty minutes the experimenter met each volunteer to record how successful she had been in selecting the items and to ask her to respond to a brief questionnaire measuring her feelings of comfort and ease in the store. To see if self-efficacy would enhance the ability to cope in the crowded store, the experimenter gave instructions to half of the volunteers that would help them label their reactions to the crowd in an adaptive manner:

> While you are carrying out this task, the store may become crowded. We know from previous research that crowding sometimes causes people to feel aroused and sometimes anxious. We just wanted you to know this so that if you feel aroused or anxious you will know why.[71]

Results of the study showed that volunteers who were given these coping instructions were significantly more efficient in filling the shopping list and rated themselves as being significantly more comfortable and at ease in the store.

We can see now that techniques for developing self-control over overt behaviors and strategies for adapting to bodily reactions can serve as coping mechanisms leading to enhanced feelings of self-efficacy and success in mastering difficult situations.

NINE

Self-Perception
and the Perception
of Others

Because we spend much of our lives interacting with other people it is interesting to ask if the factors influencing our self-perceptions are similar or different from the factors influencing our perceptions of others. We will begin our discussion of this question by evaluating the use of personality traits for explaining behavior. It seems that people usually explain their own behaviors on the basis of external factors in the situation while attributing the behaviors of others to internal traits or dispositions. However, the same fallacies that cause people to make errors in explaining their own actions also decrease their accuracy in predicting the behaviors of others. Among these fallacies are exaggerated belief in uniqueness, ignorance of probabilities in favor of intuition, underestimation of environmental forces, overestimation of consensus with one's beliefs, and bias toward plausible rather than accurate explanations for behavior. We will conclude our comparison of self-perception and the perception of others with a summary of research investigating how people react to heightened self-awareness. Studies have shown that self-awareness is related to consistency of behavior in different situations and that people vary in the amount of attention they pay to their actions.

Explaining Behavior
with Personality Traits

Most people rely on personality traits to explain the behaviors of other people. If you were attempting to understand why a particular student studied extremely hard and worked diligently on class assignments, you might conclude that the student was very competitive or had a strong need for achievement. Asked to explain why a teenager in your neighborhood consistently acted up in school, you might say that the teenager was delinquent or irresponsible. People who don't work are often considered lazy or unmotivated. People who fight with others are short tempered or aggressive. If people need approval from others it is because they are insecure. People who don't need constant approval from others are independent. People who stay by themselves and don't interact with others are shy whereas people who talk a lot in groups are outgoing and gregarious.

All of the above explanations for the behaviors in question attribute them to inherent personality traits rather than to factors or forces in the outside world. Most people who have not studied psychology have the notion that psychologists seek to understand human beings by applying labels and diagnoses, but more and more psychologists have come to emphasize the importance of environmental variables in explaining human behavior. Nonetheless, there is still a sizable number of psychologists who continue to attribute human behaviors primarily or exclusively to inner personality traits.

Psychologists who use personality traits to explain behavior come from a wide variety of schools of thought. However, all of the theories of personality that emphasize inner traits as explanations for behavior share the belief that human behaviors are manifestations of inner processes, in other words, that the inner personality exerts enduring causal effects on behavior. According to these theories, it is necessary to study behavior not for itself but rather as an indicator of the underlying personality. Some personality theories propose that inner personality traits and processes are primarily unconscious and that behavior must be carefully analyzed for its hidden meanings. In all theories of personality it is the inner personality and its underlying dynamics that serve as the primary explanation for human behavior.[1] To get an idea of how psychologists use inner traits to explain human behavior we can analyze some examples from contemporary psychoanalytic journals.

Psychoanalysts have explained the delusion of paranoia in the following manner:

> The delusion, it is theorized, is constructed to protect the individual against threatening feelings of homosexuality resulting from the negative Oedipus complex.[2]

The following is a psychoanalytic explanation for stuttering:

> Psychoanalytic theory likens the emotional dynamics of stuttering to obsessions and compulsions with similar psychosexual regression. In the obsessive–compulsive syndrome, the patient tries to avoid both masculine-aggressive and feminine-receptive behavior and, by vacillation, he avoids a fantasied consequence of either aggression or receptivity. Speech may acquire special unconscious, aggressive, and sexual properties.[3]

A psychoanalytic analysis of the 1968 student rebellion at Columbia University resulted in the following conclusions:

> "Up against the wall, motherfuckers!" became the dominant chant of the insurrectionists occupying the Columbia buildings, shouted in a great chorus of defiance especially at the police. The ubiquity of "motherfucker" as the supremely defiant insult clearly enough reveals the obsession with the Oedipal situation. Here is a ritualistic purging of Oedipal guilt, by attribution to the enemy: not we, but they, are guilty of the primal Oedipal crime.[4]

A psychoanalytic explanation argues that smoking

> . . . gratifies the need to feel the inner ego boundaries by inhalation, symbolizing introjection of the love object, which lessens fear of suffocation. The respiratory exhalation, made visible by the smoke, symbolizes a kind of projection of feared objects.[5]

Applause has been explained in this manner:

> It seems that applause is a magic, mystic, ritualistic gesture to ward off bad demons just released and to send them on their way through the ritual of noise making.[6]

Finally, for alcoholism:

> In psychoanalytic theory, alcoholics are viewed as oral and narcissistic personalities with marked oral frustration. . . .[7]

Evaluating Trait Explanations for Behavior

A comprehensive analysis of the use and misuse of personality traits and inner dynamics for explaining behavior has been provided by Walter Mischel.[8] Mischel argues that theories explaining behavior by personality traits, which are based on the assumption that personality traits cause behavior, are useful only if they satisfy at least two criteria. First, they must demonstrate that each person's behavior is relatively consistent; if people are motivated by inner personality traits it is reasonable to expect that these traits should be relatively stable. Second, the relatively stable personality traits must have utility for predicting and changing behavior; personality traits that can only be inferred to "explain" behavior after it occurs are of limited value. A scientifically useful theory of human behavior would enable us to predict behaviors before they occur. A scientifically useful theory would also suggest theoretical and practical methods for directly influencing human behavior.

Consistency of Behavior

The basic method for studying the consistency of human behavior is to put people in different situations and determine the degree to which the individual behaviors that are typically explained by trait theories are consistent. Research has shown that measures of individual intelligence and cognitive ability are *relatively* consistent when they are assessed by different instruments in different situations at different times. It is therefore reasonable to regard these attributes as *relatively* stable attributes of individuals.[9]

Measures of other behaviors that are typically explained by inferred personality traits show little individual consistency. Behaviors commonly related to personality traits such as attitudes toward authority, morality, dependency, sexual identification, aggression, authoritarianism, and anxiety vary considerably when individuals are tested in different situations. It is therefore difficult to conceive of these behaviors as a product of stable inner personality traits.[10]

Utility for Prediction

The utility of employing personality traits to predict behavior can be evaluated by determining if measures from personality tests relate in any meaningful way to people's overt behaviors. Research has shown that correlations between measures of personality and measures of overt behavior are consistently low. A person's past behavior is usually a better predictor of his or her future behavior than any existing measures of personality.[11] Since 1960 the consistent failure of personality tests to predict behavior better than knowledge of past behavior has caused disillusionment among psychologists. In 1960 Paul Meehl wrote:

Personally, I find the cultural lag between what the published research shows and what clinicians persist in claiming to do with their favorite devices even more disheartening than the adverse evidence itself.[12]

In 1964 Philip Vernon gave the following analysis of the use of personality traits to explain human behavior:

The real trouble is that it has not worked well enough, and despite the huge volume of research it has stimulated, it seems to lead to a dead end.[13]

In 1968 Walter Mischel gave the following assessment:

The initial assumptions of trait-state theory were logical, inherently plausible, and also consistent with common sense and intuitive impressions about personality. Their real limitation turned out to be empirical—they simply have not been supported adequately.[14]

Hazards of Labeling

Personality theories that are oriented toward interpreting behaviors as signs of underlying traits and inner dynamics often underemphasize the knowledge that can be gained by studying specific relationships between behavior and variables in the immediate environment. Moreover, attempts to explain behaviors by postulating underlying personality traits can result in illogical circular argument. There is nothing wrong with calling people who work hard "competitive," assessing people who give up easily as having "low self-esteem," or describing people who seek attention as having a "high need for approval." Labels for behavior often help people communicate more clearly with each other. The problem comes from giving labels to behaviors and then explaining the behaviors by using the behaviors as "proof" for the labels. It does not add to our understanding to conclude that people work hard *because* they are competitive, that giving up easily is a *sign* of low self-esteem, or that seeking attention is *caused* by a high need for approval. The causes of these behaviors are not in the labels but in the interactions between the individual people and their environments.[15]

Psychologists who attempt to understand behaviors as manifestations of inner personality traits and dynamics face the danger of using their favorite labels and theories to bias their interpretations. Left to his or her own devices, a psychologist can analyze any behavior to "discover" an expected personality trait. Professional psychotherapists were asked to look at a 15-minute segment of a videotaped interview and to give their evaluations of the man who was being interviewed.[16] The interview centered around the interviewee's feelings about his work experiences. Half of the psychotherapists were told that the man being interviewed was an applicant for a job. The remaining psychotherapists were told that the man being interviewed was a psychiatric patient. All of the videotapes were identical. Psychotherapists who thought the man was interviewing for a job described him as "realistic," "fairly sincere," "enthusiastic," "attractive," "pleasant," and "relatively bright." Psychotherapists who thought the interviewee was a patient gave the following evaluations:

> tight defensive person ... conflict over homosexuality; dependent, passive-aggressive; frightened of his own aggressive impulses ... impulsivity shows through his rigidity ... considerable hostility, repressed or channeled.[17]

These differences in evaluation arose only with psychotherapists who were oriented toward the use of psychodynamic and trait theories. Behavioral psychotherapists did not bias their evaluations of the interviewee who was described as a patient. This was presumably because behavioral psychotherapists are oriented toward describing behaviors in an objective fashion rather than using behaviors to make inferences about underlying personality dynamics or traits.

Another example of bias in labeling was shown in a study where eight professional people gained admission to mental hospitals by claiming that they were hearing voices.[18] Even though the pseudopatients did not act abnormally in the hospital, they were given the diagnosis of schizophrenia. The pseudopatients found that they could take notes quite openly without being discovered as "normal" because the hospital staff interpreted the notetaking as "a subset of behaviors correlated with schizophrenia." When the pseudopatients were finally released after an average of 19 days of hospitalization they continued to carry the diagnosis of schizophrenia "in remission."

The point of this study is that psychotherapists in the context of a mental hospital expect to see behaviors that signify underlying pathology. This expectation biases them to interpret "normal" behaviors with the labels and diagnoses they are trained to use.[19]

In another study psychotherapists at mental hospitals were told to be on the lookout for pseudopatients who might try to gain admission to their hospital.[20] In reality, *no* pseudopatients tried to gain admission to these hospitals. Because the psychotherapists were expecting pseudopatients, however, 41 out of 193 patients who were admitted to the hospitals during the period of the study were alleged by at least one member of the hospital staff to be "normal," and 19 of the 193 patients were suspected to be "normal" by a psychiatrist plus a staff member of the hospital. This study shows that expectations can influence labeling of the *same* behaviors as abnormal and normal.

Personality theories that use underlying traits and inner dynamics to explain behavior can come to terms with the fact that people's behaviors are often inconsistent by assuming that these inconsistencies reflect divergent manifestations of a fundamentally underlying personality. However, theories based on personality traits and inner dynamics are weak in their ability to accurately predict behavior, and their tendency to promote biased application and interpretation of personality and psychodynamic labels causes problems.[21]

Cognitive Social Learning Theory

It seems reasonable to assume that in order to predict behavior accurately it is necessary to take the factors and forces in a person's environment into account. The most fruitful approach is not the traditional practice of listening to a person's case history, dreams, and daily experiences and then using this information to infer inner personality traits and dynamics. A more useful cognitive social learning strategy enlists the person's assistance in determining the functional relationships between environmental conditions and the person's individual perceptions and interpretations of these conditions. This strategy is behavioristic in that it focuses on measurable relationships between environmental variables, personal interpretations, and resulting behaviors. Because of the importance of each person's *perceptions* of environmental forces, cognitive social learning theory takes full account of cognitive factors.[22]

In the discussion of self-control in Chapter Eight, we reviewed several examples showing how people's perceptions are taken into account when they are taught strategies for controlling and changing their behaviors. People who employ techniques of self-control become aware of the interaction between environmental factors and their perceptions and interpretations of these factors. If they keep a record of their behaviors they learn how variables in the environment influence them to act in different ways.

In analyzing the case of an American airman during the Second World War, Mischel makes a revealing comparison between cognitive social learning theory and personality theories that infer inner traits and dynamics.[23] During a flying mission the airman's plane was hit with a shell and he was seriously injured. After this nearly fatal experience the airman suffered fainting spells whenever his plane reached the altitude at which the accident occurred. Based on what we learned in

Chapter Three, we can surmise that the combined stimulus of flying and reaching a previously aversive altitude elicited anxiety. Our approach to treating the airman would be to teach him self-relaxation and to slowly have him associate relaxation with stimuli similar to those of flying. The airman would at first imagine flying at various altitudes and stop to relax himself whenever he began to feel anxious. After this treatment the airman could gradually begin to fly, with the opportunity to reduce altitude when necessary for self-relaxation. Gradually the airman would be able to work himself into flying at all altitudes, including the altitude at which the accident had occurred.

Because the airman was referred to a psychiatrist who used personality dynamics as explanations for behavior, that was not the treatment he received. After examining the airman, the psychiatrist attributed his fainting spells to a brittle personality structure caused by inadequate identification with his father. The psychiatrist concluded:

> The patient's maturity, achieved through identification with his grandfather and based on a rejection of his own father, was at best tenuous. It did not appear to represent an actual maturity but rather an imitation of maturity. The attempt to achieve an ego-ideal by imitation, rather than through a real identification, was characteristic of this man.[24]

Although the airman wanted to fly and felt very badly and very much like a failure because of his fainting spells, the psychiatrist decided that the airman's inner problems and psychological defenses would have to be cured before he could safely resume flying.

Perceiving Ourselves and Perceiving Others

Even though personality trait theories are of limited scientific value for predicting and controlling behavior, it is not surprising that people attempt to understand each other with labels and inferred traits. There are thousands of words in the English language that describe behaviors while at the same time implying an intrinsic quality about the behaving person. Most people think that a person who acts aggressively *is* aggressive, or that someone who behaves in a kind manner *is* a kind person. The prevalence of trait words in the English language makes it plausible to infer that people act aggressively *because* they are aggressive and that people act in a kind manner *because* they are kind. We lose sight of the fact that these explanations of behavior are based largely on circular reasoning. The tendency to seek consistency in our perceptions makes it easy to find evidence of the traits we have inferred for other people over wide ranges of their behaviors.[25]

Although most people grow up learning to use traits to explain behavior, they do this more for understanding other people than for understanding themselves. The tendency is to rely on external factors in the situation or environment to explain their own behaviors while inferring inner personality traits to explain the behaviors of others. College students observed another student agree or disagree to volunteer for a cause.[26] When the observers were asked to predict the student's future behavior they were inclined to believe that the volunteering student would volunteer for additional causes and that the nonvolunteering student would not volunteer for additional causes. The observing students apparently inferred that the volunteering student was a generally helpful or compliant person and that the nonvolunteering student was a generally unhelpful or noncompliant person. College students in a second group were asked to volunteer for a cause and then asked whether or not they would volunteer for additional causes in the future. These students did not use their own previous willingness or unwillingness to volunteer for predicting their future behavior. They were apparently more likely to perceive that their future volunteering would depend on the particular issue or situation rather than on an enduring personality trait of "helpfulness" or "compliance."

Male college students in a second study were asked to give reasons why they chose a particular girlfriend and why a friend of theirs chose a particular girlfriend.[27] In describing their own choices, the students were most likely to use external or situational explanations having to do with qualities of their girlfriend. In describing the choices of their friends the students were significantly more inclined to use explanations related to internal factors such as the friend's need for companionship or desire for someone with whom to relax.

In a third study comparing self-perception and perception of others college students were asked to choose adjectives describing themselves as well as other people including a friend, acquaintance, and well-known television personality.[28] Results of this study showed that students were far more willing to use adjectives for describing other people than for describing themselves. When describing themselves the students were more inclined to say that their behaviors "depend on the situation."

Edward E. Jones and Richard Nisbett have given a number of explanations for why people attribute their own behaviors to factors in the situation while attributing the behaviors of others to inner personality traits. Generally speaking, people view their own behaviors and the behaviors of others from two different perspectives. When they observe another person's behaviors, they become very aware of his or her facial expressions, gestures, tones of voice, and other mannerisms. The strong impressions of the other person's behaviors distract them from the variables that are present in the situation, focusing their attention on finding traits with which to label the behaviors they are observing. Once determined, the trait labels for the other person are likely to be perceived as stable. First of all, people are inclined to structure their perceptions of the other person's future behaviors in a way that corresponds with the trait labels they have chosen. In addition, because they are likely to see the same person in the same situations, that person's behaviors often appear to be more consistent than they really are. When people observe their own behaviors, they tend to underemphasize personal mannerisms because they cannot stand back and view themselves from the perspective of an outside observer. At the same time, they are highly aware of how variables in the situation and their perceptions of these variables combine to influence their actions. Personal experiences tell people that their behaviors are not consistent and depend very much on factors in the external environment.[29]

A number of research studies have investigated differences between self-perception and the perception of others. In these studies people in a position to perceive themselves are referred to as "actors" and people in a position to perceive others are referred to as "observers."

Comparing Actors and Observers

Performance on Learning Tasks

College students in two studies were asked to perform a learning task or to observe another student performing the learning task.[30] Students who worked on the task themselves felt that the external factor of the task's difficulty strongly influenced how well they did on the task. Observing students, on the other hand, viewed the performance of others as most strongly related to inner ability. Observing students were much more likely than actors to use a student's degree of success on one task as a basis for predicting the student's success on a second task. This is presumably because observers perceived the student's performance on the first task as an indication of his or her ability that would also influence performance on the second task. Actors were apparently more likely to view their own degree of success on the first and second tasks as independent and influenced primarily by the nature and difficulty of the task.

Judging Attitudes

Actors and observers also judge attitudes differently. A reader is more likely than the writer of an essay to view the essay as an expression of the writer's attitudes. This is true whether or not the writer was forced to write the essay or wrote it out of his or her own choice. People who write an essay out of their own choice are inclined to view the essay as expressing their attitudes. Observers who read the essay are even more inclined than the writer to perceive the essay as expressing the writer's attitudes. People who write an essay with little or no free choice do not view the essay as an expression of their attitudes. Observers who realize an essay was written with no choice still believe the essay reflects more of the writer's true attitudes than the writer himself.[31]

Large-Scale Behaviors

Stephen West and his colleagues have analyzed some interesting examples of how the mass media rely on personality traits to explain human behaviors taking place on a large scale.[32] The behavior of Germans in World War II has commonly been attributed to internal factors such as blind obedience, nationalism, and ethnocentrism. It is likely that observers who make such attributions for actions in Nazi Germany have neglected the importance of situational factors ranging from group censorship to fear for one's own life. Research by Stanley Milgram has shown that obedience to authority in a laboratory situation can be influenced by a number of external variables including physical distance between the experimenter and subject, proximity of the subject to the victim, and the nature of the experimenter's demands.[33] The failure of bystanders to aid a victim is commonly attributed to internal factors such as apathy, dehumanization, and alienation. Research by Latané and Darley and other psychologists has produced a long list of situational variables that influence a person's willingness or reluctance to help a victim.[34] Explanations for the Watergate affair often center around internal factors such as amorality, paranoia, and lust for power while neglecting situational factors including monetary reward, government sponsorship, and expectation of immunity from prosecution.

To gain additional information on perceptions of issues such as the Watergate burglary, West and his colleagues conducted the following experiment. Criminology students were approached by an experimenter posing as a private investigator and asked if they would be willing to participate in a special investigation that necessitated the surreptitious entry of an office building.[35] An elaborate explanation was given about sponsorship of the investigation by the Internal Revenue Service, immunity from prosecution for the illegal entry, and possible financial reward. After the students stated whether or not they would be willing to take part in the plan they were asked to specify the reasons for their decision. A second group of college students was given a detailed description of the burglary plan and was led to believe that another student had either agreed or refused to participate. These observing students were asked to give reasons for the other student's decision.

The explanations given by acting students and observing students were very different. Students who actually made the decision about whether or not to participate in the burglary were more inclined than observing students to give reasons related to external variables such as the possibility of a monetary reward, quality of the plan, and the probability of avoiding arrest. Observing students tended more than acting students to explain the decision of whether or not to participate on the basis of internal factors such as enjoyment of adventure, belief in a cause, or willingness to be persuaded.

Motivational Factors in the Perception of Self and Others

The above research studies show that people often attribute the behaviors of others to personality traits but explain their own behaviors on the basis of external forces in the environment. The explanation given earlier for this phenomenon was that people are more aware of the situational variables that affect their own behaviors than of the environmental factors that influence the behaviors of others. There are at least three other factors that cause differences between the way people perceive their own behaviors and the way they perceive the behaviors of others: the desirability of the behaviors being interpreted; the motivation to perceive one's own behaviors as internally rather than externally controlled; and the desire to appear consistent and rational.

Perceptions of Desirability

In Chapter Four we saw that people are more likely to perceive their behaviors as reflections of their true attitudes if they perceive these behaviors as internally rather than externally motivated. The same tendency applies to the perceptions of others. College students were told that someone they either liked or disliked had performed a good deed.[36] When asked to explain why they thought a person they liked had done the good deed, students said it was because the person was helpful and kind. Subjects attributed a good deed by a disliked person to external factors such as the desire to make a good impression or the lack of anything else to do. In a second experiment, college students attributed a successful performance on a skill game by someone they liked to the person's inner ability whereas they attributed a successful performance by someone they disliked to external factors such as luck or simplicity of the game. In a similar vein, poor performance by a liked person was attributed to external factors and poor performance by a disliked person was attributed to internal factors.

Another illustration of differential attributions for desirable and undesirable actions was revealed in a study showing that college students give "external" explanations for the behavior of a helpful stranger and "internal" explanations for the behavior of an unhelpful stranger.[37] This result is possibly due to the fact that helpful deeds are often motivated by the external factors of gratitude and praise. Therefore it is not clear whether helpful behavior by a stranger is due to inner qualities of "helpfulness" or to external rewards in the environment. Unhelpful behavior by a stranger is probably seen as internally motivated because a person is not likely to be rewarded by the environment for this behavior.

Behavioral desirability influences the attributions people make for their own actions as well as for those of others. When their own behaviors have positive outcomes they are likely to attribute them to personal factors and when their own behaviors have negative outcomes they are likely to attribute them to situational factors. The reverse is true with attributions for other people's behaviors.[38]

Motivation for Internal Control

People generally do not view their own behaviors as a function of enduring personality trait, because they know that they vary their actions to adapt to a particular situation. But, although they are more likely than observers to be aware of how factors in the environment influence them, they usually do not wish to acknowledge that these environmental factors might be beyond their control. The desire for a sense of personal control will sometimes motivate people to see their own behaviors as a reflection of their personality. College students who played a competitive game with another person were more likely than observers to recognize that the other person's responses in the game influenced their own responses.[39] The actors were also more likely than the observers to feel that their responses in the game reflected something about their individual personality. Interpreting their responses as a reflection of their personality apparently gave the students a greater sense of self-control.

College students who were asked to submit to a series of electric shocks were no less likely than observers to attribute their agreement to be shocked to their internal feelings.[40] Again, although the students could probably recognize the external influence of the experimenter's request, it was desirable for them to perceive their willingness to be shocked as a product of their internal motivation.

College students in a third experiment were given the task of helping another person relax.[41] When the students were expected to do

well and a physiological recording meter showed that they were successful, they were more likely than observers to attribute the success to
themselves rather than to external factors in the experiment. In this
study it was to the students' benefit to give themselves credit for successfully relaxing the other person. Observers who expected the students to succeed had no more reason to attribute the success to qualities
of the student than to factors in the experiment which led them to
expect success in the first place.

People may sometimes attribute their positive behaviors to internal
factors in order to increase their feelings of internal control, but they
are often motivated to decrease their perceptions of internal control
over other types of behavior. College students who were induced to
deliver painful electric shocks to another person were significantly less
likely to attribute this behavior to internal factors than observers of
their actions.[42] In this experiment it was to the students' advantage to
attribute their behavior of delivering shocks to the external forces of
the experimenter's request than to some aspect of their personality.

Making a Good Impression

Participants in experimental research are often motivated to make a
good impression on the experimenter. Participants in experiments may
sometimes realize that experimenters *expect* them to feel internal control over their behaviors. If participants are induced to engage in discrepant behaviors they may express attitudes that match these behaviors because they don't want to appear inconsistent and unpredictable.
The explanations people give for their behaviors are influenced by the
discriminations they make about environmental factors influencing
their actions as well as by their desire to please other people.[43]

Some Conclusions

Because of the numerous trait words in the English language and a
predisposition to seek consistency most people tend to explain the behaviors of others on the basis of personality traits and inner dynamics.
Explaining behavior through this kind of labeling is intuitively reasonable because people have a limited awareness of how environmental
variables influence other people's behavior and they lose sight of the
fallacy of "explaining" a behavior by giving it a label. When explaining
their own behaviors, however, people are much less likely to rely on
personality trait labels because they know firsthand that situational
variables directly influence their behaviors. Nevertheless, they are
prompted to attribute their own behaviors to internal causes if there

are no obvious forces in the environment influencing their actions, if they are motivated to take responsibility for a positive action, if internal attributions will enable them to achieve a feeling of self-determination, or if internal attributions will help them appear rational and consistent. Conversely, as we shall see below, they are more likely to attribute the behaviors of other people to external factors if these external factors are brought to their attention.

Increasing Observer Empathy

Empathy means to project one's consciousness into another person and to perceive the world as he or she perceives it. To become more empathic toward an actor, observers must be able to view the environmental variables affecting the actor's behavior from the same perspective as the actor. College students in one study were asked to give their impressions of a person in a videotaped discussion; students in a second study gave judgments about a person in a short story.[44] Half of the students in these studies were instructed to empathize as much as possible with the person and picture in their minds how the person was feeling. The remaining students received no instructions about empathy. The students who made a specific attempt to be empathic gave more situational explanations for the person's behaviors than the students who were not specifically attempting to be empathic. Students who did not make a special attempt to be empathic attributed the person's behaviors more to personality characteristics such as character, mood, and personal traits. Observers generally judge that a person who did an unpleasant task for low payment enjoyed it more than a person who did the unpleasant task for high payment.[45] This is presumably because observers assume that people who agreed to an unpleasant task for low payment must have "wanted" to do it. When observers are instructed to be empathic and place themselves in the other person's position, they judge the unpleasant task more favorably if it was done for high rather than low payment. The observers no longer assume that the person did the task because of internal motivation, but rather because of appreciation for the external monetary payment.

Observer empathy can also be increased through the use of videotapes. Pairs of participants in a study were introduced to each other and seated in a room so that they could talk and become acquainted.[46] Each participant was watched by an observer. In addition, a television camera was mounted directly above each participant's head to record the conversation from his or her point of view. After the conversation, the behaviors of participants were rated by themselves and by their observers. Corroborating other findings, the results showed that participants used more situational explanations and observers used more explanations based on personality traits. In a second part of the study, participants viewed themselves on videotape from the point of view of the person with whom they had been talking, essentially becoming observers of their own behaviors. As a result, they gave significantly fewer situational explanations for their behaviors. Similarly, a group of original observers had a chance to experience the conversation from the participants' point of view by watching the videotape taken by the camera over the participants' heads. After viewing the conversation as the participants had seen it, the observers gave significantly more situational explanations for the participants' behaviors. By using videotapes the author of this experiment was successful in helping observers to see an interaction from an actor's point of view and in enabling actors to look at their own behaviors from an observer's point of view. He suggested that videotapes might be useful for counseling people in their interactions with each other. We often attribute the behaviors of other people that bother us to their personal will, lack of sensitivity, or inner weaknesses. By watching our interactions with them from their perspective we can learn that the ways in which they behave are influenced by our actions just as our behaviors are influenced by their actions. Empathy is increased by experiencing an interaction from another person's point of view and by learning to understand specific variables in the situation that influence that person's behaviors.

The Fallacy of Uniqueness

Now that we are well aware of the uses and misuses of personality traits and labels for attempting to understand the behaviors of other people, it is worth pointing out that although people are often willing to use traits and labels for explaining the behaviors of others they prefer to perceive themselves as adaptable, unpredictable, and unique. The following experiment has been conducted with many different people in a wide variety of situations. Participants are given a series of personality tests and in a week or so presented with the results of the tests in the form of a personality profile. When asked to give their evaluations of the profile, the participants are almost always enthusiastic and state that the description given for them in the profile is "very good" or "excellent." In reality, the same personality profile is given to all participants and has nothing to do with the personality tests that were taken:

> You have a strong need for other people to like you and for them to admire you. You have a tendency to be critical of yourself. You have a great deal of unused capacity which you have not turned to your advan-

tage. While you have some personality weaknesses, you are generally able to compensate for them. Your sexual adjustment has presented some problems for you. Disciplined and controlled on the outside, you tend to be worrisome and insecure inside. At times you have serious doubts as to whether you have made the right decision or done the right thing. You prefer a certain amount of change and variety and become dissatisfied when hemmed in by restrictions and limitations. You pride yourself as being an independent thinker and do not accept others' opinions without satisfactory proof. You have found it unwise to be too frank in revealing yourself to others. At times you are extroverted, affable, sociable, while at other times you are introverted, wary, and reserved. Some of your aspirations tend to be pretty unrealistic.[47]

People are willing to accept the above personality profile for themselves whether or not it comes from a lay person or a professional psychologist and find it more "accurate" than descriptions from commonly used personality tests. If the above profile is changed so that it is less complimentary but still full of generalizations, people will still view it as accurate. The point is that the profile could be true for anybody, but because people feel unique they are willing to accept it as an exclusive description of themselves.[48]

The use of generalities to infer truths about a personality occurs in astrology, handwriting analysis, and fortune-telling. Whether or not these endeavors are of personal interest is a subjective judgment and outside the realm of experimental research. To be scientifically useful for predicting human behavior, personality descriptions of any sort must have incremental as well as predictive validity.

Incremental Validity

A personality profile has *incremental validity* if it adds to our knowledge by telling us something we could not have learned in an easier way.[49] Personality descriptions that use generalities are accurate, but they don't tell us anything we didn't already know. It is very easy to look at astrological charts and handwriting assessments and find a valid description of yourself. It is likely, however, that the astrological charts and handwriting assessments for someone else would also appear to describe you accurately, especially if you were led to believe that they were made for you, rather than for the other person. An experiment was conducted in which one group of people was given a horoscope that was supposedly derived from the exact day, month, and year in which they were born.[50] A second group of people received exactly the same horoscope with the explanation that it would also fit most other people in the study. Even though all of the horoscopes were identical, people who thought the horoscope had been done exclusively for them were significantly more willing to accept it as an accurate description of themselves.

A test of incremental validity was conducted by giving people personality descriptions for the twelve astrological signs and asking them to pick out the one that belonged to them.[51] When the descriptions were given without being identified by sign, the people's judgments were based purely on chance. It is easy to find personal characteristics in a handwriting sample if you know the person who wrote the sample. A test of incremental validity would have to discriminate between people on the basis of handwriting samples without knowing which person goes with which sample. People who make a living at giving personality descriptions have developed the skill of sizing up their clients in terms of sex, age, race, and socioeconomic status and giving descriptions that are stereotypic for a person with those identifiable characteristics.

Predictive Validity

A personality description has *predictive validity* if it bears some relationship to a person's actual behavior.[52] It is often intrinsically interesting to attach personality labels to people after observing how they behave. For personality descriptions to have scientific value, however, they must be useful in predicting how a person will behave. Consider the following partial transcripts of three different court cases in which a psychologist was asked to describe a defendant's personality on the basis of personality tests.[53] In each case, the psychologist (P) is being questioned by one of the acting attorneys (A):

I. A. And the House-Tree-Person Test—you handed the defendant Kent a pencil and a blank piece of paper, is that right, Doctor?

   P. That is correct.

   A. And you asked him to draw a house?

   P. Yes.

   A. And what did this tell you about Kent?

   P. The absence of a door, and the bars on the windows, indicated he saw the house as a jail, not a home. Also, you will notice it is a side view of the house; he was making it inaccessible.

   A. Isn't it normal to draw a side view of a house? You didn't ask him to draw a front view, did you?

   P. No.

   A. And those bars on the window—could they have been Venetian blinds and not bars? Who called them bars, you or Kent?

P. I did.

A. Did you ask him what they were?

P. No.

A. What else did the drawing reveal about Kent?

P. The line in front of the house runs from left to right. This indicates a need for security.

A. This line indicates insecurity! Could it also indicate the contour of the landscape, like a lawn or something?

P. This is not the interpretation I gave it.

A. And the chimney—what does it indicate?

P. You will notice the chimney is dark. This indicates disturbed sexual feelings. The smoke indicates inner daydreaming.

A. Did I understand you correctly? Did you say dark chimneys indicate disturbed sex feelings?

P. Yes.[54]

II. A. You asked the defendant to draw a human figure?

P. Yes.

A. And this is the figure he drew for you? What does it indicate to you about his personality?

P. You will note this is a rear view of a male. This is very rare, statistically. It indicates hidden guilt feelings, or turning away from reality.

A. And this drawing of a female figure, does it indicate anything to you; and, if so, what?

P. It indicates hostility towards women on the part of the subject. The pose, the hands on the hips, the hard-looking face, the stern expression.

A. Anything else?

P. The size of the ears indicates a paranoid outlook, or hallucinations. Also, the absence of feet indicates feelings of insecurity.[55]

III. A. You also administered the Draw-a-Person test?

P. Yes.

A. And what did it indicate?

P. The defendant drew the figure on the upper left-hand corner of the page. This indicates explosive feelings, insecurity, in a sense, holding onto the edges of the paper. This indicates anxiety and insecurity.

A. What if he had placed the drawing in the middle of the page—what would that indicate?

P. It would mean he is a little less insecure.[56]

The analysis of people's drawings may be intrinsically interesting and even fascinating. But does such analysis have validity for independently predicting a person's actual behaviors? Twenty clinical psychologists who were reputed experts in the analysis of human figure drawings were asked to judge the drawings made by people from five different groups.[57] One group of people had been diagnosed as schizophrenic and committed to a state hospital for most of their adult lives. People in a second group were identified as neurotics on the basis of weekly attendance at an out-patient psychiatric clinic. People in a third group were identified as mental defectives on the basis of subnormal IQ scores. The fourth group of people consisted of practicing homosexuals and people in the fifth group were "normal" college students. The task of the clinicians was to look at the drawings and independently judge which drawings corresponded with people from each of the above groups.

The results of the study were clear: Clinicians could accurately identify the drawings made by mental defectives but could not discriminate between the drawings made by people in the four remaining groups. Human figure drawings therefore have validity for predicting whether a person is labeled as mentally defective, but they do not appear to have validity for identifying people labeled as schizophrenic, neurotic, homosexual, or normal. Research has also shown that college students are just as accurate as experienced clinical psychologists in looking at human figure drawings and identifying which drawings were made by people who had been labeled mentally defective.[58]

If you are acquainted with a person who has taken a particular personality test it is easy to find things you know about the person in the test. For establishing predictive validity it is necessary to identify personality test responses without knowing ahead of time which people gave which responses. Serving as observers, psychotherapists often use personality traits to explain the behaviors of others. It is interesting to speculate whether or not psychotherapists would apply the same traits if they were giving behavioral explanations for themselves.

Other Factors Biasing Our Perceptions

We have now reviewed the perceptual and motivational factors that influence people to give internal or external explanations for their own behaviors and for the behaviors of others. We have also learned how people's feelings of uniqueness cause them to believe in personality measures that are actually stereotypic. There are a number of other factors biasing the attributions people make about themselves and others.[59] These biases (outlined below) are based more on fallacies in processing information than on personal motivation. They cause people to make errors in explaining their own actions as well as in predicting the behaviors of others.

Base Rates and the Gambler's Fallacy

Assume you are playing a roulette wheel by colors, betting whether the outcome will be red or black. You have been watching the wheel and have seen it come up red five times in a row. On the next turn you decide to place a bet. Which color would you choose: black or red? If you are convinced that the next outcome will be black you are a victim of the gambler's fallacy. In reality, the outcome of each spin of the wheel is *independent* of any outcome before it. The probability of black after five straight outcomes of red (or any other five previous outcomes) is 50 percent. Human beings have an interesting predisposition to ignore base rates and probabilities in favor of intuition and individual feelings. If you were told that 20 percent of the students at a particular university were psychology majors and were asked to guess the probability that a hypothetical student is majoring in psychology you would probably say 20 percent. Research has shown that is what most people will do. However, if the study is repeated so that participants are also given a written description of the hypothetical student (which gives no basis for judging the student's major) they will virtually ignore the knowledge that 20 percent of all students are psychology majors and use their own intuitions in predicting the student's major.[60] If we are told that 95 percent of all people act a certain way we are not likely to believe there is a 95 percent chance that *we* will act that way.

In addition to preferring intuition over base rates and probabilities, most people feel their intuitions are more accurate. The power of personal belief in intuition was pointed out by a study in which clinical psychologists and graduate students read a case history of a man and were then tested to see how accurately they could predict the man's attitudes and past behaviors on issues other than those mentioned in the case history. Participants were tested in four stages. For the first test participants had only read a brief description of the man. For the second test participants were given additional information about the man's childhood. For the third test participants read additional information about the man's high school and college years. For the fourth test they received additional information about his army service. Results showed quite clearly that no matter how much information the participants in the study received about the man, they could not accurately predict attitudes and behaviors that were not included in the case material.

When participants were asked how accurate they *thought* they were, however, the results were very different. Even though in reality the participants did not become more accurate in their judgments when they were given additional case material, their personal confidence in the judgments they made increased significantly. This was true for clinical psychologists as well as graduate students. Over 90 percent of the participants in the study felt their judgments became more accurate with each additional set of information.[61]

The Fallacy of Consensus

People overestimate the degree to which their own choices and actions are modeled by others. College students in two studies completed a series of questionnaires describing their own attitudes and actions in various situations and then predicted the attitudes and actions of their peers.[62] Results showed that the attitudes and actions students predicted for others were very similar to the ones they described for themselves. As part of the same research, college students in a third study were asked to walk around the college campus for thirty minutes wearing a large sandwich-board sign. Students who agreed to wear the sign felt that most other students would also agree to wear the sign. Students who refused to wear the sign stated that most other students would also refuse to wear the sign.

Underestimating the Power of Roles

Participants in a quiz game study were assigned randomly to one of two roles: questioner or contestant.[63] The questioner had the job of devising a series of challenging questions which the contestant then attempted to answer. After completing and answering the questions, the participants rated themselves and the other person on a measure of general knowledge. Even though it is clear that the questioner was in a position of advantage, questioners as well as contestants rated the questioner as having superior knowledge. People who observed the study from the perspective of an audience also felt that the questioner had superior knowledge. We know from our own experience that upper class people are often given the benefit of doubt in judgments of ability and intelligence. In many cases, underprivileged people are hindered because they overestimate the capabilities of more priviliged people and attribute their own disadvantaged position to personal weakness rather than social roles.

Recognizing the Causes of Behavior

Richard Nisbett and his colleagues have analyzed a large body of research and concluded that people do not have the capacity to introspect accurately about the causes of their behaviors.[64] They argue that people are aware of the factors influencing their behaviors only when the factors are obvious and plausible. When the causes of behavior are subtle and not apparent, people will give incorrect explanations for their actions that make intuitive sense. A simple example of this argument was shown in a study in which participants were given the task to tie together two cords hanging from the ceiling.[65] The cords were just far enough apart that they could not be grasped at the same time. When it was clear that participants would not solve the problem the experimenter casually put one of the cords in motion. Typically, in less than a minute the participants solved the problem by tying a weight to one cord and swinging it toward the other. When asked how they had figured out the problem the participants showed no awareness of the experimenter's subtle cue. Participants explained their solution by saying that it just dawned on them, that it was the only thing left to try, or that they had pictured a swinging pendulum in their minds. This study shows that people are sometimes not aware of what caused their behaviors. The next study indicates that people can hold explanations for their behaviors that are incorrect.

Participants watched a videotaped interview with a person who acted either in a warm and agreeable manner or in a cold and disagreeable manner, and then gave their impressions of the person on a rating form.[66] It would be reasonable for participants to like a warm interviewee more than a cold interviewee. However, there is no objective reason for thinking that a warm interviewee is more physically appealing or attractive. Participants who viewed the warm interviewee *claimed* that the warmth of the interviewee influenced their ratings of liking but not of physical appearance. *In fact,* they rated the warm interviewee as both well liked and physically attractive. Participants who viewed the cold interviewee *claimed* that they disliked him because he was physically unattractive and unappealing. *In fact,* it was the cold behavior of the interviewee that influenced participants' ratings of liking as well as physical appearance.

Another example of how incorrect but plausible cues bias behavioral explanations is seen in a study in which participants watched a film under one of three conditions.[67] Some participants watched the film with interference from a loud power saw in the outside hall. A second group of participants viewed the film while the focus was not properly adjusted. A third group of participants saw the film with no distraction. After viewing the film, participants rated it on how interesting and enjoyable it was. The experimenter then apologized to the participants who were disturbed by the noise or poor focus and asked if these disturbances had caused them to give less favorable ratings. It is plausible that the noise or poor focus would cause unfavorable ratings and many of the participants claimed that they indeed did give less favorable ratings because of these disturbances. In fact, the noise or poor focus did not influence the participants' ratings.

In summary, Nisbett and his colleagues argue that although people believe that the explanations they give for their behaviors are a product of introspection, they actually base them on salient and plausible cues in the situation. When the real causes of behavior are salient and plausible, people's explanations for their actions will be accurate. When the real causes of behavior are subtle and not apparent, people will still rely on salient and plausible cues and their explanations will be incorrect. We learned in Chapters Four and Five that people's attitudes can be influenced by changes in their behaviors attributable to their own choice. This model of attitude change is based on influencing people's behaviors with subtle requests, false feedback, or reinforcement in such a way that the people attribute their actions to free will. According to Nisbett, the real cause of the change in behavior is subtle and not apparent so the people rely on the plausible cause of "choice" to explain the change.

Objective Self-Awareness

We have gained an understanding of how observer empathy can be increased by allowing observers to view a situation from the perspective of the actor. We have also seen some of the effects of people's motivation to perceive themselves as unique and independent. We will now learn more about what happens when people become conscious observers of their own behaviors. The process of being highly aware of one's own behavior has been defined by Robert Wicklund and Shelley Duval as "objective self-awareness." Duval and Wicklund theorize that objective self-awareness is generally a negative experience because increased attention toward ourselves is likely to emphasize discrepancies between what we are and what we would like to be. However, objective self-awareness can be positive when the attention focused on oneself reveals something that is highly desirable. Most research studies have manipulated self-awareness by having people watch themselves in mirrors or on videotape or listen to tape recordings of their voices. Self-awareness could also be manipulated by having people behave in front of an audience or take special cognizance of how they are acting at a particular time. These last two methods for manipulating self-awareness are less objective because they place people in a situation in which they might be motivated to make a good impression.[68]

Self-Awareness and Negative Feelings

The self-awareness of participants in two studies was increased by tape-recordings of their voices or by a large mirror in the room where they were working.[69] In one of the studies, participants were given negative information about themselves and in the second study they were not. Participants in both studies gave themselves lower ratings on measures of self-esteem after they had been exposed to mirror images or voice recordings. The experimenters concluded that self-awareness can be an unpleasant experience even without negative feedback because people are predisposed to notice their shortcomings when they focus their attention on themselves.

The lowered self-esteem caused by increased self-awareness can be alleviated with distraction. People expressed lowered self-esteem when they viewed themselves on a television screen.[70] These same people gave significantly fewer negative ratings of their feelings when their self-focused attention was distracted with a western movie.

Self-Awareness and Positive Feelings

Increased self-awareness is likely to lower the feelings of self-esteem of people receiving either no feedback or negative feedback about themselves. When self-awareness is heightened under conditions of positive feedback, feelings of self-esteem are likely to increase. Participants in two studies, who were given information to make them feel good about themselves, rated themselves higher on self-esteem when they viewed themselves in a mirror than when they did not.[71]

Self-Awareness and Attribution

People are more likely to attribute the outcomes of their actions to themselves if their self-awareness is high rather than low. Participants in a study were asked to place themselves in hypothetical situations such as the ones below and indicate the degree to which they felt personally responsible for the outcome of each situation.[72]

You're driving down the street about five miles over the speed limit when a little kid suddenly runs out chasing a ball and you hit him.[73]

Imagine that you have selected and purchased a race horse. You enter the horse in a major race and hire a good jockey to ride him. The horse wins first place.[74]

Participants who viewed themselves in a mirror accepted the greatest responsibility for the outcome of the situations. Participants who were distracted during the study by a motor task were less likely to attribute the outcome of the situations to themselves and more likely to attribute them to external factors such as the other person. Increased self-awareness influences people to take responsibility for both behaviors with positive outcomes and behaviors with negative outcomes that are somewhat far removed. If people engage in an action resulting in a negative outcome that directly affects their lives, increased self-awareness often motivates them to protect themselves by denying personal responsibility for the action.[75]

Influencing Behavior with Self-Awareness

A number of studies have shown that it is possible to influence people to modify their behaviors by making them more self-conscious about how they are acting.

Aggression and Cheating

Participants in a study were asked to reward people by flashing a light when the people performed correctly on a learning test and to punish the people with electric shocks when they performed incorrectly on the learning test.[76] The participants had control over the intensity of the shocks that were delivered. Results showed that participants who could see themselves in a mirror delivered shocks of a significantly lower intensity than those delivered by participants who were not exposed to an image of themselves in a mirror. Participants in a second experiment reduced the intensity of the shocks they delivered if they were required to make eye contact with an audience. Participants in these experiments were required to deliver electric shocks to the learners, but they were free to decide how mild or intense the shocks would be. Increased self-awareness resulting from the mirror image of themselves or eye contact with the audience apparently made the participants more self-conscious of the fact that they were delivering electric shocks and influenced them to be less harsh with the person who was performing the learning test. Participants in a third experiment were convinced that intense electric shock would be *helpful* to the person performing the learning test.[77] In this study, increasing self-awareness with a mirror influenced participants to give shocks of greater intensity. If giving electric shocks is seen as the appropriate thing to do, increased self-awareness can also influence people to do it more often.

Participants working on a test in a situation where it was inappropriate for them to cheat engaged in significantly less cheating if their self-awareness was heightened with a mirror and recordings of their own voice.[78]

Task Performance

Heightened attention toward a task on which a person is working is likely to increase the amount of energy he or she is willing to expend. Participants in one study were significantly more productive on an assignment of copying German prose when their self-awareness during the assignment was increased with a mirror than when it was not.[79]

Performance on a task can be enhanced with heightened self-awareness up to a certain point. If people are made overly self-conscious about how they are doing on a task and feel that their responses are under close scrutiny by another person their involvement with the task will ultimately decrease.[80]

Attitude Change

We learned in Chapter Five that people will modify their attitudes if they are influenced to change their behaviors in such a way that they attribute the new behaviors to themselves. For this strategy to be successful, people must be aware of the changes in their behaviors. Participants in two studies were significantly more likely to change their attitudes in favor of an essay they wrote if their self-awareness of writing the essay was increased by the presence of a television camera.[81] People are less likely to change their attitudes if they are distracted from their behaviors by a second task on which they are working or by the passage of time.[82]

Conformity

People are more likely to agree with the opinions of others if their self-awareness is increased. Participants in one study expressed greater agreement with a group opinion when they were exposed to the sound of their own voices before giving their opinions.[83] A second study found that people conformed significantly more when they saw their images on a television monitor and when their self-awareness was increased with feedback that made them feel unique.[84]

Seeking and Avoiding Self-Awareness

We have so far studied self-awareness by reviewing research that measured people's reactions to situations in which their self-awareness was either heightened or decreased. There are two other approaches to the study of self-awareness. One is to test people's willingness to seek or avoid self-awareness in positive, neutral, and negative settings.

The other is to measure individual differences between people by evaluating how closely they attend to their own behaviors.

Because heightened self-awareness is likely to focus people's attention on their undesirable qualities they have a general predisposition to avoid it. People are most likely to seek self-awareness if they receive positive feedback or have developed a feeling of self-acceptance. Humanistic psychologists regard self-awareness as an important part of one's life. The goal of sensitivity and consciousness-raising groups is to develop self-awareness by teaching people to see themselves in a more favorable light.

Participants in a study were given positive feedback indicating that they had high scores on a measure of creativity.[85] When the self-awareness of these participants was increased with a television camera or a mirror they were more likely to use first person pronouns in a word game than when self-awareness was not increased. Because the participants had been made to feel good about themselves they were able to experience their heightened self-awareness by using a greater number of personal words such as "I," "my," and "me."

If people are not provided with positive feedback or have not achieved a feeling of self-acceptance they are likely to avoid experiences of increased self-awareness. Participants in two studies who were given negative feedback about themselves had a significant tendency to avoid being in a room with a mirror or listening to a tape-recording of their voice.[86]

Increased self-awareness without positive feedback or feelings can also lead to distraction and nervousness. In one study, people smoked more when their self-awareness was heightened with a mirror.[87] Participants in another study were significantly weaker in memorizing poetry when their self-focused attention was increased by instructions to stand still with their arms at their sides.[88] Research has also shown that stuttering is likely to occur when a speaker's self-awareness is heightened by the importance of the message and a strong desire for audience approval.[89]

Individual Differences in Self-Awareness

Measuring Individual Differences

Mark Snyder developed a scale to discriminate between people who pay close attention to their behaviors and people who do not.[90] Snyder's Self-Monitoring Scale was constructed primarily to study people's awareness of expressive behaviors that communicate emotions and feelings. Here are some of the statements on the Self-Monitoring Scale:

I guess I put on a show to impress or entertain people.

I sometimes appear to others to be experiencing deeper emotions than I actually am.

I may deceive people by being friendly when I really dislike them.

I can only argue for ideas which I already believe.

I find it hard to imitate the behavior of other people.

I have trouble changing my behavior to suit different people and different situations.[91]

People with a strong awareness of their expressive behaviors are likely to say that the first three statements are true and the last three statements are false.

People with high scores on the Self-Monitoring Scale are rated by their friends as being more self-aware and more able to adapt their behaviors to suit the social situation than people with low scores on the scale. The scores of professional stage actors on the Self-Monitoring Scale are higher than average whereas hospitalized psychiatric patients receive a lower-than-average score. People with high "self-monitoring" scores are able to communicate emotions accurately through their facial expressions and voice and are more accurate than low scorers in judging other people's facial and vocal expressions of emotions. People with high scores on the Self-Monitoring Scale are highly motivated to learn about people's opinions so that they can make their interactions appropriate and acceptable.[92] People with high self-monitoring scores are also more likely than people with low self-monitoring scores to be sensitive to group norms and behave in a socially conforming manner.[93]

Self-Awareness and Consistency of Behavior

We learned earlier that the use of personality traits for explaining behavior is challenged by the tendency of people to vary their behaviors according to factors in the environment. The study of individual differences in self-awareness has made it possible to discriminate between people who behave relatively consistently and those who behave relatively inconsistently in different situations. The behavior of people who perceive themselves as acting consistently fits the personality trait model for predicting behavior more closely than the behavior of people who see themselves as varying their actions according to the environment.[94]

People who are highly aware of their own behaviors are less consistent in how they act in different contexts than people who are not very aware of their own behaviors. This is because people who are acutely self-aware are more conscious of how they suit their behaviors to the particular demands of each interaction. From their own reports, people with high self-monitoring scores are more conscientious about fitting their behaviors of generosity, honesty, and hostility to each situation than people with low self-monitoring scores.[95] People with high self-monitoring scores have also been shown to be less influenced by an essay they were asked to write than people with low self-monitoring scores.[96] This is presumably because highly self-aware people are more likely to attribute their essay writing to factors in the situation, such as the experimenter's request. People with low self-monitoring scores pay less attention to variables affecting their behaviors in the situation and are therefore more likely to attribute the ideas in the essay to their own beliefs.

Individual differences in self-awareness can also be measured by asking people to specify how much of their behavior is consistent and how much of their behavior depends upon external factors. One study showed that people who salt their food before tasting it see their behaviors in different situations as being relatively consistent.[97] These people apparently attribute their use of salt to a personal need or preference for salt. People who salt their food after tasting it say that their behaviors generally depend upon the situation. These people apparently attribute their use of salt to the taste of the food.

Self-Awareness and Perceived Freedom

The relative importance of situational and personal factors in influencing human behavior is a topic of considerable interest among psychologists.[98] The focus of this book has been on the mechanisms whereby environmental factors and individual interpretations of these factors combine to influence people's bodily and overt behaviors as well as their self-perceptions of these behaviors. Most people learn to attribute more freedom to themselves if they perceive that their behaviors are under personal rather than environmental control. B. F. Skinner argues that people have traditionally developed a sense of personal freedom by ignoring or neglecting the effects of environmental variables on their behavior.[99] We now see that there is a second method for promoting the self-perception of freedom. As people increase their self-awareness they become more knowledgable about their responses to variables in the external environment. If they allow themselves to become aware of how these environmental variables affect their resulting behaviors and their self-perceptions of these behaviors, they will be able to enhance their personal freedom by practicing strategies of self-control.

Notes

Chapter One

1. S. Schachter, "The Interaction of Cognitive and Physiological Determinants of Emotional State," in L. Berkowitz (ed.), *Advances in Experimental Social Psychology*, Vol. 7 (New York: Academic Press, 1964), pp. 49–80; S. Schachter and J. E. Singer, "Cognitive, Social, and Physiological Determinants of Emotional State," *Psychological Review*, 1962, *69*, 379–399. This research is critically evaluated by P. G. Zimbardo, E. B. Ebbesen, and C. Maslach, *Influencing Attitudes and Changing Behavior*, 2nd ed. (Reading, Mass.: Addison-Wesley, 1977), chap. 5. Zimbardo and his colleagues argue that unexplained physiological arousal creates a negative rather than a neutral mood and that it is difficult to influence people to label unexplained arousal as a positive feeling.

2. H. S. Becker, "Becoming a Marijuana User," *American Journal of Sociology*, 1953, *59*, 235–242.

3. *Ibid.*, p. 238.

4. *Ibid.*, p. 239.

5. *Ibid.*, p. 240.

6. W. B. Plotkin, "On the Self-Regulation of the Occipital Alpha Rhythm: Control Strategies, States of Consciousness, and the Role of Physiological Feedback," *Journal of Experimental Psychology: General*, 1976, *105*, 66–99.

7. M. Zborowski, *People in Pain* (San Francisco: Jossey-Bass, 1969).

8. *Ibid.*, chap. 2.

9. *Ibid.*, chap. 3.

10. *Ibid.*, chap. 4.

11. *Ibid.*, chap. 5.

12. This quotation is cited in J. F. Chaves and T. X. Barber, "Needles and Knives: Behind the Mystery of Acupuncture and Chinese Meridians," *Human Behavior*, 1973, *2*, 19–24, p. 20.

13. R. A. Sternbach and B. Tursky, "Ethnic Differences Among Housewives in Psychophysical and Skin Potential Responses to Electric Shock," *Psychophysiology*, 1965, *1*, 241–246.

14. W. E. Lambert, E. Libman, and E. G. Posner, "The Effect of Increased Salience of a Membership Group on Pain Tolerance," *Journal of Personality*, 1960, *28*, 350–357.

15. P. G. Zimbardo, A. Cohen, M. Weisenberg, L. Dworkin, and I. Firestone, "The Control of Experimental Pain," in P. G. Zimbardo (ed.), *The Cognitive Control of Motivation* (Glenview, Ill.: Scott Foresman, 1969), pp. 100–122.

16. J. W. Brehm, "Commitment to Thirst: The Cognitive Camel Complex," in Zimbardo, *op. cit.*, pp. 55–63.

17. H. H. Mansson, "The Relation of Dissonance Reduction to Cognitive, Perceptual, Consumatory, and Learning Measures of Thirst," in Zimbardo, *op. cit.*, pp. 78–97.

18. M. L. Brehm, K. W. Back, and M. D. Bogdonoff, "A Physiological Effect of Cognitive Dissonance Under Food Deprivation and Stress," in Zimbardo, *op. cit.*, pp. 30–44.

19. S. Schachter, *Emotion, Obesity, and Crime* (New York: Academic Press, 1971).

20. *Ibid.*, p. 73.

21. *Ibid.*

22. S. Schachter, R. Goldman, and A. Gordon, "The Effects of Fear, Food Deprivation, and Obesity on Eating," *Journal of Personality and Social Psychology*, 1968, *10*, 91–97; cited in Schachter, *op. cit.*, p. 73.

23. Schachter, *Emotion, Obesity, and Crime*, p. 84.

24. S. A. Hashim and T. B. Van Italie, "Studies in Normal and Obese Subjects with a Monitored Food Dispensing Device," *Annals of the New York Academy of Sciences*, 1965, *131*, 654–661; cited in Schachter, *op. cit.*, p. 85.

25. R. E. Nisbett, "Taste, Deprivation, and Weight Determinants of Eating Behavior," *Journal of Personality and Social Psychology*, 1968, *10*, 107–116; cited in Schachter, *op. cit.*, chap. 8.

26. R. Goldman, M. Jaffa, and S. Schachter, "Yom Kippur, Air France, Dormitory Food, and the Eating Behavior of Obese and Normal Persons," *Journal of Personality and Social Psychology*, 1968, *10*, 117–123; cited in Schachter, *op. cit.*, p. 128.

27. S. Schachter and L. Gross, "Manipulated Time and Eating Behavior," *Journal of Personality and Social Psychology*, 1968, *10*, 98–106; cited in Schachter, *op. cit.*, p. 89.

28. Goldman, Jaffa, and Schachter, *op. cit.*, cited in Schachter, *op. cit.*, p. 129.

29. Schachter, *op. cit.*, p. 73.

30. R. E. Nisbett, "Determinants of Food Intake in Obesity," *Science*, 1968, *159*, 1254–1255; cited in Schachter, *op. cit.*, chap. 9.

31. S. Schachter and J. Freedman, "Effects of Work and Cue Prominence," in S. Schachter and J. Rodin (eds.), *Obese Humans and Rats* (Potomac, Md.: Erlbaum Associates, 1974).

32. D. Singh and S. Sikes, "Role of Past Experience on Food-Motivated Behavior of Obese Humans," *Journal of Comparative and Physiological Psychology*, 1974, *86*, 503–508.

33. R. E. Nisbett, "Determinants of Food Intake in Obesity;" cited in Schachter, *op. cit.*, p. 109.

34. *Ibid.*, p. 111.

35. S. Schachter and B. Latané, "Crime, Cognition, and the Autonomic Nervous System," in D. Levine (ed.), *Nebraska Symposium on Motivation* (Lincoln, Nebraska: University of Nebraska Press, 1964), pp. 221–273. This research is summarized in Schachter, *op. cit.*, chaps. 12 and 13.

36. *Ibid.*, p. 271.

37. *Ibid.*

38. *Ibid.*

39. R. A. Dienstbier and P. O. Munter, "Cheating as a Function of the Labeling of Natural Arousal," *Journal of Personality and Social Psychology*, 1971, *17*, 208–213; R. A. Dienstbier, "The Role of Anxiety and Arousal Attribution in Cheating," *Journal of Experimental Social Psychology*, 1972, *8*, 168–179.

40. R. A. Dienstbier, D. Hillman, J. Lehnhoff, J. Hillman, and M. C. Valkenaar, "An Emotion-Attribution Approach to Moral Behavior: Interfacing Cognitive and Avoidance Theories of Moral Development," *Psychological Review*, 1975, *82*, 299–315.

41. Schachter and Latané, *op. cit.*, p. 269.

42. P. Zimbardo, "Preliminary Ideas Toward a Model of Madness," unpublished notes, Stanford University, 1977.

43. B. Maher, "Delusional Thinking and Cognitive Disorder," in H. London and R. E. Nisbett (eds.), *Thought and Feeling: Cognitive Alteration of Feeling States* (Chicago: Aldine, 1974), pp. 85–103.

44. S. Valins and R. E. Nisbett, *Attribution Processes in the Development and Treatment of Emotional Disorders* (Morristown: N. J.: General Learning Press, 1971), p. 7.

45. *Ibid.*, pp. 10–11.

Chapter Two

1. D. Bramel, S. E. Bell, and S. T. Margulis, "Attributing Danger as a Means of Explaining One's Fear," *Journal of Experimental Social Psychology*, 1965, *1*, 267–281.

2. W. Wilkins, "Perceptual Distortion to Account for Arousal," *Journal of Abnormal Psychology*, 1971, *78*, 252–257.

3. R. Hirschman, "Cross-Modal Effects of Anticipatory Bogus Heart-Rate Feedback," *Journal of Personality and Social Psychology*, 1975, *31*, 13–19.

4. S. Reisman, C. A. Insko, and S. Valins, "Triadic Consistency and False Heart-Rate Feedback," *Journal of Personality*, 1970, *38*, 629–640.

5. L. Berkowitz, J. Lepinski, and E. Angulo, "Awareness of Own Anger Level and Subsequent Aggression," *Journal of Personality and Social Psychology*, 1969, *11*, 293–300.

6. D. G. Dutton and R. A. Lake, "Threat of Own Prejudice and Reverse Discrimination in Interracial Situations," *Journal of Personality and Social Psychology*, 1973, *28*, 94–100.

7. D. G. Dutton and V. L. Lennox, "Effect of Prior 'Token' Compliance on Subsequent Interracial Behavior," *Journal of Personality and Social Psychology*, 1974, *29*, 65–71.

8. M. Giesen and C. Hendrick, "Effects of False Positive and Negative Arousal Feedback on Persuasion," *Journal of Personality and Social Psychology*, 1974, *30*, 449–457.

9. V. A. Harris and J. M. Jellison, "Fear-Arousing Communcations, False Physiological Feedback, and the Acceptance of Recommendations," *Journal of Experimental Social Psychology*, 1971, *7*, 269–279.

10. P. M. Mintz and J. Mills, "Effects of Arousal and Information about Its

Source upon Attitude Change," *Journal of Experimental Social Psychology,* 1971, *7,* 561–570.

11. M. P. Zanna and J. Cooper, "Dissonance and the Pill: An Attribution Approach to Studying the Arousal Properties of Dissonance," *Journal of Personality and Social Psychology,* 1974, *29,* 703–709.

12. T. S. Pittman, "Attribution of Arousal as a Mediator in Dissonance Reduction," *Journal of Experimental Social Psychology,* 1975, *11,* 53–63.

13. M. Argyle and J. Dean, "Eye-Contact, Distance, and Affiliation," *Sociometry,* 1965, *28,* 289–304; M. L. Patterson, "Compensation in Nonverbal Immediacy Behaviors: A Review," *Sociometry,* 1973, *36,* 237–252.

14. M. L. Patterson, "An Arousal Model of Interpersonal Intimacy," *Psychological Review,* 1976, *83,* 235–254.

15. A. Schiffenbauer and R. S. Schiavo, "Physical Distance and Attraction: An Intensification Effect," *Journal of Experimental Social Psychology,* 1976, *12,* 274–282; M. D. Storms and G. C. Thomas, "Reactions to Physical Closeness," *Journal of Personality and Social Psychology,* 1977, *35,* 412–418.

16. R. D. Middlemist, E. S. Knowles, and C. F. Matter, "Personal Space Invasion in the Lavatory: Suggestive Evidence for Arousal," *Journal of Personality and Social Psychology,* 1976, *33,* 541–546.

17. P. C. Ellsworth and J. M. Carlsmith, "Effects of Eye Contact and Verbal Content on Affective Response to a Dyadic Interaction," *Journal of Personality and Social Psychology,* 1968, *10,* 15–20; L. Scherwitz and R. Helmreich, "Interactive Effects of Eye Contact and Verbal Content on Interpersonal Attraction in Dyads," *Journal of Personality and Social Psychology,* 1973, *25,* 6–14.

18. P. C. Ellsworth and E. J. Langer, "Staring and Approach: An Interpretation of the Stare as a Nonspecific Activator," *Journal of Personality and Social Psychology,* 1976, *33,* 117–122.

19. H. T. Reis and A. Werner, "Some Inter- and Intrapersonal Consequences of Eye Contact," paper presented at the meeting of the Eastern Psychological Association, Philadelphia, April 1974.

20. P. C. Ellsworth, J. M. Carlsmith, and A. Henson, "The Stare as a Stimulus for Flight in Human Subjects: A Series of Field Experiments," *Journal of Personality and Social Psychology,* 1972, *21,* 302–311.

21. C. L. Kleinke, "Interaction Between Gaze and Legitimacy on Compliance with Requests in a Field Setting," unpublished paper, 1977.

22. E. Berscheid and E. Walster, "A Little Bit about Love," in T. L. Huston (ed.), *Foundations of Interpersonal Attraction* (New York: Academic Press, 1974), pp. 355–381; E. Walster, "Passionate Love," in B. Murstein (ed.), *Theories of Attraction and Love* (New York: Springer, 1971), pp. 85–99.

23. This quotation is cited by Walster, *op. cit.,* p. 87.

24. This quotation is cited by Walster, *op. cit.,* p. 97.

25. Walster, *op. cit.,* p. 97.

26. S. Valins, "Cognitive Effects of False Heart-Rate Feedback," *Journal of Personality and Social Psychology,* 1966, *4,* 400–408; D. Goldstein, D. Fink, and D. R. Mettee, "Cognition of Arousal and Actual Arousal as Determinants of Emotion," *Journal of Personality and Social Psychology,* 1972, *21,* 41–51.

27. S. Misovich and P. C. Charis, "Information Need, Affect, and Cognition of Autonomic Activity," *Journal of Experimental Social Psychology,* 1974, *10,* 274–283.

28. N. A. Walsh, L. A. Meister, and C. L. Kleinke, "Interpersonal Attraction and Visual Behavior as a Function of Perceived Arousal and Evaluation by an Opposite Sex Person," *Journal of Social Psychology,* 1977, *103,* 65–74.

29. A. M. Isen, "Success, Failure, and Reaction to Others: The Warm Glow of Success," *Journal of Personality and Social Psychology,* 1970, *15,* 294–301.

30. A. M. Isen and P. F. Levin, "Effects of Feeling Good on Helping: Cookies and Kindness," *Journal of Personality and Social Psychology,* 1972, *3,* 384–388.

31. *Ibid.*

32. A. J. Lott and B. E. Lott, "The Formation of Positive Attitudes toward Group Members," *Journal of Abnormal and Social Psychology,* 1960, *61,* 297–300.

33. A. J. Lott and B. E. Lott, "A Learning Theory Approach to Interpersonal Attitudes," in A. G. Greenwald, T. C. Brock, and T. M. Ostrom (eds.), *Psychological Foundations of Attitudes* (New York: Academic Press, 1968).

34. A. J. Lott, B. E. Lott, and G. Matthews, "Interpersonal Attraction among Children as a Function of Vicarious Reward," *Journal of Educational Psychology,* 1969, *60,* 274–282.

35. W. B. Griffitt, "Attraction toward a Stranger as a Function of Direct and Associated Reinforcement," *Psychonomic Science,* 1968, *11,* 147–148.

36. W. B. Griffitt and P. Guay, "'Object' Evaluation and Conditioned Affect," *Journal of Experimental Research in Personality,* 1969, *4,* 1–8.

37. C. Gouaux, "Induced Affective States and Interpersonal Attraction," *Journal of Personality and Social Psychology,* 1971, *20,* 37–43.

38. D. Aderman, "Elation, Depression, and Helping Behavior," *Journal of Personality and Social Psychology,* 1972, *24,* 91–101.

39. W. Stephan, E. Berscheid, and E. Walster, "Sexual Arousal and Heterosexual Perception," *Journal of Personality and Social Psychology,* 1971, *20,* 93–101.

40. G. L. Clore and J. B. Gormly, "Knowing, Feeling, and Liking: A Psychophysiological Study of Attraction," *Journal of Research in Personality,* 1974, *8,* 218–230.

41. L. Jacobs, E. Berscheid, and E. Walster, "Self-Esteem and Attraction," *Journal of Personality and Social Psychology,* 1971, *17,* 84–91.

42. W. B. Griffitt, J. May, and R. Veitch, "Sexual Stimulation and Interpersonal Behavior: Heterosexual Evaluative Responses, Visual Behavior, and Physical Proximity," *Journal of Personality and Social Psychology,* 1974, *30,* 367–377.

43. H. A. Hornstein, *Cruelty and Kindness: A New Look at Aggression and Altruism* (Englewood Cliffs, New Jersey: Prentice-Hall, 1976), chap. 9.

44. L. S. Wrightsman and F. C. Noble, "Reactions to the President's Assassination and Changes in Philosophy of Human Nature," *Psychological Reports,* 1965, *16,* 159–162.

45. H. A. Hornstein, E. LaKind, G. Frankel, and S. Manne, "The Effects of

Knowledge about Remote Social Events on Prosocial Behavior, Social Conception, and Mood," *Journal of Personality and Social Psychology*, 1975, *32*, 1038–1046.

46. *Ibid.*, p. 1040.

47. *Ibid.*

48. Hornstein, *op. cit.*, p. 122.

49. D. T. Kenrick and R. B. Cialdini, "Romantic Attraction: Misattribution versus Reinforcement Explanations," *Journal of Personality and Social Psychology*, 1977, *35*, 381–391.

50. J. W. Brehm, M. Gatz, G. Goethals, J. McCrommon, and L. Ward, "Psychological Arousal and Interpersonal Attraction," cited in Berscheid and Walster, *op. cit.*

51. D. G. Dutton and A. P. Aron, "Some Evidence for Heightened Sexual Attraction under Conditions of High Anxiety," *Journal of Personality and Social Psychology*, 1974, *30*, 510–517.

52. E. Walster, G. Walster, J. Piliavin, and L. Schmidt, "'Playing Hard-to-Get': Understanding an Elusive Phenomenon," *Journal of Personality and Social Psychology*, 1973, *26*, 113–121. This research is also summarized in Berscheid and Walster, *op. cit.*

53. Xenophon, *Memorabilia* (London: Heinemann, 1923), p. 48; cited in Walster, Walster, Piliavin, and Schmidt, *op. cit.*

54. Ovid, *The Art of Love* (Bloomington: University of Indiana Press, 1963), pp. 65–66; cited in Walster, Walster, Piliavin, and Schmidt, *op. cit.*

55. A. M. Kirch (ed.), *The Anatomy of Love* (New York: Dell, 1960); cited in Berscheid and Walster, *op. cit.*

56. Walster, Walster, Piliavin, and Schmidt, *op. cit.*

57. *Ibid.*, p. 115.

58. *Ibid.*, p. 116.

59. R. Driscoll, K. E. Davis, and M. E. Lipitz, "Parental Interference and Romantic Love," *Journal of Personality and Social Psychology*, 1972, *24*, 1–10.

60. The issue of basing marriage on love is discussed more fully by Z. Rubin in *Liking and Loving: An Invitation to Social Psychology* (New York: Holt, Rinehart and Winston, 1973), p. 191.

61. J. R. Udry, *The Social Context of Marriage*, 2d ed. (Philadelphia: Lippincott, 1974), p. 163; cited in Rubin, *op. cit.*, p. 190.

62. D. de Rougemont, "The Crisis of the Modern Couple," in R. N. Anshem (ed.), *The Family: Its Function and Destiny* (New York: Harper & Row, 1949); cited in Rubin, *op. cit.*, p. 191.

63. Rubin, *op. cit.*, p. 188.

64. *Ibid.*

65. *Ibid.*, p. 190.

66. P. C. Rosenblatt, "Cross-Cultural Perspective on Attraction," in T. L. Huston (ed.), *Foundations of Interpersonal Attraction* (New York: Academic Press, 1974), pp. 79–95.

67. This notion is suggested by Berscheid and Walster, *op. cit.*, p. 375; see also Rubin, *op. cit.*, p. 207.

68. Rubin, *op. cit.*, p. 195.

69. *Ibid.*, p. 196.

70. A. C. Kerckhoff and K. E. Davis, "Value Consensus and Need Complementarity in Mate Selection," *American Sociological Review*, 1962, *27*, 295–303.

71. D. Byrne, C. R. Ervin, and J. Lamberth, "Continuity between the Experimental Study of Attraction and Real-Life Computer Dating," *Journal of Personality and Social Psychology*, 1970, *16*, 157–165.

72. This notion is suggested by Berscheid and Walster, *op. cit.*, p. 374. The importance of physical attractiveness on first impressions of other people is discussed in C. L. Kleinke, *First Impressions: The Psychology of Encountering Others* (Englewood Cliffs, N.J.: Prentice-Hall, 1975).

73. R. Linton, *The Study of Man* (New York: Appleton-Century Co., 1936); cited in Berscheid and Walster, *op. cit.*, p. 374.

74. This notion is suggested by Berscheid and Walster, *op. cit.*, p. 376.

75. K. Miles, personal communication in course on marriage and the family, California State University, Los Angeles, 1965.

76. W. M. Kephart, "Some Correlates of Romantic Love," *Journal of Marriage and the Family*, 1967, *29*, 470–474.

77. K. K. Dion and K. L. Dion, "Self-Esteem and Romantic Love," *Journal of Personality*, 1975, *43*, 39–57.

78. K. L. Dion and K. K. Dion, "Correlates of Romantic Love," *Journal of Consulting and Clinical Psychology*, 1973, *41*, 51–56.

79. Berscheid and Walster, *op. cit.*, p. 378.

80. *Ibid.*, p. 377.

Chapter Three

1. S. Valins and A. A. Ray, "Effects of Cognitive Desensitization on Avoidance Behavior," *Journal of Personality and Social Psychology*, 1967, *7*, 345–350.

2. T. D. Borkovec, R. L. Wall, and N. M. Stone, "False Physiological Feedback and the Maintenance of Speech Anxiety," *Journal of Abnormal Psychology*, 1974, *83*, 164–168.

3. R. E. Nisbett and S. Schachter, "Cognitive Manipulation of Pain," *Journal of Experimental Social Psychology*, 1966, *2*, 227–236.

4. G. C. Davison and S. Valins, "Maintenance of Self-Attributed and Drug-Induced Behavior Change," *Journal of Personality and Social Psychology*, 1969, *11*, 25–33.

5. L. Ross, J. Rodin, and P. G. Zimbardo, "Toward an Attribution Therapy: The Reduction of Fear through Induced Cognitive-Emotional Misattribution," *Journal of Personality and Social Psychology*, 1969, *12*, 279–288.

6. J. Rodin, "Menstruation, Reattribution, and Competence," *Journal of Personality and Social Psychology*, 1976, *33*, 345–353.

7. M. Zukerman, "Attribution Processes, Placebo Effect, and Anxiety over Dental Treatment," *Representative Research in Social Psychology*, 1974, *5*, 35–46.

8. M. D. Storms and R. E. Nisbett, "Insomnia and the Attribution Process," *Journal of Personality and Social Psychology*, 1970, *16*, 319–328.

9. R. Kellogg and R. S. Baron, "Attribution Theory, Insomnia, and the Reverse Placebo Effect: A Reversal of Storms and Nisbett's Findings," *Journal of Personality and Social Psychology*, 1975, *32*, 231–236.

10. *Smoking and Health, Report of the Advisory Committee to the Surgeon General of the Public Health Service* (Washington, D. C.: Public Health Service Publication No. 1103, 1964); cited in P. D. Nesbitt, "Smoking, Physiological Arousal, and Emotional Response," *Journal of Personality and Social Psychology*, 1974, *25*, 137–144.

11. Nesbitt, *op. cit.*

12. Federal Trade Commission, "Results of Cigarette Tests," *New York Times*, March 8, 1969, p. 85; cited in Nesbitt, *op. cit.*

13. J. C. Barefoot and M. Girodo, "The Misattribution of Smoking Cessation Symptoms," *Canadian Journal of Behavioral Science*, 1972, *4*, 358–363.

14. S. E. Taylor, "On Inferring One's Attitude from One's Behavior: Some Delimiting Conditions," *Journal of Personality and Social Psychology*, 1975, *31*, 126–131.

15. D. Goldstein, D. Fink, and D. R. Mettee, "Cognition of Arousal and Actual Arousal as Determinants of Emotion," *Journal of Personality and Social Psychology*, 1972, *21*, 41–51.

16. C. L. Kleinke, "Self-Labeling of Bodily States," Journal Supplement Abstract Service, *Catalog of Selected Documents in Psychology*, 1977, *7*, Ms. 1468, p. 18.

17. R. R. Bootzin, C. P. Herman, and P. Nicassio, "The Power of Suggestion: Another Explanation of Misattribution and Insomnia," *Journal of Personality and Social Psychology*, 1976, *34*, 673–679.

18. Kleinke, *op. cit.*

19. E. Jacobson, *Progressive Relaxation* (Chicago: University of Chicago Press, 1938); J. Wolpe, *The Practice of Behavior Therapy* (New York: Pergamon Press, 1969).

20. Wolpe, *Ibid.*, pp. 100–107.

21. *Ibid.*, p. 109.

22. *Ibid.*, p. 117.

23. *Ibid.*, p. 118.

24. An excellent summary of systematic desensitization techniques can be found in G. L. Paul and D. A. Bernstein, *Anxiety and Clinical Problems: Systematic Desensitization and Related Techniques* (Morristown, N. J.: General Learning Press, 1973).

25. M. R. Goldfried, "Systematic Desensitization as Training in Self-Control," *Journal of Consulting and Clinical Psychology*, 1971, *37*, 228–234.

26. M. R. Goldfried and C. S. Trier, "Effectiveness of Relaxation as an Active Coping Skill," *Journal of Abnormal Psychology*, 1974, *83*, 348–355.

27. G. Weil and M. R. Goldfried, "Treatment of Insomnia in an Eleven-Year-Old Child Through Self-Relaxation," *Behavior Therapy*, 1973, *4*, 282–284.

28. A. Ellis, *Reason and Emotion in Psychotherapy* (New York: Lyle Stuart, 1962).

29. *Ibid.*, p. 50.

30. *Ibid.*

31. *Ibid.*, p. 38.

32. *Ibid.*, chap. 3.

33. M. R. Goldfried, E. T. Decenteceo, and L. Weinberg, "Systematic Rational Restructuring as a Self-Control Technique," *Behavior Therapy*, 1974, *5*, 247–254.

34. M. R. Goldfried and D. Sobocinski, "Effect of Irrational Beliefs on Emotional Arousal," *Journal of Consulting and Clinical Psychology*, 1975, *43*, 504–510.

35. E. J. Langer, I. L. Janis, and J. A. Wolfer, "Reduction of Psychological Stress in Surgical Patients," *Journal of Experimental Social Psychology*, 1975, *11*, 155–165.

36. D. H. Meichenbaum, "Cognitive Modification of Test Anxious College Students," *Journal of Consulting and Clinical Psychology*, 1972, *39*, 370–380; D. H. Meichenbaum, J. B. Gilmore, and A. Fedoravicius, "Group Insight versus Group Desensitization in Treating Speech Anxiety," *Journal of Consulting and Clinical Psychology*, 1971, *36*, 410–421.

37. D. H. Meichenbaum, *Cognitive Behavior Modification* (Morristown, N. J.: General Learning Press, 1974).

38. T. X. Barber, N. P. Spanos, and J. F. Chaves, *Hypnotism, Imagination, and Human Potentialities* (New York: Pergamon Press, 1974).

39. T. X. Barber and D. S. Caverley, "The Definition of the Situation as a Variable Affecting 'Hypnotic-Like' Suggestibility," *Journal of Clinical Psychology*, 1964, *20*, 438–440; cited in Barber, Spanos, and Chaves, *op. cit.*, p. 53.

40. T. X. Barber and D. S. Caverley, "Empirical Evidence for a Theory of 'Hypnotic' Behavior: Effects of Pretest Instructions on Response to Primary Suggestions," *Psychological Reports*, 1964, *14*, 457–467; cited in Barber, Spanos, and Chaves, *op. cit.*, p. 53.

41. *Ibid.*

42. Barber, Spanos, and Chaves, *op. cit.*, p. 51.

43. *Ibid.*

44. N. P. Spanos and T. X. Barber, "Cognitive Activity During 'Hypnotic' Suggestibility: Goal-Directed Fantasy and the Experience of Non-Volition," *Journal of Personality*, 1972, *40*, 510–524; cited in Barber, Spanos, and Chaves, p. 132.

45. N. P. Spanos and M. L. Ham, "Cognitive Activity in Response to Hypnotic Suggestions: Goal-Directed Fantasy and Selective Amnesia," *American Journal of Clinical Hypnosis*, 1973, *15*, 191–198; cited in Barber, Spanos, and Chaves, *op. cit.*, p. 133.

46. Barber, Spanos, and Chaves, *op. cit.*, p. 115.

47. *Ibid.*, p. 134.

48. *Ibid.*, p. 112.

49. C. L. Tuckey, "Psychotherapeutics; or Treatment by Hypnotism" *Woods*

Medical and Surgical Monographs, 1889, *3,* 721–795; cited in Barber, Spanos, and Chaves, *op. cit.,* p. 80.

50. Barber, Spanos, and Chaves, *op. cit.,* chap. 8.

51. *Ibid.,* p. 83.

52. *Ibid.,* p. 84.

53. *Ibid.,* p. 87.

54. *Ibid.,* p. 95.

55. L. E. Klausman, "Reduction of Pain in Childbirth by the Alleviation of Anxiety during Pregnancy," *Journal of Consulting and Clinical Psychology,* 1975, *43,* 162–165.

56. F. H. Kanfer and D. A. Goldfoot, "Self-Control and Tolerance of Noxious Stimulation," *Psychological Reports,* 1966, *18,* 79–85. A similar case in which attempted self-distraction was not successful in reducing attention to pain is reported by B. K. Houston and D. S. Holmes, "Effect of Avoidant Thinking and Reappraisal for Coping with Threat Involving Temporal Uncertainty," *Journal of Personality and Social Psychology,* 1974, *30,* 382–388.

57. T. X. Barber and B. J. Cooper, "Effects on Pain of Experimentally Induced and Spontaneous Distraction," *Psychological Reports,* 1972, *31,* 647–651.

58. Barber, Spanos, and Chaves, *op. cit.,* p. 94.

59. L. J. Bloom, B. K. Houston, D. S. Holmes, and T. G. Burish, "The Effectiveness of Attentional Diversion and Situation Redefinition for Reducing Stress Due to a Nonambiguous Threat," *Journal of Research in Personality,* 1977, *11,* 83–94.

60. P. Levendusky and L. Pankratz, "Self-Control Techniques as an Alternative to Pain Medication," *Journal of Abnormal Psychology,* 1975, *11,* 155–165.

61. Barber, Spanos, and Chaves, *op. cit.,* p. 95.

62. D. S. Holmes and B. K. Houston, "Effectiveness of Situation Redefinition and Affective Isolation in Coping with Stress," *Journal of Personality and Social Psychology,* 1974, *29,* 212–218.

63. J. F. Chaves and T. X. Barber, "Cognitive Strategies, Experimenter Modeling, and Expectation in the Attenuation of Pain," *Journal of Abnormal Psychology,* 1974, *83,* 356–363. Another study showing the effectiveness of positive expectations in reducing stress is reported by R. W. J. Neufeld, "Evidence of Stress as a Function of Experimentally Altered Appraisal of Stimulus Aversiveness and Coping Adequacy," *Journal of Personality and Social Psychology,* 1976, *33,* 632–646.

64. Bloom, Houston, Holmes, and Burish, *op. cit.*

65. Barber, Spanos, and Chaves, *op. cit.,* p. 153.

66. *Ibid.,* Appendix B.

67. J. F. Chaves and T. X. Barber, "Needles and Knives: Behind the Mystery of Acupuncture and Chinese Meridians," *Human Behavior,* 1973, *2,* 19–24.

68. *Ibid.*

69. *Ibid.*

70. *Ibid.*

71. *Ibid.*

72. S. N. Berk, M. E. Moore, and J. H. Resnick, "Psychosocial Factors as Mediators of Acupuncture Therapy," *Journal of Consulting and Clinical Psychology,* 1977, *45,* 612–619.

73. A. C. Kinsey, W. B. Pomeroy, C. E. Martin, and P. H. Gebhard, *Sexual Behavior in the Human Female* (New York: Simon and Schuster, 1965).

74. E. B. Hariton and J. L. Singer, "Women's Fantasies during Sexual Intercourse: Normative and Theoretical Implications," *Journal of Consulting and Clinical Psychology,* 1974, *42,* 313–322.

75. J. H. Geer and R. Fuhr, "Cognitive Factors in Sexual Arousal: The Role of Distraction," *Journal of Consulting and Clinical Psychology,* 1976, *44,* 238–243.

76. G. H. Bower, "Imagery as a Relational Organizer in Associative Learning," *Journal of Verbal Learning and Verbal Behavior,* 1970, *9,* 529–533.

77. A. Paivio, *Imagery and Verbal Processes* (New York: Holt, Rinehart and Winston, 1971).

78. J. L. Singer, *The Inner World of Daydreaming* (New York: Harper & Row, 1975).

79. J. F. Rychlak, "Time Orientation in the Positive and Negative Free Phantasies of Mildly Abnormal versus Normal High School Males," *Journal of Consulting and Clinical Psychology,* 1973, *41,* 175–180.

80. J. L. Singer, *Imagery and Daydream Methods in Psychotherapy and Behavior Modification* (New York: Academic Press, 1974).

Chapter Four

1. D. J. Bem, "Self-Perception Theory," in L. Berkowitz (ed.), *Advances in Experimental Social Psychology,* Vol. 6 (New York: Academic Press, 1972), pp. 1–62; D. J. Bem, *Beliefs, Attitudes, and Human Affairs* (Belmont, Calif.: Brooks/Cole, 1970).

2. Further discussion of this point can be found in W. Mischel, *Personality and Assessment* (New York: Wiley, 1968).

3. A similar point is made by H. H. Kelley, "Attribution Theory in Social Psychology," in D. Levine (ed.) *Nebraska Symposium on Motivation,* Vol. 15 (Lincoln: University of Nebraska Press, 1967), pp. 192–238.

4. D. J. Bem, "An Experimental Analysis of Self-Persuasion," *Journal of Experimental Social Psychology,* 1965, *1,* 199–218.

5. Bem, *Beliefs, Attitudes, and Human Affairs,* pp. 61–66.

6. C. A. Kiesler, R. E. Nisbett, and M. P. Zanna, "On Inferring One's Beliefs from One's Behavior," *Journal of Personality and Social Psychology,* 1969, *11,* 321–327.

7. D. J. Bem, "Inducing Beliefs in False Confessions," *Journal of Personality and Social Psychology,* 1966, *3,* 707–710.

8. C. Maslach, "The 'Truth' about False Confessions," *Journal of Personality and Social Psychology,* 1971, *20,* 141–146.

9. D. E. Linder and R. A. Jones, "Discriminative Stimuli as Determinants of

Consonance and Dissonance," *Journal of Experimental Social Psychology,* 1969, *5,* 467–482.

10. P. G. Zimbardo, "The Psychology of Police Confessions," *Psychology Today,* June, 1967, p. 16.

11. Bem, *Beliefs, Attitudes, and Human Affairs,* p. 65.

12. Zimbardo, *op. cit.;* P. G. Zimbardo, "Toward a More Perfect Justice," *Psychology Today,* July, 1967, p. 44.

13. C. L. Kleinke, K. S. Gitlin, and H. A. Segal, "Effect of Perceived Looking Time on Evaluation of Paintings," *Perceptual and Motor Skills,* 1973, *37,* 421–422.

14. C. L. Kleinke, "Effects of False Feedback about Response Lengths on Subjects' Perception of an Interview," *Journal of Social Psychology,* 1975, *95,* 99–104.

15. M. Ross, C. A. Insko, and H. S. Ross, "Self-Perception of Attitude," *Journal of Personality and Social Psychology,* 1971, *17,* 292–297.

16. C. L. Kleinke, A. A. Bustos, F. B. Meeker, and R. A. Staneski, "Effects of Self-Attributed and Other-Attributed Gaze on Interpersonal Evaluations between Males and Females," *Journal of Experimental Social Psychology,* 1973, *9,* 154–163.

17. P. Munson and C. A. Kiesler, "The Role of Attributions by Others in the Acceptance of Persuasive Communications," *Journal of Personality,* 1974, *42,* 453–466.

18. A. Bavelas, A. H. Hastorf, A. E. Gross, and W. R. Kite, "Experiments in the Alteration of Group Structure," *Journal of Experimental Social Psychology,* 1965, *1,* 55–70; A. H. Hastorf, "The 'Reinforcement' of Individual Actions in a Group Discussion," in L. Krasner and L. P. Ullmann (eds.), *Research in Behavior Modification* (New York: Holt, Rinehart and Winston, 1968).

19. C. L. Kleinke, R. A. Staneski, and D. E. Berger, "Evaluation of an Interviewer as a Function of Interviewer Gaze, Reinforcement of Subject Gaze, and Interviewer Attractiveness," *Journal of Personality and Social Psychology,* 1975, *31,* 115–122.

20. L. Festinger, *A Theory of Cognitive Dissonance* (Evanston, Ill.: Row-Peterson, 1957). A good summary of cognitive dissonance research can be found in J. W. Brehm and A. R. Cohen, *Explorations in Cognitive Dissonance* (New York: Wiley, 1962).

21. L. Festinger and J. M. Carlsmith, "Cognitive Consequences of Forced Compliance," *Journal of Abnormal and Social Psychology,* 1959, *58,* 203–210.

22. D. J. Bem, "Self-Perception: An Alternative Interpretation of Cognitive Dissonance Phenomena," *Psychological Review,* 1967, *74,* 183–200.

23. The reader wishing to learn more about the conceptual differences between Festinger's theory of cognitive dissonance and Bem's theory of self-perception is referred to Bem, "Self-Perception Theory."

24. B. E. Collins and M. F. Hoyt, "Personal Responsibility-for-Consequences: An Integration and Extension of 'Forced Compliance' Literature," *Journal of Experimental Social Psychology,* 1972, *8,* 558–593. The importance of when we learn the consequences of an act is elaborated by G. R. Goethals and J. Cooper, "When Dissonance is Reduced: The Timing of Self-

Justificatory Attitude Change," *Journal of Personality and Social Psychology,* 1975, *32,* 361–367.

25. Collins and Hoyt, *op. cit.*

26. B. J. Calder, M. Ross, and C. A. Insko, "Attitude Change and Attitude Attribution: Effects of Incentive, Choice, and Consequences in the Festinger and Carlsmith Paradigm," *Journal of Personality and Social Psychology,* 1973, *25,* 84–99.

27. J. Cooper, M. P. Zanna, and G. R. Goethals, "Mistreatment of an Esteemed Other as a Consequence Affecting Dissonance Reduction," *Journal of Experimental Social Psychology,* 1974, *10,* 224–233.

28. This section is based on an article by E. Walster, E. Berscheid, and G. W. Walster, "New Directions in Equity Research," *Journal of Personality and Social Psychology,* 1973, *25,* 151–176.

29. J. W. Regan, "Guilt, Perceived Injustice, and Altruistic Behavior," *Journal of Personality and Social Psychology,* 1971, *18,* 124–132.

30. J. L. Freedman, S. A. Wallington, and E. Bless, "Compliance Without Pressure: The Effect of Guilt," *Journal of Personality and Social Psychology,* 1967, *7,* 117–124.

31. E. I. Rawlings, "Witnessing Harm to Other: A Reassessment of the Role of Guilt in Altruistic Behavior," *Journal of Personality and Social Psychology,* 1968, *10,* 377–380; J. M. Carlsmith and A. E. Gross, "Some Effects of Guilt on Compliance," *Journal of Personality and Social Psychology,* 1969, *11,* 232–239; R. B. Darlington and C. E. Macker, "Displacement of Guilt-Produced Altruistic Behavior," *Journal of Personality and Social Psychology,* 1966, *4,* 442–443.

32. D. Regan, M. Williams, and S. Sparling, "Voluntary Expiation of Guilt: A Field Experiment," *Journal of Personality and Social Psychology,* 1972, *24,* 42–45.

33. Carlsmith and Gross, *op. cit.,* p. 238.

34. K. E. Davis and E. E. Jones, "Changes in Interpersonal Perception as a Means of Reducing Cognitive Dissonance," *Journal of Abnormal and Social Psychology,* 1960, *61,* 402–410.

35. G. M. Sykes and D. Matza, "Techniques of Neutralization: A Theory of Delinquency," *American Sociological Review,* 1957, *22,* 664–670.

36. W. Ryan, *Blaming the Victim* (New York: Random House, 1971).

37. M. Lerner, "The Desire for Justice and Reactions to Victims," in J. Macaulay and L. Berkowitz (eds.), *Altruism and Helping Behavior: Social Psychological Studies of Some Antecedents and Consequences* (New York: Academic Press, 1970), pp. 205–229.

38. T. C. Brock and A. H. Buss, "Dissonance, Aggression, and Evaluation of Pain," *Journal of Abnormal and Social Psychology,* 1962, *65,* 192–202.

39. B. Harris and J. H. Harvey, "Self-Attributed Choice as a Function of the Consequence of a Decision," *Journal of Personality and Social Psychology,* 1975, *31,* 1013–1019.

40. C. Mynatt and S. J. Sherman, "Responsibility Attribution in Groups and Individuals: A Direct Test of the Diffusion of Responsibility Hypothesis," *Journal of Personality and Social Psychology,* 1975, *32,* 1111–1118.

41. J. Mills and R. Egger, "Effects on Derogation of a Victim of Choosing to Reduce His Distress," *Journal of Personality and Social Psychology*, 1972, *23*, 405–408.

42. E. Aronson and J. Mills, "The Effects of Severity of Initiation on Liking for a Group," *Journal of Abnormal and Social Psychology*, 1959, *59*, 177–181.

43. J. W. Brehm, "Attitudinal Consequences of Commitment to Unpleasant Behavior," *Journal of Abnormal and Social Psychology*, 1960, *60*, 379–383.

44. R. Comer and J. D. Laird, "Choosing to Suffer as a Consequence of Expecting to Suffer: Why do People do it?" *Journal of Personality and Social Psychology*, 1975, *32*, 92–101.

45. E. E. Smith, "The Power of Dissonance Techniques to Change Attitudes," *Public Opinion Quarterly*, 1961, *25*, 626–639.

46. S. A. Darley and J. Cooper, "Cognitive Consequences of Forced Non-compliance," *Journal of Personality and Social Psychology*, 1972, *24*, 321–326; M. P. Zanna, "Inference of Belief From Rejection of an Alternative Action," *Representative Research in Social Psychology*, 1972, *3*, 85–95.

47. J. W. Brehm, "Post-Decision Changes in the Desirability of Alternatives," *Journal of Abnormal and Social Psychology*, 1956, *52*, 384–389.

48. J. W. Brehm and A. R. Cohen, "Re-Evaluation of Choice Alternatives as a Function of their Number and Qualitative Similarity," *Journal of Abnormal and Social Psychology*, 1959, *58*, 373–378.

49. C. L. Kleinke, A. A. Bustos, F. B. Meeker, and R. A. Staneski, unpublished data, Claremont, California, 1973.

50. S. E. Taylor, "On Inferring One's Attitudes From One's Behavior: Some Delimiting Conditions," *Journal of Personality and Social Psychology*, 1975, *31*, 126–131.

Chapter Five

1. N. Chapanis and A. Chapanis, "Cognitive Dissonance: Five Years Later," *Psychological Bulletin*, 1964, *61*, 1–22. An integration of dissonance and self-perception theories can be found in R. H. Fazio, M. P. Zanna, and J. Cooper, "Dissonance and Self-Perception: An Integrative View of Each Theory's Proper Domain of Application," *Journal of Experimental Social Psychology*, 1977, *13*, 464–479.

2. J. Schopler and J. S. Compere, "Effects of Being Kind or Harsh to Another on Liking," *Journal of Personality and Social Psychology*, 1971, *20*, 155–159.

3. J. Jecker and D. Landy, "Liking a Person as a Function of Doing Him a Favor," *Human Relations*, 1969, *22*, 371–378.

4. D. C. Glass, "Changes in Liking as a Means of Reducing Cognitive Discrepancies Between Self-Esteem and Aggression," *Journal of Personality*, 1964, *32*, 530–549.

5. R. J. Bandler, G. R. Madaras, and D. J. Bem, "Self-Observation as a Source of Pain Perception," *Journal of Personality and Social Psychology*, 1968, *9*, 205–209.

6. N. L. Corah and J. Boffa, "Perceived Control, Self-Observation, and Response to Aversive Stimulation," *Journal of Personality and Social Psychology*, 1970, *16*, 1–4.

7. S. A. Kopel and H. S. Arkowitz, "Role Playing as a Source of Self-Observation and Behavior Change," *Journal of Personality and Social Psychology,* 1974, *29,* 677–686.

8. J. T. Lanzetta, J. Cartwright-Smith, and R. E. Kleck, "Effects of Nonverbal Dissimulation on Emotional Experience and Autonomic Arousal," *Journal of Personality and Social Psychology,* 1976, *33,* 354–370.

9. J. D. Laird, "Self-Attribution of Emotion: The Effects of Expressive Behavior on the Quality of Emotional Experience," *Journal of Personality and Social Psychology,* 1974, *29,* 475–486.

10. *Ibid.,* p. 480.

11. H. Leventhal and W. Mace, "The Effect of Laughter on Evaluation of a Slapstick Movie," *Journal of Personality,* 1970, *38,* 16–30.

12. G. C. Cupchik and H. Leventhal, "Consistency between Expressive Behavior and the Evaluation of Humorous Stimuli: The Role of Sex and Self-Observation," *Journal of Personality and Social Psychology,* 1974, *30,* 429–442.

13. E. Aronson and J. M. Carlsmith, "Effect of Severity of Threat on the Evaluation of a Forbidden Behavior," *Journal of Abnormal and Social Psychology,* 1963, *66,* 584–588. The results of this experiment have been replicated in the following investigations: J. L. Freedman, "Long-Term Behavioral Effects of Cognitive Dissonance," *Journal of Experimental Social Psychology,* 1965, *1,* 145–155; A. Pepitone, C. McCauley, and P. Hammond, "Changes in Attractiveness of Forbidden Toys as a Function of Severity of Threat," *Journal of Experimental Social Psychology,* 1967, *3,* 221–229; E. A. Turner and J. Wright, "Effects of Severity of Threat and Perceived Availability on the Attractiveness of Objects," *Journal of Personality and Social Psychology,* 1965, *2,* 128–132.

14. J. M. Carlsmith, E. B. Ebbesen, M. R. Lepper, M. P. Zanna, A. J. Joncas, and R. P. Abelson, "Dissonance Reduction Following Forced Attention to Dissonance," *Proceedings of the 77th Annual Convention of the American Psychological Association,* 1969, 321–322; M. P. Zanna, R. P. Abelson, and M. R. Lepper, "Attentional Mechanisms in Children's Devaluation of a Forbidden Activity in a Forced-Compliance Situation," *Journal of Personality and Social Psychology,* 1973, *28,* 355–359.

15. E. B. Ebbesen, R. J. Bowers, S. Phillips, and M. Snyder, "Self-Control Processes in the Forbidden Toy Paradigm," *Journal of Personality and Social Psychology,* 1975, *31,* 442–452.

16. M. R. Lepper, M. P. Zanna, and R. P. Abelson, "Cognitive Irreversibility in a Dissonance-Reduction Situation," *Journal of Personality and Social Psychology,* 1970, *16,* 191–198.

17. M. R. Lepper, "Dissonance, Self-Perception, and Honesty in Children," *Journal of Personality and Social Psychology,* 1973, *25,* 65–74.

18. R. E. Kraut, "Effects of Social Labeling on Giving to Charity," *Journal of Experimental Social Psychology,* 1973, *9,* 551–562.

19. L. A. McArthur, C. A. Kiesler, and B. P. Cook, "Acting on an Attitude as a Function of Self-Percept and Inequity," *Journal of Personality and Social Psychology,* 1969, *12,* 295–302.

20. R. L. Miller, P. Brickman, and D. Bolen, "Attribution versus Self-

Persuasion as a Means for Modifying Behavior," *Journal of Personality and Social Psychology*, 1975, *31*, 430–431.

21. *Ibid.*

22. *Ibid.*, p. 434.

23. *Ibid.*

24. J. R. Salancik, "Inference of One's Attitude from Behavior Recalled under Linguistically Manipulated Cognitive Sets," *Journal of Experimental Social Psychology*, 1974, *10*, 415–427.

25. *Ibid.*, p. 421.

26. In E. T. Webb and J. B. Morgan, *Strategy in Handling People* (Garden City, N. Y.: Garden City Publishing Co., 1930) p. 8; this quotation is also cited in G. L. Clore, *Interpersonal Attraction—An Overview* (Morristown, N. J.: General Learning Press, 1975), p. 24.

27. J. L. Freedman and S. C. Fraser, "Compliance without Pressure: The Foot-in-the-Door Technique," *Journal of Personality and Social Psychology*, 1966, *4*, 195–202.

28. *Ibid.*

29. *Ibid.*, p. 201.

30. M. B. Harris, "The Effects of Performing One Altruistic Act on the Likelihood of Performing Another," *Journal of Social Psychology*, 1972, *88*, 65–73.

31. P. Pliner, H. Hart, J. Kohl, and D. Saari, "Compliance without Pressure: Some Further Data on the Foot-in-the-Door Technique," *Journal of Experimental Social Psychology*, 1974, *10*, 17–22.

32. M. Snyder and M. R. Cunningham, "To Comply or Not Comply: Testing the Self-Perception Explanation of the 'Foot-in-the-Door' Phenomenon," *Journal of Personality and Social Psychology*, 1975, *31*, 64–67.

33. R. B. Cialdini, J. E. Vincent, S. K. Lewis, J. Catalan, D. Wheeler, and B. L. Darby, "Reciprocal Concessions Procedure for Inducing Compliance: The Door-in-the-Face Technique," *Journal of Personality and Social Psychology*, 1975, *31*, 206–215.

34. A. Cann, S. J. Sherman, and R. Elkes, "Effects of Initial Request Size and Timing of a Second Request on Compliance: The Foot in the Door and the Door in the Face," *Journal of Personality and Social Psychology*, 1975, *32*, 774–782.

35. S. W. Uranowitz, "Helping and Self-Attributions: A Field Experiment," *Journal of Personality and Social Psychology*, 1975, *31*, 852–854.

36. J. Cooper, J. M. Darley, and J. E. Henderson, "On the Effectiveness of Deviant- and Conventional-Appearing Communicators: A Field Experiment," *Journal of Personality and Social Psychology*, 1974, *29*, 752–757.

37. Boston: Ginn and Company, 1940.

38. For a discussion of these ideas, see D. J. Bem, *Beliefs, Attitudes, and Affairs* (Belmont, Calif.: Brooks/Cole, 1970), p. 1.

39. P. B. Sheatsley, "White Attitudes toward the Negro," *Daedalus*, 1966, *95*, 217–238.

40. G. Saenger and E. Gilbert, "Customer Reactions to the Integration of Negro Sales Personnel," *International Journal of Opinion and Attitude Research*, 1950, *4*, 57–76.

41. J. Harding and R. Hogrefe, "Attitudes of White Department Store Employees toward Negro Co-Workers," *Journal of Social Issues,* 1952, *8,* 18–28.

42. B. MacKenzie, "The Importance of Contact in Determining Attitudes toward Negroes," *Journal of Abnormal and Social Psychology,* 1948, *43,* 417–441.

43. M. Deutsch and M. E. Collins, *Interracial Housing, a Psychological Evaluation of a Social Experiment* (Minneapolis: University of Minnesota Press, 1951).

44. M. Jahoda and P. S. West, "Race Relations in Public Housing," *Journal of Social Issues,* 1951, 7, 132–138.

45. D. M. Wilner, R. P. Walkley, and S. W. Cook, "Residential Proximity and Intergroup Relations in Public Housing Projects," *Journal of Social Issues,* 1952, *8,* 45–69; E. Works, "The Prejudice-Interaction Hypothesis from the Point of View of the Negro Minority Group," *American Journal of Sociology,* 1961, *67,* 47–52.

46. S. A. Star, R. M. Williams, and S. A. Stouffer, "Negro Infantry Platoons in White Companies," in E. E. Maccoby, T. M. Newcomb, and E. L. Hartley (eds.), *Readings in Social Psychology* (New York: Holt, Rinehart and Winston, 1958), pp. 596–601.

47. *Ibid.,* p. 598.

48. R. D. Minard, "Race Relationships in the Pocahontas Field," *Journal of Social Issues,* 1952, *8,* 29–44.

49. S. Cook, "Motives in a Conceptual Analysis of Attitude-Related Behavior," in W. Arnold and D. Levine (eds.), *Nebraska Symposium on Motivation* (Lincoln: University of Nebraska Press, 1969), pp. 179–231. A good summary of this study can be found in L. S. Wrightsman, *Social Psychology in the Seventies* (Belmont, Calif.: Brooks/Cole, 1972), pp. 324–337.

50. W. O. Eaton and G. L. Clore, "Interracial Imitation at a Summer Camp," *Journal of Personality and Social Psychology,* 1975, *32,* 1099–1105.

51. Y. Amir, "Contact Hypothesis in Ethnic Relations," *Psychological Bulletin,* 1969, *71,* 319–342. Other important discussions of this issue can be found in the following references: J. Harding, H. Proshansky, B. Kutner, and I. Chein, "Prejudice and Ethnic Relations," in G. Lindzey and E. Aronson (eds.), *The Handbook of Social Psychology,* 2nd Edition, Vol. 5 (Reading, Mass.: Addison-Wesley, 1969), pp. 1–76; T. F. Pettigrew, "Social Psychology and Desegregation Research," *American Psychologist,* 1961, *16,* 105–112; T. F. Pettigrew, "Racially Separate or Together?" *Journal of Social Issues,* 1969, *25,* 43–69.

52. This point is also made by Bem, *op. cit.,* p. 76.

53. B. Bettelheim, "Individual and Mass Behavior in Extreme Situations," *Journal of Abnormal and Social Psychology,* 1943, *38,* 417–452.

54. E. H. Schein, "The Chinese Indoctrination Program for Prisoners of War: A Study of Attempted 'Brainwashing,'" *Psychiatry,* 1956, *19,* 149–172; E. H. Schein, "Reaction Patterns to Severe, Chronic Stress in American Prisoners of War of the Chinese," *Journal of Social Issues,* 1957, *13,* 21–30.

55. J. Segal, "Correlates of Collaboration and Resistance Behavior among U. S. Army POWs in Korea," *Journal of Social Issues,* 1957, *13,* 31–40.

56. R. A. Bauer, "Brainwashing: Psychology or Demonology?" *Journal of Social Issues,* 1957, *13,* 41–47.

57   Schein, *op. cit.*

58.   A somewhat different orientation toward this issue is taken by J. G. Miller, "Brainwashing: Present and Future," *Journal of Social Issues,* 1957, *13,* 48–55.

Chapter Six

1.   The following discussion about internal and external control is based on E. J. Phares, *Locus of Control in Personality* (Morristown, N. J.: General Learning Press, 1976).

2.   The above six statements are from Rotter's Scale, cited in *ibid.,* pp. 178–180.

3.   J. B. Rotter, "Generalized Expectancies for Internal versus External Control of Reinforcement," *Psychological Monographs,* 1966, *80,* (No. 1, Whole No. 609).

4.   M. Seeman and J. W. Evans, "Alienation and Learning in a Hospital Setting," *American Sociological Review,* 1962, *27,* 772–783.

5.   M. Seeman, "Alienation and Social Learning in a Reformatory," *American Journal of Sociology,* 1963, *69,* 270–284.

6.   E. J. Phares, "Differential Utilization of Information as a Function of Internal-External Control," *Journal of Personality,* 1968, *36,* 649–662.

7.   E. J. Phares, D. E. Ritchie, and W. L. Davis, "Internal-External Control and Reaction to Threat," *Journal of Personality and Social Psychology,* 1968, *10,* 402–405.

8.   J. DuCette and S. Wolk, "Cognitive and Motivational Correlates of Generalized Expectancies for Control," *Journal of Personality and Social Psychology,* 1973, *26,* 420–426; S. Wolk and J. Ducette, "Intentional Performance and Incidental Learning as a Function of Personality and Task Dimensions," *Journal of Personality and Social Psychology,* 1974, *29,* 90–101.

9.   Phares, *Locus of Control in Personality,* pp. 66–67.

10.   R. B. Cialdini and H. L. Mirels, "Sense of Personal Control and Attributions about Yielding and Resisting Persuasion Targets," *Journal of Personality and Social Psychology,* 1976, *33,* 395–402.

11.   Phares, *Locus of Control in Personality,* pp. 74–78.

12.   D. P. Crowne and S. Liverant, "Conformity under Varying Conditions of Personal Commitment," *Journal of Abnormal and Social Psychology,* 1963, *66,* 547–555.

13.   Phares, *Locus of Control in Personality,* pp. 84–86.

14.   E. Ritchie and E. J. Phares, "Attitude Change as a Function of Internal-External Control and Communicator Status," *Journal of Personality,* 1969, *37,* 429–443.

15.   R. M. Ryckman, W. C. Rodda, and M. F. Sherman, "Locus of Control and Expertise Relevance as Determinants of Changes in Opinion about Student Activism," *Journal of Social Psychology,* 1972, *88,* 107–114.

16.   S. C. Jones and J. S. Shrauger, "Locus of Control and Interpersonal Evaluations," *Journal of Consulting and Clinical Psychology,* 1968, *32,* 664–668; C. R. Snyder and G. R. Larson, "A Further Look at Student Acceptance of General Personality Interpretations," *Journal of Consulting and Clinical Psychology,* 1972, *38,* 384–388.

17. S. J. Sherman, "Internal-External Control and Its Relationship to Attitude Change under Different Social Influence Techniques," *Journal of Personality and Social Psychology,* 1973, *23,* 23–29.

18. Phares, *Locus of Control in Personality,* pp. 68–70.

19. *Ibid.,* pp. 93–100.

20. *Ibid.,* pp. 108–110.

21. *Ibid.,* pp. 113–118.

22. *Ibid.,* chap. 8.

23. *Ibid.,* pp. 145–150.

24. B. K. Bryant and J. F. Trockel, "Personal History of Psychological Stress Related to Locus of Control Orientation among College Women," *Journal of Consulting and Clinical Psychology,* 1976, *44,* 266–271.

25. Phares, *Locus of Control in Personality,* pp. 151–155.

26. *Ibid.,* pp. 164–167; R. deCharms, "Personal Causation Training in the Schools," *Journal of Applied Social Psychology,* 1972, *2,* 95–113; G. Reimanis, "Effects of Experimental IE Modification Techniques and Home Environmental Variables on IE," paper presented at the annual meeting of the American Psychological Association, Washington, D.C., 1971.

27. B. S. Gorman, "An Observation of Altered Locus of Control following Political Disappointment," *Psychological Reports,* 1968, *23,* 1094.

28. L. A. McArthur, "Luck is Alive and Well in New Haven," *Journal of Personality and Social Psychology,* 1970, *16,* 316–318.

29. M. Brecher and F. L. Denmark, "Locus of Control: Effects of a Serendipitous Manipulation," *Psychological Reports,* 1971, *30,* 461–462.

30. Phares, *Locus of Control in Personality,* p. 160.

31. J. M. Henslin, "Craps and Magic," *American Journal of Sociology,* 1967, *73,* 316–330.

32. L. H. Strickland, R. J. Lewicki, and A. M. Katz, "Temporal Orientation and Perceived Control as Determinants of Risk-Taking," *Journal of Experimental Social Psychology,* 1966, *2,* 143–151.

33. E. J. Langer, "The Illusion of Control," *Journal of Personality and Social Psychology,* 1975, *32,* 311–328.

34. *Ibid.*

35. C. B. Wortman, "Some Determinants of Perceived Control," *Journal of Personality and Social Psychology,* 1975, *31,* 282–294.

36. Langer, *op. cit.*

37. F. Ayeroff and R. P. Abelson, "ESP & ESB: Belief in Personal Success at Mental Telepathy," *Journal of Personality and Social Psychology,* 1976, *34,* 240–247.

38. E. J. Langer and J. Roth, "Heads I Win, Tails It's Chance: The Illusion of Control as a Function of the Sequence of Outcomes in a Purely Chance Task," *Journal of Personality and Social Psychology,* 1975, *32,* 951–955.

39. Langer, *op. cit.*

40. An overview of intrinsic motivation is provided by E. L. Deci, *Intrinsic Motivation* (New York: Plenum Press, 1975).

41. E. L. Deci, "Effects of Externally Mediated Rewards on Intrinsic Motiva-

tion," *Journal of Personality and Social Psychology*, 1971, *18*, 105–115; E. L. Deci, "Intrinsic Motivation, Extrinsic Reinforcement, and Inequity," *Journal of Personality and Social Psychology*, 1972, *22*, 113–120.

42. E. L. Deci, "The Effects of Contingent and Noncontingent Rewards and Controls on Intrinsic Motivation," *Organizational Behavior and Human Performance*, 1972, *8*, 217–229.

43. A. W. Kruglanski, A. Riter, D. Arazi, R. Agassi, J. Monteqio, I. Peri, and M. Peretz, "Effects of Task-Intrinsic Rewards upon Extrinsic and Intrinsic Motivation," *Journal of Personality and Social Psychology*, 1975, *31*, 699–705.

44. K. Bogart, A. Loeb, and I. D. Rutman, "A Dissonance Approach to Behavior Modification," paper presented at the meeting of the Eastern Psychological Association, Philadelphia, 1969; cited in Deci, *Intrinsic Motivation*, p. 167.

45. D. Greene and M. R. Lepper, "Effects of Extrinsic Rewards on Children's Subsequent Intrinsic Interest," *Child Development*, 1974, *45*, 1141–1145; M. R. Lepper, D. Greene, and R. E. Nisbett, "Undermining Children's Intrinsic Interest With Extrinsic Rewards: A Test of the 'Overjustification' Hypothesis," *Journal of Personality and Social Psychology*, 1973, *28*, 129–137.

46. M. R. Lepper and D. Greene, "Turning Play into Work: Effects of Adult Surveillance and Extrinsic Rewards on Children's Intrinsic Motivation," *Journal of Personality and Social Psychology*, 1975, *31*, 479–486.

47. A. W. Kruglanski, I. Freedman, and G. Zeevi, "The Effects of Extrinsic Incentive on Some Qualitative Aspects of Task Performance," *Journal of Personality*, 1971, *39*, 606–617.

48. A. W. Kruglanski, S. Alon, and T. Lewis, "Retrospective Misattribution and Task Enjoyment," *Journal of Experimental Social Psychology*, 1972, *8*, 493–501.

49. M. Ross, "Salience of Reward and Intrinsic Motivation," *Journal of Personality and Social Psychology*, 1975, *32*, 245–254.

50. *Ibid.*

51. E. L. Deci and W. F. Cascio, "Changes in Intrinsic Motivation as a Function of Negative Feedback and Threats," paper presented at the meeting of the Eastern Psychological Association, Boston, 1972; cited in Deci, *Intrinsic Motivation*, p. 139.

51. E. L. Deci, W. F. Cascio, and J. Krusell, "Sex Difference, Verbal Reinforcement, and Intrinsic Motivation," paper presented at the meeting of the Eastern Psychological Association, Washington, D.C., 1973; cited in Deci, *Intrinsic Motivation*, pp. 143–147.

53. R. Anderson, S. T. Manoogian, and J. J. Reznick, "The Undermining and Enhancing of Intrinsic Motivation in Preschool Children," *Journal of Personality and Social Psychology*, 1976, *34*, 915–922.

54. A. W. Kruglanski, A. Riter, A. Amitai, B. Margolin, L. Shabtai, and D. Zaksh, "Can Money Enhance Intrinsic Motivation?: A Test of the Content-Consequence Hypothesis," *Journal of Personality and Social Psychology*, 1975, *31*, 744–750.

55. B. J. Calder and B. M. Staw, "Self-Perception of Intrinsic and Extrinsic Motivation," *Journal of Personality and Social Psychology*, 1975, *31*, 599–605; B. M. Staw, *Intrinsic and Extrinsic Motivation* (Morristown, N. J.: General Learning Press, 1976).

56. J. W. Brehm, *A Theory of Psychological Reactance* (New York: Academic Press, 1966); I. D. Steiner, "Perceived Freedom," in L. Berkowitz (ed.), *Advances in Experimental Social Psychology,* Vol. 5 (New York: Academic Press, 1970).

57. S. Reiss and L. W. Sushinsky, "Overjustification, Competing Responses, and the Acquisition of Intrinsic Interest," *Journal of Personality and Social Psychology,* 1975, *31,* 1116–1125; S. Reiss and L. W. Sushinsky, "The Competing Response Hypothesis of Decreased Play Effects: A Reply to Lepper and Greene," *Journal of Personality and Social Psychology,* 1976, *33,* 233–244.

58. K. McGraw and J. C. McCullers, "The Distracting Effect of Material Reward: An Alternative Explanation for the Superior Performance of Reward Groups in Probability Learning," *Journal of Experimental Child Psychology,* 1974, *18,* 149–158.

59. J. Garbarino, "The Impact of Anticipated Reward Upon Cross-Age Tutoring," *Journal of Personality and Social Psychology,* 1975, *32,* 421–428.

60. Deci, *Intrinsic Motivation,* chap. 7.

61. M. R. Lepper and D. Greene, "On Understanding 'Overjustification': A Reply to Reiss and Sushinsky," *Journal of Personality and Social Psychology,* 1976, *33,* 25–35; Reiss and Sushinsky, 1975, *op. cit.;* Reiss and Sushinsky, 1976, *op. cit.* A review of research related to this issue can be found in J. Condry, "Enemies of Exploration: Self-Initiated Versus Other-Initiated Learning," *Journal of Personality and Social Psychology,* 1977, *35,* 459–477.

62. S. Reiss and L. W. Sushinsky, "Undermining *Extrinsic* Interest," *American Psychologist,* 1975, *30,* 782–783.

63. W. L. Hodges, "The Role of Rewards and Reinforcement in Early Education Programs: I External Reinforcement in Early Education," *Journal of School Psychology,* 1972, *10,* 233–241.

64. J. E. Brophy, "The Role of Rewards and Reinforcements in Early Education Programs: II Fostering Intrinsic Motivation to Learn," *Journal of School Psychology,* 1972, *10,* 243–251.

65. Staw, *Intrinsic and Extrinsic Motivation.*

66. *Ibid.*

Chapter Seven

1. B. Weiner, I. Frieze, A. Kukla, L. Reed, S. Rest, and R. M. Rosenbaum, *Perceiving the Causes of Success and Failure* (Morristown, N. J.: General Learning Press, 1971).

2. E. E. Jones, L. Rock, K. G. Shaver, G. R. Goethals, and L. M. Ward, "Pattern of Performance and Ability Attribution: An Unexpected Primacy Effect," *Journal of Personality and Social Psychology,* 1968, *10,* 317–340.

3. L. J. Beckman, "Effects of Students' Performance on Teachers' and Observers' Attributions of Causality," *Journal of Educational Psychology,* 1970, *61,* 76–82.

4. N. T. Feather and J. G. Simon, "Attribution of Responsibility and Valence of Outcome in Relation to Initial Confidence and Success and Failure of Self and Other," *Journal of Personality and Social Psychology,* 1971, *18,* 173–188; I. Frieze and B. Weiner, "Cue Utilization and Attributional Judgments for Success and Failure," *Journal of Personality,* 1971, *39,* 591–

605; I. D. McMahan, "Relationships Between Causal Attributions and Expectancy of Success," *Journal of Personality and Social Psychology*, 1973, *28*, 108–114.

5.   Weiner, Frieze, Kukla, Reed, Rest, and Rosenbaum, *op. cit.*, p. 22.

6.   N. T. Feather, "Attribution of Responsibility and Valence of Success and Failure in Relation to Initial Confidence and Task Performance," *Journal of Personality and Social Psychology*, 1969, *13*, 129–144; D. Weaver and P. Brickman, "Expectancy, Feedback, and Disconfirmation as Independent Factors in Outcome Satisfaction," *Journal of Personality and Social Psychology*, 1974, *30*, 420–428.

7.   W. C. House and V. Perney, "Valence of Expected and Unexpected Outcomes as a Function of Locus of Control and Type of Expectancy," *Journal of Personality and Social Psychology*, 1974, *29*, 454–463.

8.   J. E. R. Luginbuhl, "Role of Choice and Outcome on Feelings of Success and Estimates of Ability," *Journal of Personality and Social Psychology*, 1972, *22*, 121–127.

9.   N. T. Feather, "Change in Confidence following Success or Failure as a Predictor of Subsequent Performance," *Journal of Personality and Social Psychology*, 1968, *9*, 38–46.

10. P. Brickman and M. Hendricks, "Expectancy for Gradual or Sudden Improvement and Reaction to Success and Failure," *Journal of Personality and Social Psychology*, 1975, *32*, 893–900.

11. P. Brickman, J. A. W. Linsenmeier, and A. G. McCareins, "Performance Enhancement by Relevant Success and Irrelevant Failure," *Journal of Personality and Social Psychology*, 1976, *33*, 149–160.

12. G. Fontaine, "Causal Attribution in Simulated versus Real Situations: When Are People Logical, When Are They Not?" *Journal of Personality and Social Psychology*, 1975, *32*, 1021–1029.

13. *Ibid.*

14. I. Frieze and B. Weiner, "Cue Utilization and Attributional Judgments for Success and Failure," *Journal of Personality*, 1971, *39*, 591–605.

15. B. Weiner, H. Heckhausen, W. U. Meyer, and R. C. Cook, "Causal Ascriptions and Achievement Behavior: A Conceptual Analysis of Effort and Reanalysis of Locus of Control," *Journal of Personality and Social Psychology*, 1972, *21*, 239–248.

16. G. Fontaine, "Social Comparison and Some Determinants of Expected Personal Control and Expected Performance in a Novel Task Situation," *Journal of Personality and Social Psychology*, 1974, *29*, 487–496.

17. P. Brickman, "Adaptation Level Determinants of Satisfaction with Equal and Unequal Outcome Distributions in Skill and Chance Situations," *Journal of Personality and Social Psychology*, 1975, *32*, 191–198.

18. G. Fitch, "Effects of Self-Esteem, Perceived Performance, and Choice on Causal Attributions," *Journal of Personality and Social Psychology*, 1970, *16*, 311–315; Frieze and Weiner, *op. cit.*; Weiner, Frieze, Kukla, Reed, Rest, and Rosenbaum, *op. cit.*, p. 22.

19. Beckman, *op. cit.*

20. C. B. Wortman, P. R. Costanzo, and T. R. Witt, "Effect of Anticipated Performance on the Attributions of Causality to Self and Others," *Journal of Personality and Social Psychology*, 1973, *27*, 372–381.

21. B. R. Schlenker, "Self-Presentation: Managing the Impression of Consistency When Reality Interferes with Self-Enhancement," *Journal of Personality and Social Psychology,* 1975, *32,* 1030–1037.

22. J. W. Regan, H. Gosselink, J. Hubsch, and E. Ulsh, "Do People Have Inflated Views of Their Own Ability?" *Journal of Personality and Social Psychology,* 1975, *31,* 295–301.

23. D. R. Mettee, "Rejection of Unexpected Success as a Function of the Negative Consequences of Accepting Success," *Journal of Personality and Social Psychology,* 1971, *17,* 332–341.

24. J. Marecek and D. R. Mettee, "Avoidance of Continued Success as a Function of Self-Esteem, Level of Esteem Certainty, and Responsibility for Success," *Journal of Personality and Social Psychology,* 1972, *22,* 98–107.

25. J. E. R. Luginbuhl, D. H. Crowe, and J. P. Kahan, "Causal Attributions for Success and Failure," *Journal of Personality and Social Psychology,* 1975, *31,* 86–93.

26. A. L. Chaikin, "The Effects of Four Outcome Schedules on Persistence, Liking for the Task, and Attributions of Causality," *Journal of Personality,* 1971, *39,* 512–526.

27. Brickman and Hendricks, *op. cit.*

28. B. Weiner and A. Kukla, "An Attributional Analysis of Achievement Motivation," *Journal of Personality and Social Psychology,* 1970, *15,* 1–20; B. Weiner and P. A. Potepan, "Personality Characteristics and Affective Reactions toward Exams of Superior and Failing College Students," *Journal of Educational Psychology,* 1970, *61,* 144–151.

29. A. Kukla, "Attributional Determinants of Achievement-Related Behavior," *Journal of Personality and Social Psychology,* 1972, *21,* 166–174.

30. K. Kjerulff and N. H. Wiggins, "Graduate Student Styles for Coping with Stressful Situations," *Journal of Educational Psychology,* 1976, *68,* 247–254.

31. Weiner, Frieze, Kukla, Reed, Rest, and Rosenbaum, *op. cit.,* p. 13.

32. S. Rest, R. Nierenberg, B. Weiner, and H. Heckhausen, "Further Evidence concerning the Effects of Perceptions of Effort and Ability on Achievement Evaluation," *Journal of Personality and Social Psychology,* 1973, *28,* 187–191; Weiner and Kukla, *op. cit.*

33. Weiner, Heckhausen, Meyer, and Cook, *op. cit.*

34. B. Weiner and J. Sierad, "Misattribution for Failure and Enhancement of Achievement Strivings," *Journal of Personality and Social Psychology,* 1975, *31,* 415–421.

35. P. Rosenkrantz, S. Vogel, H. Bee, I. Broverman, and D. M. Broverman, Sex-Role Stereotypes and Self-Concepts in College Students," *Journal of Consulting and Clinical Psychology,* 1968, *32,* 287–295.

36. J. Z. Rubin, F. J. Provenzano, and Z. Luria, "The Eye of the Beholder: Parents Views on Sex of Newborns," *American Journal of Orthopsychiatry,* 1974, *44,* 512–519.

37. M. S. Horner, "Toward an Understanding of Achievement-Related Conflicts in Women," *Journal of Social Issues,* 1972, *28,* 157–175.

38. *Ibid.,* p. 161.

39. *Ibid.*

40. M. Zuckerman and L. Wheeler, "To Dispel Fantasies about the Fantasy-

Based Measure of Fear of Success," *Psychological Bulletin*, 1975, *82*, 932–946.

41. N. T. Feather, "Positive and Negative Reactions to Male and Female Success and Failure in Relation to the Perceived Status and Sex-Typed Appropriateness of Occupations," *Journal of Personality and Social Psychology*, 1975, *31*, 536–548.

42. M. Zuckerman and S. N. Allison, "An Objective Measure of Fear of Success: Construction and Validation," *Journal of Personality Assessment*, 1976, *40*, 422–430; the quoted statements appear on pp. 423–424 of the article.

43. *Ibid.*

44. A more detailed discussion of this issue can be found in D. Tresemer, "The Cumulative Record of Research on 'Fear of Success,'" *Sex Roles*, 1976, *2*, 217–236. Another relevant article is E. Lenny, "Women's Self-Confidence in Achievement Settings," *Psychological Bulletin*, 1977, *84*, 1–43.

45. K. Deaux and J. Taynor, "Evaluation of Male and Female Ability: Bias Works Two Ways," *Psychological Reports*, 1973, *32*, 261–262.

46. J. T. Spence and R. Helmreich, "Who Likes Competent Women? Competence, Sex-Role Congruence of Interests, and Subjects' Attitudes toward Women as Determinants of Interpersonal Attraction," *Journal of Applied Social Psychology*, 1972, *2*, 197–213.

47. D. Shaffer and C. Wegley, "Success Orientation and Sex-Role Congruence as Determinants of the Attractiveness of Competent Women," *Journal of Personality*, 1974, *42*, 586–600.

48. J. Taynor and K. Deaux, "When Women Are More Deserving Than Men: Equity, Attribution, and Perceived Sex Differences," *Journal of Personality and Social Psychology*, 1973, *28*, 360–367.

49. R. Winchel, D. Fenner, and P. Shaver, "Impact of Coeducation on 'Fear of Success' Imagery Expressed by Male and Female High School Students," *Journal of Educational Psychology*, 1974, *66*, 726–730.

50. W. C. House, "Actual and Perceived Differences in Male and Female Expectancies and Minimal Goal Levels as a Function of Competition," *Journal of Personality*, 1974, *42*, 493–509.

51. K. L. Dion, "Women's Reactions to Discrimination from Members of the Same or Opposite Sex," *Journal of Research in Personality*, 1975, *9*, 294–306.

52. Zuckerman and Allison, *op. cit.*

53. K. Deaux and T. Emswiller, "Explanations of Successful Performance on Sex-Linked Tasks: What Is Skill for the Male Is Luck for the Female," *Journal of Personality and Social Psychology*, 1974, *29*, 80–85.

54. K. Deaux and E. Farris, "Attributing Causes for One's Own Performance: The effects of Sex, Norms and Outcomes," *Journal of Research in Personality*, 1977, *11*, 59–72.

55. J. G. Nicholls, "Causal Attributions and Other Achievement-Related Cognitions: Effects of Task Outcomes, Attainment Value, and Sex," *Journal of Personality and Social Psychology*, 1975, *31*, 379–389.

56. K. Deaux, L. White, and E. Farris, "Skill versus Luck: Field and Laboratory Studies of Male and Female Preferences," *Journal of Personality and Social Psychology*, 1975, *32*, 629–636.

57. *Ibid.*

58. An excellent bibliography on research in sex differences can be found in E. E. Maccoby and C. N. Jacklin, *The Psychology of Sex Differences* (Stanford, Calif.: Stanford University Press, 1974).

59. A. H. Stein and M. M. Bailey, "The Socialization of Achievement Orientation in Females," *Psychological Bulletin,* 1973, *80,* 345–366.

60. A. H. Stein, "The Effects of Sex-Role Standards for Achievement and Sex-Role Preference on Three Determinants of Achievement Motivation," *Developmental Psychology,* 1971, *4,* 219–231.

61. Stein and Bailey, *op. cit.*

62. C. S. Dweck, "Sex Differences in the Meaning of Negative Evaluation in Achievement Situations: Determinants and Consequences," paper presented at the meeting of the Society for Research in Child Development, Denver, Colorado, 1974.

63. C. S. Dweck and E. S. Bush, "Sex Differences in Learned Helplessness: I. Differential Debilitation with Peer and Adult Evaluators," *Developmental Psychology,* 1976, *12,* 147–156.

64. L. Weitzman, D. Eifler, E. Hokada, and C. Ross, "Sex-Role Socialization in Picture Books for Pre-School Children," *American Journal of Sociology,* 1972, *77,* 1125–1150.

65. L. Z. McArthur and S. V. Eisen, "Achievements of Male and Female Storybook Characters as Determinants of Achievement Behavior by Boys and Girls," *Journal of Personality and Social Psychology,* 1976, *33,* 467–473.

Chapter Eight

1. W. B. Cannon, "'Voodoo' Death," *American Anthropologist,* 1942, *44,* 169–181 (reprint in *Psychosomatic Medicine,* 1957, *19,* 182–190); this quotation was compiled from Cannon's writings by C. P. Richter, "On the Phenomenon of Sudden Death in Animals and Man," *Psychosomatic Medicine,* 1957, *19,* 191–198, p. 191.

2. R. H. Basedow, *The Australian Aboriginal* (Adelaide, Australia, 1925), pp. 178–179; this passage is quoted in Cannon, *op. cit.,* p. 172 (reprint, p. 184), and in Richter, *op. cit.,* p. 191.

3. B. Bettelheim, *The Informed Heart—Autonomy in a Mass Age* (Glencoe, Ill.: The Free Press, 1960), pp. 151–152.

4. N. A. Ferrari, "Institutionalization and Attitude Change in an Aged Population: A Field Study and Dissidence Theory," unpublished doctoral dissertation, Western Reserve University, 1962; cited in M. E. P. Seligman, *Helplessness—On Depression, Development, and Death* (San Francisco: W. H. Freeman and Company, 1975), p. 185.

5. N. Boureston and S. Tars, "Alterations in Life Patterns following Nursing Home Relocation," *The Gerontologist,* 1974, *14,* 506–509.

6. Seligman, *op. cit.,* p. 74.

7. *Ibid.,* chap. 3.

8. *Ibid.,* chap. 4.

9. *Ibid.,* chap. 4.

10. E. J. Phares, "Perceptual Threshold Decrements as a Function of Skill and Chance Expectancies," *Journal of Personality,* 1962, *53,* 399–407.

11. E. J. Phares, "Expectancy Changes in Skill and Chance Situations," *Journal of Abnormal and Social Psychology,* 1957, *54,* 339–342.

12. R. S. Lazarus, *Psychological Stress and the Coping Process* (New York: McGraw-Hill, 1966).

13. J. R. Averill, "Personal Control over Aversive Stimuli and Its Relationship to Stress," *Psychological Bulletin,* 1973, *80,* 286–303.

14. E. J. Phares, *Locus of Control in Personality* (Morristown, N. J.: General Learning Press, 1976), pp. 33–34.

15. D. S. Hiroto and M. E. P. Seligman, "Generality of Learned Helplessness in Man," *Journal of Personality and Social Psychology,* 1975, *31,* 311–327.

16. *Ibid.*

17. *Ibid.*

18. S. Roth and L. Kubal, "Effects of Noncontingent Reinforcement on Tasks of Differing Importance: Facilitation and Learned Helplessness," *Journal of Personality and Social Psychology,* 1975, *32,* 680–391; C. B. Wortman, L. Panciera, L. Shusterman, and J. Hibscher, "Attributions of Causality and Reactions to Uncontrollable Outcomes," *Journal of Experimental Social Psychology,* 1976, *12,* 301–316.

19. C. S. Dweck and N. D. Reppucci, "Learned Helplessness and Reinforcement Responsibility in Children," *Journal of Personality and Social Psychology,* 1973, *25,* 109–116.

20. R. J. Gatchel, P. B. Paulus, and C. W. Maples, "Learned Helplessness and Self-Reported Affect," *Journal of Abnormal Psychology,* 1975, *84,* 732–734.

21. R. J. Gatchel and J. D. Proctor, "Physiological Correlates of Learned Helplessness in Man," *Journal of Abnormal Psychology,* 1976, *85,* 27–34.

22. W. B. Miller and M. E. P Seligman, "Depression and Learned Helplessness in Man," *Journal of Abnormal Psychology,* 1975, *84,* 228–238; D. C. Klein, E. Fencil-Morse, and M. E. P. Seligman, "Learned Helplessness, Depression, and the Attribution of Failure," *Journal of Personality and Social Psychology,* 1976, *33,* 508–546.

23. A. T. Beck, M. Kovacs, and A. Weissman, "Hopelessness and Suicidal Behavior," *Journal of the American Medical Association,* 1975, *234,* 1146–1149; A. T. Beck, A. Weissman, D. Lester, and L. Trexler, "The Measurement of Pessimism: The Hopelessness Scale," *Journal of Consulting and Clinical Psychology,* 1974, *42,* 861–865.

24. J. W. Pennebaker, M. A. Burnam, M. A. Schaeffer, and D. C. Harper, "Lack of Control as a Determinant of Perceived Physical Symptoms," *Journal of Personality and Social Psychology,* 1977, *35,* 167–174.

25. Seligman, *op. cit.,* p. 34.

26. R. Eisenberger, R. M. Kaplan, and R. D. Singer, "Decremental and Non-decremental Effects of Noncontingent Social Approval," *Journal of Personality and Social Psychology,* 1974, *30,* 716–722.

27. C. B. Ferster, "A Functional Analysis of Depression," *American Psychologist,* 1973, *28,* 857–870.

28. This argument was given by John R. Surber in a colloquium at Claremont Men's College, 1972.

29. D. C. Klein and M. E. P. Seligman, "Reversal of Performance Deficits and Perceptual Deficits in Learned Helplessness and Depression," *Journal of Abnormal Psychology,* 1976, *85,* 11–26.

30. C. S. Dweck, "The Role of Expectations and Attributions in the Alleviation of Learned Helplessness," *Journal of Personality and Social Psychology*, 1975, *31*, 674–685: M. Chapin and D. G. Dyck, "Persistence in Children's Reading Behavior as a Function of N Length and Attribution Retraining," *Journal of Abnormal Psychology*, 1976, *85*, 511–515.

31. R. Schultz, "The Effects of Control and Predictability on the Physical and Psychological Well-Being of the Institutionalized Aged," *Journal of Personality and Social Psychology*, 1976, *33*, 563–573.

32. E. J. Langer and J. Rodin, "The Effects of Choice and Enhanced Personal Responsibility for the Aged: A Field Experiment in an Institutional Setting," *Journal of Personality and Social Psychology*, 1976, *34*, 191–198.

33. J. P. McKee and A. C. Sherriffs, "The Differential Evaluation of Males and Females," *Journal of Personality*, 1957, *25*, 356–371.

34. P. Rosenkrantz, S. Vogel, H. Bee, I. Broverman, and D. M. Broverman, "Sex-Role Stereotypes and Self-Concepts in College Students," *Journal of Consulting and Clinical Psychology*, 1968, *32*, 287–295.

35. P. A. Goldberg, "Are Women Prejudiced against Women?" *Transaction*, 1968, *5*, 28–30.

36. G. I. Pheterson, S. B. Kiesler, and P. A. Goldberg, "Evaluation of the Performance of Women as a Function of Their Sex, Achievement, and Personal History," *Journal of Personality and Social Psychology*, 1971, *19*, 114–118.

37. C. L. Kleinke, "Knowledge and Favorability of Descriptive Sex Names for Males and Females," *Perceptual and Motor Skills*, 1974, *39*, 419–422; F. B. Meeker and C. L. Kleinke, "Knowledge of Names for In- and Outgroup Members of Different Sex and Ethnic Groups," *Psychological Reports*, 1972, *31*, 832–834.

38. P. A. Goldberg, M. Gottesdiener, and P. R. Abramson, "Another Put-Down of Women?: Perceived Attractiveness as a Function of Support for the Feminist Movement," *Journal of Personality and Social Psychology*, 1975, *32*, 113–115.

39. I. K. Broverman, D. M. Broverman, F. E. Clarkson, P. S. Rosenkrantz, and S. R. Vogel, "Sex-Role Stereotypes and Clinical Judgments of Mental Health," *Journal of Consulting and Clinical Psychology*, 1970, *34*, 1–7.

40. J. D. Coie, B. F. Pennington, and H. H. Buckley, "Effects of Situational Stress and Sex Roles on the Attribution of Psychological Disorder," *Journal of Consulting and Clinical Psychology*, 1974, *42*, 559–568.

41. U. S. Department of Labor, *Manpower Report of the President* (Washington, D. C.: U. S. Government Printing Office, 1974); cited in S. L. Cohen and K. A. Bunker, "Subtle Effects of Sex Role Stereotypes on Recruiters' Hiring Decisions," *Journal of Applied Psychology*, 1975, *60*, 566–572.

42. E. A. Cecil, R. M. Paul, and R. A. Olins, "Perceived Importance of Selected Variables Used to Evaluate Male and Female Job Applicants," *Personnel Psychology*, 1973, *26*, 397–404.

43. V. E. Schein, "The Relationship between Sex-Role Stereotypes and Requisite Management Characteristics," *Journal of Applied Psychology*, 1973, *57*, 95–100.

44. Cohen and Bunker, *op. cit.*

45. L. S. Fidell, "Empirical Verification of Sex Discrimination in Hiring Practice in Psychology," *American Psychologist*, 1970, *25*, 1094–1098.

46. B. Rosen and T. H. Jerdee, "Effects of Applicant's Sex and Difficulty of Job on Evaluations of Candidates for Managerial Positions," *Journal of Applied Psychology,* 1974, *59,* 511–512; E. A. Shaw, "Differential Impact of Negative Stereotyping in Employee Selection," *Personnel Psychology,* 1972, *25,* 333–338.

47. B. Rosen and T. H. Jerdee, "Influence of Sex-Role Stereotype on Personnel Decisions," *Journal of Applied Psychology,* 1974, *59,* 9–14.

48. The following books will be of value for readers wishing to learn more about self-control: M. R. Goldfried and G. C. Davison, *Clinical Behavior Therapy* (New York: Holt, Rinehart and Winston, 1976); C. E. Thoresen and M. J. Mahoney. *Behavioral Self-Control* (New York: Holt, Rinehart and Winston, 1974).

49. R. M. McFall and C. T. Twentyman, "Four Experiments on the Relative Contributions of Rehearsal, Modeling, and Coaching to Assertion Training," *Journal of Abnormal Psychology,* 1973, *81,* 199–218.

50. D. P. Holmes and J. J. Horan, "Anger Induction in Assertion Training," *Journal of Counseling Psychology,* 1976, *23,* 108–111.

51. R. M. McFall, "The Effects of Self-Monitoring on Normal Smoking Behavior," *Journal of Consulting and Clinical Psychology,* 1970, *34,* 135–142.

52. H. D. Kunzelmann (ed.), *Precision Teaching* (Seattle: Special Child Publications, 1970); cited in Thoresen and Mahoney, *op. cit.,* p. 59.

53. Kunzelmann (ed.), *op. cit.,* cited in Thoresen and Mahoney, *op. cit.,* p. 60.

54. E. J. Thomas, K. S. Abrams, and J. B. Johnson, "Self-Monitoring and Reciprocal Inhibition in the Modification of Multiple Tics of Gilles de la Tourette's Syndrome," *Journal of Behavior Therapy and Experimental Psychiatry,* 1971, *2,* 159–171.

55. M. Broden, R. V. Hall, and B. Mitts, "The Effect of Self-Recording on the Classroom Behavior of Two Eighth-Grade Students," *Journal of Applied Behavior Analysis,* 1971, *4,* 191–199; S. M. Johnson and G. White, "Self-Observation as an Agent of Behavioral Change," *Behavior Therapy,* 1971, *2,* 488–497; M. J. Mahoney, B. S. Moore, T. C. Wade, and N. G. M. Moura, "The Effects of Continuous and Intermittent Self-Monitoring on Academic Behavior," *Journal of Consulting and Clinical Psychology,* 1973, *41,* 65–69; C. S. Richards, "Behavior Modification of Studying through Study Skills Advice and Self-Control Procedures," *Journal of Counseling Psychology,* 1975, *22,* 431–436.

56. A more detailed analysis of self-observation can be found in A. E. Kazdin, "Self-Monitoring and Behavior Change," in M. J. Mahoney and C. E. Thoresen (eds.), *Self-Control: Power to the Person* (Belmont, Calif.: Brooks/Cole, 1974), pp. 218–246.

57. R. B. Stuart and B. Davis, *Slim Chance in a Fat World: Behavioral Control of Obesity* (Champaign, Ill.: Research Press, 1972); cited in Mahoney and Thoresen (eds.), *op. cit.,* p. 41.

58. Thoresen and Mahoney, *op. cit.,* pp. 19–20.

59. L. Fox, "Effecting the Use of Efficient Study Habits," *Journal of Mathetics,* 1962, *1,* 76–86.

60. I. Goldiamond, "Self-Control Procedures in Personal Behavior Problems," *Psychological Reports,* 1965, *17,* 851–868.

61. J. W. Hannum, C. E. Thoresen, and D. R. Hubbard, "A Behavioral Study of Self-Esteem with Elementary Teachers," in Mahoney and Thoresen (eds.), *op. cit.*, pp. 144–155.

62. A more detailed summary of self-reward is provided in Thoresen and Mahoney, *op. cit.*, chap. 4.

63. A more detailed summary of self-punishment is provided in Thoresen and Mahoney, *op. cit.*, chap. 5.

64. J. R. Cautela, "Covert Conditioning" in A. Jacobs and L. B. Sachs (eds.), *The Psychology of Private Events: Perspective on Covert Response Systems* (New York: Academic Press, 1971), p. 121.

65. S. B. Penick, R. Filion, S. Fox, and A. J. Stunkard, "Behavior Modification in the Treatment of Obesity," *Psychosomatic Medicine,* 1971, *33,* 49–55.

66. A. Bandura, "Self-Efficacy: Toward a Unifying Theory of Behavioral Change," *Psychological Review,* 1977, *84,* 191–215.

67. T. J. D'Zurilla and M. R. Goldfried, "Cognitive Processes, Problem Solving, and Effective Behavior," *Journal of Abnormal Psychology,* 1971, *78,* 107–126.

68. A. Bandura, N. E. Adams, and J. Beyer, "Cognitive Processes Mediating Behavioral Change," *Journal of Personality and Social Psychology,* 1977, *35,* 125–139.

69. R. W. Hovaco, "Stress Inoculation: A Cognitive Therapy for Anger and Its Application to a Case of Depression," *Journal of Consulting and Clinical Psychology,* 1977, *45,* 600–608.

70. E. J. Langer and S. Saegert, "Crowding and Cognitive Control," *Journal of Personality and Social Psychology,* 1977, *35,* 175–182.

71. *Ibid.,* p. 178.

Chapter Nine

1. W. Mischel, *Personality and Assessment* (New York: Wiley, 1968), chap. 1.

2. L. Diamant (ed.), *Case Studies in Psychopathology* (Columbus, Ohio: Charles E. Merrill Publishing Co., 1971), p. 109.

3. *Ibid.,* p. 260.

4. R. Endleman, "Oedipal Elements in Student Rebellions," *Psychoanalytic Review,* 1970, *57,* 442–471.

5. M. Grotjahn, "Smoking, Coughing, Laughing and Applause: A Comparative Study of Respiratory Symbolism," *International Journal of Psychoanalysis,* 1972, *53,* 345–349.

6. *Ibid.*

7. Diamant (ed.), *op. cit.,* p. 216.

8. Mischel, *Personality and Assessment;* W. Mischel, "On the Empirical Dilemmas of Psychodynamic Approaches," *Journal of Abnormal Psychology,* 1973, *82,* 335–344; W. Mischel, "Toward a Cognitive Social Learning Reconceptualization of Personality," *Psychological Review,* 1973, *80,* 252–283.

9. Mischel, *Personality and Assessment,* chap. 2.

10. *Ibid.*

11. *Ibid.,* chap. 5.

12. P. E. Meehl, "The Cognitive Activity of the Clinician," *American Psychologist*, 1960, *15*, 19–27; cited in Mischel, *Personality and Assessment*, p. 146.

13. P. E. Vernon, *Personality Assessment: A Critical Survey* (New York: Wiley, 1964), p. 239; cited in Mischel, *Personality and Assessment*, p. 146.

14. Mischel, *Personality and Assessment*, p. 147.

15. *Ibid.*, pp. 94–100.

16. E. J. Langer and R. P. Abelson, "A Patient by Any Other Name . . . : Clinician Group Difference in Labeling Bias," *Journal of Consulting and Clinical Psychology*, 1974, *42*, 4–9.

17. *Ibid.*, p. 8.

18. D. Rosenhan, "On Being Sane in Insane Places," *Science*, 1973, *179*, 250–258.

19. D. Rosenhan, "The Contextual Nature of Psychiatric Diagnosis," *Journal of Abnormal Psychology*, 1975, *84*, 462–474.

20. Rosenhan, "On Being Sane in Insane Places,"

21. Mischel, "On the Empirical Dilemmas of Psychodynamic Approaches."

22. Mischel, *Personality and Assessment*, chap. 8; Mischel, "Toward a Cognitive Social Learning Reconceptualization of Personality."

23. Mischel, *Personality and Assessment*, pp. 264–272.

24. *Ibid.*, p. 270.

25. E. E. Jones and R. E. Nisbett, *The Actor and the Observer: Divergent Perceptions of the Causes of Behavior* (Morristown, N. J.: General Learning Press, 1971).

26. R. E. Nisbett, C. Caputo, P. Legant, and J. Marecek, "Behavior as Seen by the Actor and as Seen by the Observer," *Journal of Personality and Social Psychology*, 1973, *27*, 154–164.

27. *Ibid.*

28. *Ibid.*

29. Jones and Nisbett, *op. cit.*

30. A. G. Miller, "Actor and Observer Perceptions of the Learning of a Task," *Journal of Experimental Social Psychology*, 1975, *11*, 95–111; D. Bar-Tel and I. H. Frieze, "Attributions of Success and Failure for Actors and Observers," *Journal of Research in Personality*, 1976, *20*, 256–265.

31. M. Snyder and E. E. Jones, "Attitude Attribution When Behavior Is Constrained," *Journal of Experimental Social Psychology*, 1974, *10*, 585–600.

32. S. G. West, S. P. Gunn, and P. Chernicky, "Ubiquitous Watergate: An Attributional Analysis," *Journal of Personality and Social Psychology*, 1975, *32*, 55–65.

33. *Ibid.*

34. *Ibid.*

35. *Ibid.*

36. D. T. Regan, E. Straus, and R. Fazio, "Liking and the Attribution Process," *Journal of Experimental Social Psychology*, 1974, *10*, 385–397.

37. W. G. Stephan, "Actor vs. Observer: Attributions to Behavior with Positive or Negative Outcomes and Empathy for the Other Role," *Journal of Experimental Social Psychology*, 1975, *11*, 205–214.

38. S. E. Taylor and J. H. Koivumaki, "The Perception of Self and Others: Acquaintanceship, Affect, and Actor-Observer Differences," *Journal of Personality and Social Psychology*, 1976, *33*, 403–408.

39. D. T. Miller and S. A Norman, "Actor-Observer Differences in Perceptions of Effective Control," *Journal of Personality and Social Psychology*, 1975, *31*, 503–515.

40. R. J. Wolosin, J. Esser, and G. A. Fine, "Effects of Justification and Vocalization on Actors' and Observers' Attributions of Freedom," *Journal of Personality*, 1975, *43*, 612–633.

41. J. H. Harvey, R. M. Arkin, J. M. Gleason, and S. Johnston, "Effect of Expected and Observed Outcome of an Action on the Differential Causal Attributions of Actor and Observer," *Journal of Personality*, 1974, *42*, 62–77.

42. J. H. Harvey, B. Harris, and R. D. Barnes, "Actor-Observer Differences in the Perceptions of Responsibility and Freedom," *Journal of Personality and Social Psychology*, 1975, *32*, 22–28.

43. B. R. Schlenker, "Liking for a Group Following an Initiation: Impression Management or Dissonance Reduction?" *Sociometry*, 1975, *38*, 99–118; J. T. Tedeschi, B. R. Schlenker, and T. V. Bonoma, "Cognitive Dissonance: Private Ratiocination or Public Spectacle?" *American Psychologist*, 1971, *26*, 685–695.

44. D. T. Regan and J. Totten, "Empathy and Attribution: Turning Observers into Actors," *Journal of Personality and Social Psychology*, 1975, *32*, 850–856; R. E. Galper, "Turning Observers into Actors: Differential Causal Attributions as a Function of 'Empathy,'" *Journal of Research in Personality*, 1976, *10*, 328–335.

45. D. M. Wegner and K. Finstuen, "Observers' Focus of Attention in the Simulation of Self-Perception," *Journal of Personality and Social Psychology*, 1977, *35*, 56–62.

46. M. D. Storms, "Videotape and the Attribution Process: Reversing Actors' and Observers' Points of View," *Journal of Personality and Social Psychology*, 1973, *27*, 165–175.

47. B. R. Forer, "The Fallacy of Personal Validation: A Classroom Demonstration of Gullibility," *Journal of Abnormal and Social Psychology*, 1949, *44*, 118–123; the quotation appears on p. 120 of the article.

48. V. M. Dmitruk, R. W. Collins, and D. L. Clinger, "The 'Barnum Effect' and Acceptance of Negative Personal Evaluation," *Journal of Consulting and Clinical Psychology*, 1973, *41*, 192–194; E. J. Manning, "Personal Validation: Replication of Forer's Study," *Psychological Reports*, 1968, *23*, 181–182; M. R. Merrens and W. S. Richards, "Acceptance of Generalized versus 'Bona Fide' Personality Interpretation," *Psychological Reports*, 1970, *27*, 691–694; C. R. Snyder and G. R. Larson, "A Further Look at Student Acceptance of General Personality Interpretations," *Journal of Consulting and Clinical Psychology*, 1972, *38*, 384–388; R. Stagner, "The Gullibility of Personnel Managers," *Personnel Psychology*, 1958, *11*, 347–352; R. E. Ulrich, T. J. Stachnik, and N. R. Stainton, "Student Acceptance of Generalized Personality Interpretations," *Psychological Reports*, 1963, *13*, 831–834; C. R. Snyder, R. J. Shenker, and C. R. Lowery, "Acceptance of Personality Interpretations: The 'Barnum Effect' and Beyond," *Journal of Consulting and Clinical Psychology*, 1977, *45*, 104–114.

49. Mischel, *Personality and Assessment*, chap. 5.

50. C. R. Snyder, "Why Horoscopes Are True: The Effects of Specificity on Acceptance of Astrological Interpretations," *Journal of Clinical Psychology,* 1974, *30,* 577–580.

51. C. L. Kleinke, unpublished data, Claremont, Calif., 1971.

52. This issue is discussed in greater detail by Mischel, *Personality and Assessment.*

53. R. Jeffery, "The Psychologist as an Expert Witness on the Issue of Insanity," *American Psychologist,* 1964, *19,* 838–843.

54. *Ibid.,* p. 839.

55. *Ibid.,* p. 840.

56. *Ibid.,* p. 842.

57. Z. W. Wanderer, "Validity of Clinical Judgments Based on Human Figure Drawings," *Journal of Consulting and Clinical Psychology,* 1969, *33,* 143–150.

58. I. Lublin and S. Lublin, "The Draw-A-Person Test: A Minimal Validity Investigation," paper presented at the meeting of the Western Psychological Association, San Francisco, 1967.

59. A more detailed discussion of this issue can be found in L. Ross, "The Intuitive Psychologist and His Shortcomings: Distortions in the Attribution Process," in L. Berkowitz (ed.), *Advances in Experimental Social Psychology,* Vol. 10 (New York: Academic Press, 1977), pp. 173–220.

60. D. Kahneman and A. Tversky, "On the Psychology of Prediction," *Psychological Review,* 1973, *80,* 237–251; R. E. Nisbett and E. Borgida, "Attribution and the Psychology of Prediction," *Journal of Personality and Social Psychology,* 1975, *32,* 932–943.

61. S. Oskamp, "Overconfidence in Case-Study Judgments," *Journal of Consulting Psychology,* 1965, *29,* 261–265.

62. L. Ross, D. Greene, and P. House, "The 'False Consensus Effect': An Egocentric Bias in Social Perception and Attribution Processes," *Journal of Experimental Social Psychology,* 1977, *13,* 279–301.

63. L. Ross, T. M. Amabile, and J. L. Steinmetz, "Social Roles, Social Control, and Biases in Social-Perception Processes," *Journal of Personality and Social Psychology,* 1977, *35,* 485–494.

64. R. E. Nisbett and T. D. Wilson, "Telling More Than We Can Know: Verbal Reports on Mental Processes," *Psychological Review,* 1977, *84,* 231–259.

65. N. R. F. Maier, "Reasoning in Humans: II. The Solution of a Problem and Its Appearance in Consciousness," *Journal of Comparative Psychology,* 1931, *12,* 181–194.

66. R. E. Nisbett and T. D. Wilson, "The Halo Effect: Evidence for Unconscious Alteration of Judgments," *Journal of Personality and Social Psychology,* 1977, *35,* 250–256.

67. Nisbett and Wilson, "Telling More Than We Can Know," p. 245.

68. R. A. Wicklund, "Objective Self-Awareness," in L. Berkowitz (ed.), *Advances in Experimental Social Psychology,* Vol. 9 (New York: Academic Press, 1975), pp. 233–275.

69. W. J. Ickes, R. A. Wicklund, and C. B. Ferris, "Objective Self-Awareness, Choice, and Dissonance," *Journal of Personality and Social Psychology,* 1973, *28,* 262–269.

70. Wicklund, *op. cit.,* p. 242.

71. Ickes, Wicklund, and Ferris, *op. cit.;* Wicklund, *op. cit.,* p. 247.

72. S. Duval and R. A. Wicklund, "Effects of Objective Self-Awareness on Attribution of Causality," *Journal of Experimental Social Psychology,* 1973, *9,* 17–31.

73. *Ibid.,* p. 21.

74. *Ibid.,* p. 26.

75. N. A. Federoff and J. H. Harvey, "Focus of Attention, Self-Esteem, and the Attribution of Causality," *Journal of Research in Personality,* 1976, *10,* 336–345.

76. M. F. Scheier, A. Fenigstein, and A. H. Buss, "Self-Awareness and Physical Aggression," *Journal of Experimental Social Psychology,* 1974, *10,* 264–273.

77. C. S. Carver, "Facilitation of Physical Aggression through Objective Self-Awareness," *Journal of Experimental Social Psychology,* 1974, *10,* 365–370.

78. E. Diener and M. Wallbom, "Effects of Self-Awareness on Antinormative Behavior," *Journal of Research in Personality,* 1976, *10,* 107–111,

79. R. A. Wicklund and S. Duval, "Opinion Change and Performance Facilitation as a Result of Objective Self-Awareness," *Journal of Experimental Social Psychology,* 1971, *7,* 319–342.

80. B. A. Liebling and P. Shaver, "Evaluation, Self-Awareness, and Task Performance," *Journal of Experimental Social Psychology,* 1973, *9,* 297–306.

81. C. A. Insko, S. Worchel, E. Songer, and S. T. Arnold, "Effort, Objective Self-Awareness, Choice, and Dissonance," *Journal of Personality and Social Psychology,* 1973, *28,* 262–269; Wicklund and Duval, *op. cit.*

82. V. L. Allen, "Effect of Extraneous Cognitive Activity on Dissonance Reduction," *Psychological Reports,* 1965, *16,* 1145–1151.

83. Wicklund and Duval, *op. cit.*

84. S. Duval, "Conformity on a Visual Task as a Function of Personal Novelty on Attitudinal Dimensions and Being Reminded of the Object Status of Self," *Journal of Experimental Social Psychology,* 1976, *12,* 87–98.

85. D. Davis and T. C. Brock, "Use of First Person Pronouns as a Function of Increased Objective Self-Awareness and Performance Feedback," *Journal of Experimental Social Psychology,* 1975, *11,* 381–388.

86. F. X. Gibbons and R. A. Wicklund, "Selective Exposure to Self," *Journal of Research in Personality,* 1976, *10,* 98–106; Wicklund, 'Objective Self-Awareness," p. 250.

87. B. A. Liebling, M. Seiler, and P. Shaver, "Self-Awareness and Cigarette-Smoking Behavior," *Journal of Experimental Social Psychology,* 1974, *10,* 325–332; R. A. Wicklund, "Discrepancy Reduction or Attempted Distraction? A Reply to Liebling, Seiler, and Shaver," *Journal of Experimental Social Psychology,* 1974, *11,* 78–81.

88. Wicklund, "Objective Self-Awareness," p. 256.

89. *Ibid.,* p. 255.

90. M. Snyder, "Self-Monitoring of Expressive Behavior," *Journal of Personality and Social Psychology,* 1974, *30,* 526–537.

91. *Ibid.,* p. 531.

92. M. Snyder, *op. cit.*

93. M. Snyder and T. C. Monson, "Persons, Situations, and the Control of Social Behavior," *Journal of Personality and Social Psychology,* 1975, *32,* 637–644.

94. D. J. Bem and A. Allen, "On Predicting Some of the People Some of the Time: The Search for Cross-Situational Consistencies in Behavior," *Psychological Review,* 1974, *81,* 506–520.

95. Snyder and Monson, *op. cit.*

96. M. Snyder and E. D. Tanke, "Behavior and Attitude: Some People Are More Consistent than Others," *Journal of Personality,* 1976, *44,* 501–517.

97. M. G. McGee and M. Snyder, "Attribution and Behavior: Two Field Studies," *Journal of Personality and Social Psychology,* 1975, *32,* 185–190.

98. Two excellent reviews of this issue can be found in Bem and Allen, *op. cit.* and K. S. Bowers, "Situationism in Psychology: An Analysis and a Critique," *Psychological Review,* 1973, *80,* 307–336.

99. B. F. Skinner, *Beyond Freedom and Dignity* (New York: Knopf, 1971).

Subject Index

Author Index